FROM BOMBAY TO BOLLYWOOD

POSTMILLENNIAL POP

General Editors: Karen Tongson and Henry Jenkins

From Bombay to Bollywood

The Making of a Global Media Industry

Aswin Punathambekar

NEW YORK UNIVERSITY PRESS

New York and London

NEW YORK UNIVERSITY PRESS
New York and London
www.nyupress.org

References to Internet Websites (URLs) were accurate at the time of writing.
Neither the author nor New York University Press is responsible for URLs that
may have expired or changed since the manuscript was prepared.

Library of Congress Cataloging-in-Publication Data
Punathambekar, Aswin.
From Bombay to Bollywood : the making of a global media industry /
Aswin Punathambekar.
pages cm
Includes bibliographical references and index.
ISBN 978-0-8147-7189-1 (cl : alk. paper) — ISBN 978-0-8147-2949-6 (pb : alk. paper)
1. Motion picture industry—India. 2. Motion pictures—India. I. Title.
PN1993.5.I8P86 2013
791.430954—dc23   2013011871

New York University Press books are printed on acid-free paper, and their binding materials
are chosen for strength and durability. We strive to use environmentally responsible suppliers
and materials to the greatest extent possible in publishing our books.

Manufactured in the United States of America
c 10 9 8 7 6 5 4 3 2 1

p 10 9 8 7 6 5 4 3 2 1

For my mother,
and in fond memory of my father

CONTENTS

ACKNOWLEDGMENTS

This is a book about connections and networks that span multiple spaces and places in the world. Through the long process of reading, learning, and writing about transnational media spaces, the numerous material, intellectual, and emotional debts I have accrued also span many places and times.

Thanks first of all to Anandam Kavoori, whose kindness and encouragement gave me the confidence to embark on an academic career and begin the work that would lead to this book. The groundwork for this book was laid under the guidance of Henry Jenkins, William Uricchio, Michael Fischer, and Tuli Banerjee in the Comparative Media Studies program at MIT. In particular, I want to thank Henry Jenkins for his advice, unwavering support, zany humor, and showing me how to read, write, and teach with kindness and generosity. Several other teachers and friends at MIT also played a crucial role in my early years in graduate school: David Thorburn, Joe Dumit, Ken Keniston, Sangita Shresthova, Zhan Li, Stephanie Davenport, Philip Tan, Wally Banks, Alex Chisholm, Sanjit Sethi, Robin Hauck, Margaret Weigel, Anita Chan, Candis Callison, Susannah Mandel, Aparna Das, and Sajan Saini. I have also had the good fortune of staying connected with the CMS-MIT community through the Convergence Culture Consortium. Among others involved with C3, I would like to thank Sam Ford, Ivan Askwith, Ana Domb, Xiaochang Li, and Joshua Green for the many conversations about media cultures and for creating opportunities to engage with media industry professionals.

This book would not have been possible without the advice and encouragement of teachers and fellow students in the Department of Communication Arts at the University of Wisconsin-Madison. I feel very fortunate to have had a chance to learn from and work with Shanti Kumar, Julie D'acci, Michele Hilmes, Michael Curtin, Lisa Nakamura, and Mary Beltran. I would like to thank all of them for their many kindnesses, advice, and research and teaching opportunities. Most of all, I would like to thank Shanti Kumar and Michael Curtin. I could not have begun and completed this book without their encouragement, support, and inspiration over the years. I am also grateful to Hemant Shah and Kirin Narayan for many conversations on South Asia and South Asian diasporic cultures.

My colleagues in the Department of Communication Studies at the University of Michigan provided the intellectual environment as well as everyday support that made it possible to rethink and complete this book.

Amanda Lotz, Robin Coleman, Susan Douglas, and Derek Vaillant have been eager mentors and I am deeply grateful to them for helping me negotiate the ups and downs of academic life. My intellectual and academic debts to Paddy Scannell are simply too numerous. I can only hope that the conversation we have been having over the past few years continues well into the future. A number of friends and colleagues at Michigan have listened, read, critiqued, and helped make this a better book. In particular, I would like to thank Dan Herbert, Sheila Murphy, Mrinalini Sinha, Ram Mahalingam, Lee Schlesinger, Matthew Hull, Rebecca Grapevine and others in the Kitabmandal group, Shazia Iftkhar, Will Glover, Farina Mir, Juan Cole, Sunil Agnani, Nadine Naber, Evelyn Alsultany, and Sean Jacobs. I am also grateful for the material support that I have received from the University of Michigan: start-up research funds from the College of Literature Science and Arts, a junior faculty research grant from the Rackham Graduate School, a travel grant from the Center for International Business Education, and a publication subvention from the Office of the Vice President for Research. I am also grateful to Susan Douglas for organizing a manuscript workshop at a crucial stage, and to John Caldwell and Radhika Parameswaran for being such terrific interlocutors. Two graduate students in Communication Studies exceeded all my expectations and taught me a great deal as they helped me with various aspects of research toward this book: many thanks to Lia Wolock and Brad Jones. I should also make public my indebtednes to Shevon Desai, a wonderful librarian at Michigan who listened patiently to many a research query and pointed me in just the right directions.

At Michigan and beyond, an ever-expanding network of friends and colleagues have helped, in ways both direct and subtle, shape many of the ideas in this book: thanks to Marwan Kraidy, Sreya Mitra, Josh Jackson, Megan Ankerson, Russ Neuman, Joseph Straubhaar, Nancy Baym, Yeidy Rivero, Madhavi Mallapragada, Joseph Turow, Monroe Price, Katherine Sender, Paula Chakravarty, Sangeet Kumar, Bill Kirkpatrick, Serra Tinic, Tim Havens, Nitin Govil, Sudhir Mahadevan, Bhaskar Sarkar, Rohit Chopra, Manan Ahmed, S V Srinivas, Lawrence Liang, Ravi Sundaram, Miranda Banks, Vicki Mayer, Ranjani Mazumdar, Ratheesh Radhakrishnan, Rosie Thomas, Daya Kishan Thussu, Tarik Sabry, Zeynep Gursel, Navaneetha Mokkil-Marathur, Pavitra Sundar, Sugi Ganeshananthan, Nilanjana Bhattacharjya, Neepa Majumdar, William Mazzarella, Amit Rai, and Carolina Acosta-Alzuru.

In Bombay, New Delhi, New York, and Los Angeles, I am indebted to all those who took time away from their busy work schedules to talk to me. In particular, I would like to thank Shashank Saksena, Parmesh Shahani, Gargi

Mukherjee, and Advait Shelke for inviting me into their workplaces. Thanks also to Amlu and Girish Vidyanath for their warm hospitality in Bombay. My editor Eric Zinner's patience and faith in the project has meant a lot to me all along. And to Ciara McLaughlin and Alicia Nadkarni at NYU Press, whose care and diligence kept everything moving forward, thanks in no small measure.

I have been fortunate to have the love and support of friends and relatives too numerous to mention. Without their care and affection, not to mention the countless phone calls and emails some endured, it would have been impossible to write this book. Some of them are: Parmesh Shahani, Shashank Saksena, Mobina Hashmi, Swati Bandi, Vikas John, Samina Raja, Chris Lee, Niharika Banerjee, Amrita Chanda, Ben Aslinger, Derek Johnson, Jonathan Gray, Manishita Dass, Varuni Bhatia, Toy (Sharmadip Basu), Sri Nair, and Ram Mahalingam. My family provides the kind of everyday care and love that makes all this possible: thanks to Anita, Arvind, Mahika, Kavel, and Vanur; Mihir and Geeta Banerjee, Somnath, Sramana, Priya, and Dhruv; and most of all, Mandira Banerjee and Ameya Punathambekar, without whom I would be deprived of the pleasures that make this vocation possible and meaningful. Finally, I would not have been able to accomplish this without my parents' blessings. I would like to dedicate this book to my mother and in loving memory of my father.

In May 1998, the Indian government transformed world media by granting Bombay cinema "industry" status. It was a remarkable decision, given the history of the state's relationship with popular cinema. Even though Bombay had emerged as a major center of film production during the 1930s and 1940s, the Indian state did not regard filmmaking as an important industrial activity or as central to the project of defining national culture. As a consequence, filmmaking did not receive the concessions and support that media—including radio and television—did. Punitive taxation, licensing, and censorship codes defined the state's approach to cinema for nearly five decades.

Ascribing industry status to filmmaking in 1998 was, at one level, an intervention in film financing. The government framed the decision as an attempt to rid the film business of "black money" (untaxed/unaccounted) as well as the involvement of the mafia/underworld, and to encourage transparent accounting practices. More broadly, this moment of reform also generated a discourse of "corporatization," a set of changes deemed necessary for the film industry to shed its image as a dysfunctional "national" cinema and assume its place as a global media industry. Corporatizing the film business seemed all the more urgent given the phenomenal growth of other media sectors in India (television and telecommunications in particular) and the emergence of a globally competitive IT and software services sector in cities like Bangalore and Hyderabad during the 1990s. Narratives of India Inc. confidently and triumphantly navigating the global economy were not lost on either the state or those in the film industry. This process of reform has by no means been smooth or uncontested. There has been much disagreement and confusion regarding the many institutional, creative, and social transitions under way within the film industry and the media industries at large in Bombay and other cities across India. And media industry professionals remain deeply ambivalent about changes that a decade of reform has wrought and what it means to adopt and perform globally recognizable practices of organization and management. This sense of uncertainty and ambivalence about "going global" notwithstanding, two things are clear.

First, the spatial coordinates and geographic reach of Bollywood have changed dramatically over the past decade. The answer to the question, "Where in the world is Bollywood?" is, to be sure, "Bombay." However, Bombay's emergence as a global media capital cannot be grasped without mapping the city's links with other centers of finance, technology, the South Asian diaspora, and creative work such as New York, Los Angeles, and London, among others.[1] Second, it is neither possible nor productive to conceptualize Bollywood as a *film* industry. Television and digital media have been central to the circulation of Bollywood content across the world, in expanding and redefining sites and modes of consumption, and enabling filmmakers and stars to envision overseas markets and audiences.

This book focuses on these and other transitions to analyze the transformation of the Bombay film industry into a transnational and multimedia cultural industry that the world has come to recognize as Bollywood. Bringing together in-depth interviews with a range of media industry professionals, ethnographic accounts of industry conventions and sites of media production, and trade-press materials, my central goal in this book is to capture the dynamics of a media industry in formation and thereby analyze how a media industry in the postcolonial world imagines and claims the global as its scale of operations. Scale, as the anthropologist Anna Tsing observes, is the "spatial dimensionality necessary for a particular kind of view, whether up close or from a distance, microscopic or planetary."[2] Tsing further argues that a scale needs to be understood not just as a "neutral frame for viewing the world," but rather as something that "must be brought into being—proposed, practiced, evaded, as well as taken for granted."[3] Drawing on Tsing's reflections on scale and scale-making, I approach the transition from Bombay cinema to Bollywood as a particularly rich conjuncture for analyzing how the "global" is variously imagined, acted upon, contested, and rearticulated. Thus at a broader level, this book presents an analysis of globalization, especially as it pertains to media and communications, and the capitalist frameworks within which a majority of the world's media systems have come to operate.

Of course, there is no denying that Bollywood has come to occupy a privileged position in the study of media in India and processes of media globalization more generally. Scholars including Shanti Kumar and S. V. Srinivas are surely right to point out that this focus on Bollywood provides too partial a view of media globalization and marginalizes other centers of media production that are also enmeshed in transnational circuits.[4] In the Indian context, the Tamil and Telugu language film and television industries based in Chennai and Hyderabad, for instance, are anything but "local." The establishment of powerful television corporations such as Sun TV and Eenadu TV during the mid-1990s led to the creation of a translocal network of audiences based not only in India and the "first world" diaspora in countries like the United States, U.K., and Canada, but also brought in Tamil- and Telugu-speaking communities in countries like Malaysia, Singapore, and South Africa. As in the case of Hindi-language television channels like Star and ZEE, film-based content constitutes a major part of these television channels' programming. The use of the term "regional" to mark these industries' position within the Indian mediascape and the Indian state's material and symbolic investments in Bollywood certainly underscore the continued relevance of the "national" as a scale where the politics of media globalization play out.[5]

However, I would argue that one way to address this problem is to make Bollywood more specific. In other words, in addition to developing accounts of media industries in other cities within India, we also need to map the many forces that produced Bollywood as *the* Indian global media industry in order to reveal the presentist and limited nature of that globalism. Brian Larkin's careful mapping of circuits and patterns of distribution of Bombay cinema in Nigeria, and Sudha Rajagopalan's analysis of the circulation and consumption of Indian cinema in the erstwhile Soviet Union are important reminders of other trajectories and articulations of the "global" in the history of the Bombay film industry.[6] Further, as Ravi Vasudevan observes, when we consider the fact that "regional distribution offices across the Middle East, North, East, and South Africa date back to the 1940s and were feeding into a particular market for 'Arabian night stories' and Laila Majnu, Shireen Farhad style love legends," it becomes clear that we need to be far more grounded and precise in our use of terms like global and transnational.[7]

My analysis of the transition from Bombay cinema to Bollywood is thus set within the sociohistorical conjuncture of the past two decades—from 1991, when economic reforms initiated by the Indian government led to large-scale political and sociocultural transitions across the country, to the present. I argue that the emergence of Bollywood as a global media industry rests on profoundly uneven and contested spatial transformations across three interrelated fields: first, the reconfiguration of national space in transnational terms, marked in particular by the state's creative responses and efforts to refigure its relationship with the diaspora as well as the media and entertainment industries; second, the reinvention of Bombay as a global city in this period of economic and cultural globalization, and its position as a key node in multiple transnational networks of capital and cultural production; and third, the phenomenal expansion of India's mediaspace, characterized by the rapid development of the television, advertising, Internet, and mobile phone industries as well as increasing levels of technological and industrial convergence among them.

In relation to these broader shifts, chapters in this book tackle several other questions, themes, and issues. Tracing changes in state policy toward media and entertainment, I explore how various people and groups associated with Bollywood negotiated and articulated what it meant to "go global." How was the notion of corporatization, for instance, normalized as exactly what the industry needed in order to refashion itself as Bollywood? Exploring the world of marketing and promotions, I analyze the ways in which the film industry responded to new circuits of capital that became available in Bombay following the establishment of transnational television and advertising corporations. Situating the workings of the film industry within the broader mediaspace of Bombay, my approach opens up an opportunity to understand, for example, how family-run businesses like Dharma Productions (Karan Johar) tackled the challenges and opportunities that this period of transition presented. Moving beyond questions of reception in diasporic contexts, I examine how digital media companies established by South Asian American entrepreneurs in New York have forged relations with Bollywood to create new and unexpected trajectories of media circulation.

Overall, I conceptualize Bollywood as a zone of cultural production shaped by multiple sites of mediation, including the operations and social worlds of industry professionals, state policies, technological and industrial shifts, and audience practices—all simultaneously dependent on, yet not completely determining one another. While my primary orientation is in the field of media and cultural studies, in the course of writing this book I have drawn from a range of disciplines and in particular, recent historical and ethnographic work on media cultures outside Anglo American contexts. In doing so, I hope to contribute not only to scholarship on media and public culture in India and the Indian diaspora but more broadly, to expand our understanding of the histories and patterns of media convergence as well as the spatial dynamics of media globalization.

Beyond Film, Toward a History of Media Convergence

In 2003, the New Delhi-based *Seminar* magazine invited a group of media scholars to "unsettle cinema." The objective, as Bhrigupati Singh outlined in his opening essay, was to grapple with the question: What sort of an object is cinema in India? Singh went on to situate this question in relation to the transformation of India's mediaspace since the early 1990s and to assert that Ashis Nandy's view of popular cinema being a "slum's eye view of Indian politics" had become nearly impossible to sustain.[8] Writing in the mid-1990s, Nandy had famously argued that "both the cinema and the slum in India show the same impassioned negotiation with everyday survival."[9] Arguing that this articulation was no longer possible, Singh wrote: "The object that Nandy, even till as recently as 1995, could refer to as 'cinema' has completely changed in its shape, form and mode of dispersal."[10] So what does cinema post-1995 look like? The snapshot that Singh presented is worth quoting:

> Take the case of a recent film, *Kabhi Khushi Kabhie Gham* (*K3G*). Alongside his transnational presence in the film, Shahrukh Khan flows uninterrupted and simultaneous into a Pepsi ad on Star Plus, a rerun of *Baazigar* on Sony TV into an Ericsson ad in the *Times of India*, only to reappear on the upper left corner of the MSN Hotmail India screensaver. Amitabh Bachchan plays an aging corporate scion and benevolently distributes money and a few minutes of fame to the Indian middle class on *Kaun Banega Crorepati?* (Who Wants to Be a Crorepati?). *K3G* the film, itself appears in only a fraction of the cinema halls in any of the big Indian cities on the day of its release, simultaneously screened with a shaky and uncertain print on TV by various cablewallahs (cable TV entrepreneurs), flooding various electronic bazaars soon after as an easily copied VCD, its songs long-since released (and "pirated") on CD and cassette.[11]

To this account, we could add that *K3G*'s songs were available on various peer-to-peer networks and websites like raaga.com and smashits.com the day after the music was officially released. Web portals such as rediff.com created slideshows (offering behind-the-scenes stills, interviews, gossip, etc.) and hosted online chat sessions with the stars that were attended by fans across the world. Within a few days of the film's release, pirated copies were in circulation all over the world and available, for instance, at South Asian grocery stores across North America. And at the cinema hall in Boston where I saw the film (first day first show, no less), the audience, comprised mostly of Indian immigrants, stood up reverentially when Krish (Shahrukh Khan's son in *K3G*) led his British schoolmates in a rendition of the Indian national anthem.

Snapshots such as these are interesting not only because they serve as useful entry points for thinking about the ways in which the object that we term "cinema" has changed dramatically. More important, they highlight how India's mediaspace is defined by rapidly evolving, complex, and often surprising connections within and among industry practices, state policy, new media technologies and platforms, and spaces of consumption and participation that criss-cross regional, national, and transnational boundaries and affiliations. In this context, to suggest that film shares deep connections with radio, television, and digital media seems to state the obvious. Yet, apart from brief mentions of radio and television as important sites for audiences' engagement with film music, there is no sustained historical study of how broadcasting, for instance, may have shaped the workings of the film industry or vice versa. Film and media scholars have yet to pay close attention to the ways in which relations among the media industries in Bombay have defined circuits of capital, production cultures, and policy decisions, among other things.[12] Singh's essay in *Seminar* was, in many respects, among the first to call for a move away from conceiving of cinema in purely textual terms.[13]

Thus far, scholars have approached cinema in India as a profoundly important "national-popular" domain that has negotiated various transitions and conflicts in the sociocultural and political fabric of India for over a century now, focusing in particular on the politics of representation in Indian cinema.[14] Juxtaposing readings of films' narrative and representational strategies with the sociocultural and political context within which they were produced, circulated, and debated, these studies help us understand how cinema mediates ideas regarding nation, gender, caste, class, community, and sexuality. Over the past decade, others have built on this work and focused attention on a range of filmic and extrafilmic sites—stardom, censorship, style and visual culture, and gender and queer politics—to explore how cinema relates in complex ways to the civic and the political.[15] However, as Ranjani Mazumdar points out, analyses have so far placed cinema "within a framework of either 'dominant ideology' or the 'nation' and 'state,' thus situating cinema within networks that constitute nationalist and ideological closure."[16] Further, the study of cinema has been dominated by a focus on the formal properties of film and the narrative form.

In contrast, this book looks beyond the film text and the cinema hall to examine film's relations with other media. I argue that historically informed institutional and ethnographic analyses of intermedia relations are crucial for developing more complex and textured cultural genealogies of Bollywood's global flows and influences. As the chapters that follow show, by focusing on intermedia relations in the Indian context, I also hope to broaden scholarly discussions of media convergence that are informed primarily by developments in Anglo American media cultures. In one respect, my understanding of media convergence is shaped by Henry Jenkins' approach, which moves beyond a focus on technological dimensions to explore the industrial and cultural dimensions of what he calls convergence culture. For Jenkins, convergence refers to "the flow of content across multiple media platforms, the cooperation between multiple media industries, and the migratory behavior of media audiences who will go almost anywhere in search of the kinds of entertainment experiences they want."[17] Paying close attention to relations between "old" and "new" media technologies, Jenkins explores changes in the operations of the media industries in the United States as well as the ways in which participatory cultures that cohere around media and popular culture shape this rapidly evolving media terrain in important ways.

This framework for thinking about convergence is certainly useful for understanding processes of technological and industrial convergence in the Indian mediaspace. Moreover, any account of the emergence of Bollywood as a global media industry has to acknowledge the defining role played by a vast, networked, and often "pirate" realm of fandom and participation that ensures the circulation of Bollywood content across the world. However, the pace of media development and change in countries like India over the past two decades confound notions of "old" and "new" media that inform discussions of media convergence. As Ravi Sundaram's scholarship on relations between media and urban infrastructures has shown, cultures of copying and recycling built on low-cost technologies of reproduction have, since the early 1990s, "blurred the distinctions between producers and consumers of media, adding to the diffusion of both media infrastructures—video stores, photocopy and design shops, bazaars, cable networks, piracy—and media forms (images, video, phone sms/txt, sounds)."[18] To put it simply, media convergence takes different trajectories and forms in varied sociocultural contexts.

Further, I am interested here in situating the contemporary period of media convergence within a longer history of interrelationships between film, broadcasting, and other emerging media platforms and institutions.[19] I argue that at issue is our understanding of the role that "new media" play at different historical conjunctures in enabling media producers in established industries to imagine and mobilize national and transnational markets, fortifying, in the process, certain cities' positions as influential media capitals. In other words, a central part of developing an account of how Bombay has emerged as an important center of media production even as it forges connections with an ever-expanding network of places worldwide involves deepening and refining our understanding of the interwoven histories of different media technologies and institutions. While a comprehensive analysis of intermedia relations is beyond the scope of my analysis here, let me offer a brief account of the relationship between Radio Ceylon, a commercial broadcasting station based in Sri Lanka, and the Bombay film industry during the 1950s as a way to situate contemporary media dynamics in Bombay within a broader historical and comparative framework.[20]

The story of film songs and broadcasting has been narrated mainly from the perspective of All India Radio and nationalist elites' interventions in the realm of cultural policy. As the story goes, Dr. B. V. Keskar, Minister of Information & Broadcasting (1950–1962), deemed film songs "cheap and vulgar" and brought about a nearly complete ban on film songs.[21] While Keskar attempted to create "light music"—with lyrics of "high literary and moral quality" and music that would steer away from the "tendency to combine western and eastern music as was done in Hindi films"—listeners began to tune in to Radio Ceylon for Indian film songs.[22] As one oft-quoted survey of listener preferences noted, "out of ten households with licensed radio sets, nine were tuned to Radio Ceylon and the tenth set was broken."[23] Recognizing the enduring popularity of film songs and acknowledging the difficulties involved in forging a new "taste public," Keskar relented and on October 28, 1957 announced the launch of a new variety program called *Vividh Bharati* that would "consist of popular music and other light items."[24] The press release also pointed out that of five hours' programming on week days, nearly four hours would be dedicated to film songs.

This was, without doubt, a struggle over defining "national culture," and as David Lelyveld points out, government-controlled All India Radio was expected to play "a leading role in integrating Indian culture and raising standards."[25] However, this narrative, in which Radio Ceylon makes a brief appearance, does not shed light on any other aspect of the film industry's relationship with radio. How did producers, music directors, and playback singers react to All India Radio's policies? How exactly did the overseas programming division of a commercially operated broadcasting station from Colombo establish ties with the Bombay film industry? What role did advertisers play? And what was the production process for various film-based radio programs?

In 1951, Radio Ceylon established an agency in the Colaba area of downtown Bombay—Radio Advertising Services—in order to attract advertising revenue and recruit professional broadcasters who could record both commercials and programs. It was through this agency, headed by Dan Molina, an American entrepreneur who had lived and traveled across the subcontinent, that Ameen Sayani and a small group of producers and writers created a number of film-based radio programs, including the hit countdown show *Binaca Geet Mala*. Sponsored by a Swiss company named CIBA and using two powerful shortwave transmitters located in Colombo, *Geet Mala* was initially produced as a half-hour competition program in which seven random film songs were broadcast each week with audiences invited to rearrange the songs chronologically. With a hundred rupees as the jackpot each week, the show attracted immediate attention and, according to Ameen Sayani, "the very first program, broadcast on December 3, 1952, brought in a mail of 9,000 letters and within a year, the mail shot up to 65,000 a week." Recognizing the difficulties of the competition format, Sayani and other producers decided to transform *Binaca Geet Mala* into a one-hour "hit parade" in December 1954. While continuing to encourage audiences to write in with song requests, CIBA, after consultations with their sales personnel, identified forty record stores across India that would send weekly sales reports to be used as the basis for the countdown show. However, when it became clear that some film producers and music directors were involved in rigging record sales, *Geet Mala* producers decided to set up Radio Clubs (*srota sangh*) across the country as a "popular" counterweight. Each week, representatives from CIBA would collect sales figures and fan letters and develop a countdown that Ameen Sayani would use to produce a show. Each week's show, recorded in Bombay, would be flown to Colombo and broadcast from 8:00 to 9:00 p.m. on Wednesdays. As Sayani reminisced, "[T]he streets would be empty on Wednesday nights . . . in fact, Wednesday nights came to be known as *Geet Mala* day."

I wish to draw attention here to the ways in which the film industry became involved with *Geet Mala*. The overwhelming popularity of *Geet Mala* led to complaints from music directors when their songs did not feature in the weekly countdown. Sayani suggested appointing "an ombudsman from the film industry" who would check the countdown list. With established film producers and directors like G. P. Sippy and B. R. Chopra assuming this role, producers and music directors seemed satisfied with the process. And according to Sayani, information regarding record sales and popularity among audiences in different parts of the country began circulating in the film industry. By the mid-1950s, directors and stars from the film industry were participating in other weekly sponsored shows on Radio Ceylon (such as *Lipton Meet Your Stars*) and film publicity quickly became a central aspect of Radio Ceylon's programs. As Sayani recalled, no film was ever released without a huge publicity campaign over Radio Ceylon and later, All India Radio's *Vividh Bharati*. Radio, in other words, provided film stars, directors, music directors, and playback singers with the opportunity to listen, speak to, and imagine an audience in a fundamentally novel way.

I do not wish to suggest that the picture of the audience conjured by radio programs carried greater weight than box-office considerations and the information that producers, directors, and stars in Bombay received through production and distribution networks. But it is possible to open up a new framework of inquiry by considering radio's role in making the films, songs, and stars of Bombay cinema a part of the daily life of listeners across India and elsewhere, in creating a shared space for listeners in locations as diverse as the southern metropolis of Madras and a small mining town like Jhumri Tilaiya in the northern state of Bihar, binding together the nation-as-audience, and enabling the Bombay film industry to imagine a "national audience."[26] It also encourages us to ponder how marketing and promotions, stardom, conceptions of the audience, fan cultures, and other aspects of cinema in India have been profoundly shaped by technological, business, and creative developments in broadcasting and other media technologies and institutions (VCRs and the video business, cable and satellite television, and so on). It is this broader historical and spatial understanding of media convergence that guides my analysis of how relations among the film, television, and digital media industries have shaped the refashioning of the Bombay film industry as Bollywood and, in the process, positioned Bombay as a key node in an emergent cultural geography.

Spaces of Media Production

If thinking beyond film to account for intermedia relations and processes of media convergence constitutes one of the significant interventions this book makes, the other involves bringing an emerging industry studies/production cultures framework to bear on the operations of the media industries. My analysis of the ongoing restructuring of the media industries in India thus proceeds from the understanding that industry professionals play a central role in shaping both everyday practices and the larger project of imagining Bollywood as a global media industry. Of course, a few scholars writing about film and television in India have addressed these issues. Madhava Prasad, for instance, has analyzed how relations of production shape the film form by examining the fragmented nature of the production apparatus, the centrality of kinship loyalties within the industry, the reliance on merchant capital, the influence that distributors wield in every aspect of the filmmaking process, and so on.[27] Among other essays, Ashish Rajadhyaksha's account of links between the film industry, particularly in the distribution and exhibition sector, and various forms of speculative capital in Bombay has also been immensely valuable.[28] However, as Tejaswini Ganti has pointed out, such analyses "that try to 'read' or infer production practices from the finished film cannot access or do justice to the complexity, the negotiations, the idiosyncrasies and frequent chaos that characterizes filmmaking."[29]

This gap that Ganti identifies in the scholarship on cinema does, in fact, characterize the majority of studies on media and public culture in India and diasporic contexts as well. While scholars have analyzed the globalization of Bollywood through critical readings of films and ethnographic studies of audiences in different locations, they have yet to pay close attention to industry dynamics. Moreover, as Michael Curtin points out, media industries research remains focused on film and television in the United States and where scholars have looked beyond that country, they have been concerned primarily with issues of media/cultural imperialism, national policy, and aesthetics.[30]

In contrast, this book pays close attention to how exactly Bollywood's spatial expansion is being achieved and what business practices and strategies underpin the creation of a new scale of operations. I certainly do not wish to neglect the importance of audience practices or the role that state institutions continue to play in shaping the ways in which professionals associated with Bollywood respond to the challenges and opportunities of globalization. Rather, the objective is to build on the work of scholars who have moved past center-periphery models and notions of cultural homogenization to acknowledge the emergence of multiple centers of media production and increasingly complex patterns of media circulation. Understanding media industry dynamics calls for a focus on the changing relations between economy, culture, and space that in turn requires moving beyond theoretical and methodological frameworks that tend to privilege the national as the dominant, pregiven, and uniformly imagined framework and scale of analysis.

In particular, I draw inspiration from Serra Tinic and Michael Curtin who have brought insights from political economy, cultural studies, and geography to bear on the spatial dynamics of media production.[31] Examining the worlds of Canadian television and Chinese film and television, respectively, Tinic and Curtin have developed detailed analyses of the forces that led to the emergence of cities like Vancouver and Hong Kong as key nodes or "switching points" for flows of capital and labor. More broadly, they demonstrate that the dynamics of media production in these locations are defined by complex articulations of finance, state policy, technological advances, the built environment, media policy, the desires and ambitions of media moguls, migration patterns, and audience practices that cannot be grasped through a macrolevel political economy approach. Without a doubt, an account of the structural and regulatory foundations upon which media industries in such cities rest would be crucial, as would details of media ownership. However, such an approach would not foreground issues of industrial identity and work at the level of the everyday or, for that matter, spaces such as industry conventions where various imaginations of the "national," "global," and "diasporic" come into play. The challenge, as Curtin suggests, is to capture the ways in which media capitals like Bombay are now "bound up in a web of relations that exist at the local, regional, and global levels, as well as the national level."[32]

To be sure, there are a number of particularities to Bollywood that need to be elaborated: the history of state-cinema relations; shifts from a "national development"-oriented and state-run broadcasting sector to an advertising-based, decidedly commercial and consumerist television industry; the sheer pace of media transitions (the emergence of satellite television, Internet, and mobile phones in a span of ten to fifteen years); vibrant "pirate networks," and so on. Building on ethnographic and historical work on market cultures in South Asia, I show that media industries in formation like Bollywood do not fit neatly within dominant narratives of post-Fordist modes of capital accumulation, deterritorialization, and media production and circulation.[33] Arjun Appadurai's observation that cities like Bombay are characterized by "disjunct, yet adjacent histories and temporalities," where "Fordist manufacture, craft and artisanal production, service economies involving law, leisure, finance, biotechnology, and banking and virtual economies involving global finance capital and local stock markets live in an uneasy mix," is an appropriate description of the uneven, incomplete, and seemingly contradictory nature of Bombay cinema's refashioning as Bollywood.[34] Consider the inaugural session of FRAMES 2009, a media convention organized by the Federation of Indian Chambers of Commerce and Industry (FICCI) and held in Bombay over a span of three days (February 21–23).

Organized in collaboration with the U.S. Department of Commerce, FRAMES 2009 brought together nearly three thousand individuals—media executives, directors and producers, policymakers, bureaucrats, and others involved with the media industries—from over twenty countries. Held annually since the year 2000, the overarching goal for this tenth edition of the FRAMES convention was to "celebrate a decade" of the corporatization and globalization of Bollywood. However, with the worldwide financial crisis looming large over the gathering, the celebration was a bit subdued. Every speaker at the inaugural session felt compelled to remind the audience that the media and entertainment industries were not recession-proof. At the same time, these prominent government and industry figures also framed the downturn as a brief interval in what was otherwise a smooth and at times spectacular period of transformation and growth for Bollywood. This framing narrative was further reinforced with the official release of the Media and Entertainment Industry Report prepared by the consultancy firm KPMG, entitled "In the interval . . . But ready for the next act." But this narrative, which elided the complex manner in which the Bombay film industry's transformation into Bollywood had unfolded over the past decade, could not be sustained even during the inaugural session.

The second speaker to address the gathering was Yash Chopra, cochairman of the FICCI Entertainment Committee. Chopra is also one of the most prominent and influential producer-directors in Bollywood who has, with his son Aditya Chopra's assistance, transformed his production company into a powerful family-owned studio that now has stakes in film production, film distribution, home entertainment, television, and music (Yash Raj Films). A few minutes into his address, after exhorting everyone in the media and entertainment industries to consider the economic downturn as an opportunity to reflect on their business practices, Chopra announced that he wanted to invite "a very, very talented writer, producer and director, someone who is like a son to me . . . Karan Johar, onto the stage." And to thunderous applause from the audience, Chopra declared: "Karan, who is very dear to me, will from today serve as co-chairman of the FICCI Entertainment Committee along with me and Kunal Dasgupta." Karan Johar represents another powerful family in Bollywood. He has also, since 2000, refashioned a small-scale production company that his father had established in 1976 into a "corporatized" set up (Dharma Productions). Thanking "Yash Uncle" and touching his feet in a gesture of respect, Karan Johar went on to remark that his father, producer-director Yash Johar, had always dreamed of a platform like FICCI-FRAMES, an organization that could "put Indian entertainment on the global map."

Yash Chopra's presence on this stage and Karan Johar's induction into FICCI were striking reminders to everyone present of the enduring power of long-standing social and kinship relationships in the Bombay film industry and, equally important, the creative ways in which small-scale, family-run businesses have responded to changes in the global media landscape and calls for corporatization. For all their confidence in market cycles, risk management techniques, and Hollywood-style film marketing, corporate executives had come to acknowledge, if only grudgingly, that established family-run companies had considerable experience in gauging audience tastes and expectations. By the same token, prominent figures like Yash Chopra had been pointing out over the past few years that corporatization had led to greater transparency and changes in business practices. Every panel at FRAMES 2009 that I attended featured interactions between representatives of large media corporations (including Hollywood studios) and producers who were grappling with the challenges of transforming their family-run businesses, production cultures, and outlooks to fit visions of a corporatized media industry.

Such interactions suggest that processes of corporatization and the emergence of new circuits of global capital in Bombay did not result in the delegitimization of existing relations of media production or kinship-based capitalist networks more generally. In fact, the influence that small-scale and family-owned production companies wield in Bollywood indicates novel social and institutional arrangements and adaptations that theories of media globalization have yet to take into account. As I show in chapter 2, positing the world of kinship-based media production as a domain opposed to and incommensurable with an industrialized and purportedly rational model fails to account for the kinds of exchanges and relationships upon which Bollywood's production dynamics rest. But this does not imply documenting a set of practices that are somehow essentially *Indian*. The more relevant task remains, as Kajri Jain observes in her study of the production and circulation of calendar images in India, accounting for the "distinctive character that . . . capitalist networks take on through being forged in articulation with existing economic, political, and social formations."[35] Steering clear of narratives of homogenization and, at the other extreme, celebrations of local difference, this book thus aims to develop a nuanced account of relations between capital, space, and cultural production as they play out in Bollywood.

In doing so, it joins a growing body of literature that decenters Hollywood to highlight new directions and patterns of media circulation that define our world today. To be sure, this is not simply a question of assessing the *extent* of Bombay, Hong Kong, or Seoul's global reach. Media capital, as Curtin reminds us, is a "relational concept, not simply an acknowledgment of dominance."[36] In other words, we need to analyze the reconfiguration of the Bombay film industry's spatial reach while maintaining an awareness of how established centers like Hollywood respond to and reflect on their own position in the midst of considerable social, technological, and institutional change. Consider, for instance, this image that appeared in the *Wall Street Journal* in 2008.

The image accompanied an article that provided a survey of Hollywood's changing relations with India, and focused in particular on a recent deal between the Bombay-based company Reliance Entertainment and the Hollywood company DreamWorks SKG. Reliance Entertainment's investment of $500 million allowed DreamWorks, led by Steven Spielberg, to leave Viacom's Paramount Pictures and launch a new venture. As the story noted, for Hollywood studios struggling to raise finances in the midst of a major economic crisis, pursuing opportunities in India seemed to make sense.[37] It was to be a new beginning.

It was only fitting, then, that the new figure occupying the director's seat was a twenty-first-century incarnation of Lord Ganesha, the androgynous, light-skinned, four-armed Hindu god who is typically invoked to bless new

An image that captures Hollywood's anxieties and the emergence of Bombay as a global media capital.

ventures and remove obstacles. However, this incarnation of Lord Ganesha suggests more than just the act of seeking blessings for a new beginning. Let's take a closer look, then, beginning with the body of the new deity whom I shall name, at the risk of incurring his wrath, Anilesha, after the CEO of Reliance Entertainment Mr. Anil Ambani.

In keeping with the times, Anilesha, as we can see, has cast aside the trident and the small axe in favor of the more modern and task-appropriate mobile phone and the megaphone. The lotus remains in place, as does the other hand held up to bless devotees. The plush throne and cushions apart, he is also more austere and understated, leaving behind the intricately designed headgear (*mukut*), necklaces, rings, and gold-embroidered (*zari*) lower-body garment (*dhoti*) for a few tasteful bracelets and a simple, almost Buddha-like ochre robe. One must not, after all, offend the sensibilities of devotees struggling in a harsh economic climate. And perhaps as a sign of affection toward Steven Spielberg, surely his most ardent devotee now, Anilesha too wears a sports cap. A closer look at his lips, hands, and feet suggest delicate features and perhaps even a certain degree of androgyny, which is not surprising given the long history of Indian men being rendered effeminate in colonial discourse or, for that matter, in American film and television.[38] The plate of sweets and other offerings have been replaced by a film reel and pictures of

Hollywood and Bollywood stars Sylvester Stallone, Mallika Sherawat, and Tom Hanks strewn about. And it is probably safe to assume that Anilesha now has many other stars' phone numbers on speed dial. But the biggest and arguably most significant difference that sets Anilesha apart from Ganesha is his gaze. Looking askance, behind dark glasses, Anilesha refuses to exchange looks with the readers of the *Wall Street Journal*.

At one level, it is possible to interpret this image as a telling expression of Hollywood's (and America's) anxiety about a future in which it may no longer hold the pursestrings or, even more ominously, remain in the director's seat. It is simply too wrenching to gaze into the eyes of a foreign deity and contemplate a multipolar media landscape. When placed in the broader context of the financial crisis and the economic recession in the United States, such an interpretation would not be far off the mark. At the same time, it is difficult to completely ignore other ideas that this image mobilizes. Anilesha could also be seen as an effeminate and nonthreatening figure who could easily be displaced in the near future should Viacom or some other media conglomerate come courting Spielberg again. Let us also not forget that Hollywood and American culture have dealt with such anxieties in the past. During the 1980s and early 1990s, the acquisition of American businesses by Japanese conglomerates like Sony and Matsushita sparked discussions about foreign influence, especially when it came to the cultural industries, and led to protectionist measures that imposed limits on foreign ownership in the media and communication sectors.[39] The director's chair could be moved, as it were, from this throne to another.

However, if we were to set aside Hollywood's anxiety, a different set of possibilities emerges. Does Anilesha really care about presiding over Hollywood? Perhaps he regards the deal with DreamWorks more as an opportunity that allows him to expand his own company's sphere of influence and in the process strengthen his position in Bombay. Rajesh Sawhney, the president of Reliance Big Entertainment, the division that brokered the deal with DreamWorks, is on record saying: "If you have global ambitions, then Hollywood is the right starting point."[40] But while this deal garnered all the media attention, it is worth noting that it was part of a much larger gambit. At least eight months before initiating talks with Spielberg and co., Reliance Entertainment bought stakes in Phoenix Theatres, a Knoxville (Tennessee)-based film management company, acquired a chain of 250 theaters across the United States, bought a Burbank (California)-based postproduction unit called Lowry Digital Images, and also expanded into Malaysia with the goal of targeting not only the Indian diaspora beyond the Anglo American centers but also other Asian audiences.[41]

Without a doubt, the image above does speak to the influence that Hollywood continues to exert on cultural policy, production practices, and, more broadly, Bombay-based media industries' imaginations of "going global" since the early 1990s. And given the long and complex history of the Bombay film industry looking toward Hollywood, it is not surprising that recent changes in the Bombay film industry have also been inspired, certainly in rhetorical terms if not in practice, by Hollywood.[42] On the other hand, Reliance Entertainment's moves over the past few years also indicate that it would be a mistake to characterize Bollywood's relationship with Hollywood as one of mere imitation. In the image above, Anilesha is positioned behind the spotlights and the action, looking away, calm and detached. Is Hollywood now merely another locale of media production for deities like Anilesha? Perhaps Anilesha's strategic moves over the past few years can also be read as a striking assertion of Bombay's reinvention as a media capital with global reach and ambitions and, by the same token, a clear sign that Hollywood's position as the preeminent center of transnational media flows can no longer be presumed. It is this complex and ongoing transition in the global media landscape at the turn of the twenty-first century that this book tackles.

Sites, Access, and Limits: A Note on Studying Emergent Media

In recent years a growing number of scholars have turned their attention to the media industries and their production cultures and, in the process, to questions of methodology in general and ethnographic approaches in particular. Recently published anthologies, including *Media Industries: History, Theory, and Method* and *Production Studies: Cultural Studies of Media Industries*, have been immensely valuable in bringing together essays that draw on a range of disciplines to reflect on problems unique to the study of media industries.[43] In addition to the question of access to various sites within the world of media production, there is also the vexing problem of analyzing and representing industry practices, given the self-reflexivity that marks media industries today. These and other concerns have been most clearly elaborated in John Caldwell's ethnography of film and television industry professionals in Los Angeles.[44]

Indeed, one way to describe my own approach here would be in terms of what Caldwell calls an "integrated cultural-industrial method of analysis" that involves examining "data from four registers or modes of analysis: textual analysis of trade and worker artifacts; interviews with film/television workers; ethnographic field observation of production spaces and professional gatherings; and economic/industrial analysis."[45] But this book is also a multisited and transnational ethnography, given the multiple sites that I map and analyze. This does not simply mean, as George Marcus and Michael Fischer argue, an increase in the number of sites that one observes.[46] Rather, it is to recognize the difficulties of defining a particular field site for understanding the operations of media industries like Bollywood. It also involves being attuned to how each site—an industry convention such as FICCI-FRAMES, for example—is embedded within and shaped by larger economic, political, and cultural systems. In this book, this has meant moving across national spaces (India and the United States) and media spaces (film, television, advertising and marketing, and digital media companies).

The chapters that follow thus draw on in-depth interviews with a range of media industry professionals, participant observation in various production settings as well as industry conventions, and textual materials (largely unexamined trade-press sources such as *TV and Video World*, and industry artifacts such as press kits and materials circulated at industry conventions). I read all these materials critically and in relation to one another, attentive to the relationship between the production of press kits and media journalists' coverage of industry-related topics (particularly writers at trade magazines), and aware of the risks and limitations of interviews with industry professionals, particularly high-level executives.[47] This involves, as Caldwell writes, keeping these different research materials "in check" by "placing the discourses and results of any one register in critical tension or dialogue with the others."[48]

Further, studying the media industries in a context where access to industry archives and trade artifacts remains limited meant developing a few industry contacts and relying on them to establish more connections and to gain access to various sites in Bombay and New Delhi. Not surprisingly, I had a range of experiences in various media companies and with different industry professionals. In some instances, it became clear that the people I was speaking with were not willing to offer anything more than what one could glean from the PR materials that their companies had developed. In other cases, my initial conversation led to subsequent meetings and invitations to spend as many days as I would like observing production practices, attending staff meetings, and so on. Differences in levels of openness notwithstanding, it is worth mentioning that gaining access to a range of sites in Bombay—sets of films and television shows in production, staff meetings at a dot-com company, publicity events for films, and so on—as well as across different levels of the media industries (executives, middle-management, and entrepreneurs) was not as fraught as it may have been in, say, Hollywood.

These issues of access and openness played out very differently, however, as my "field" expanded beyond Bombay and New Delhi to include the worlds of diasporic media professionals in the United States. My analysis of the role that diasporic media entrepreneurs in cities like New York and Los Angeles play in reconfiguring Bollywood's sphere of operations is based, therefore, on in-depth interviews and participant observation at publicity events as well as key industry conventions such as the one organized by the South Asians in Media and Marketing Association (SAMMA-Summit).

In general, "studying up" did not pose the kinds of issues that Sherry Ortner, for instance, describes in her account of the challenges of conducting ethnographic research in Hollywood.[49] At the same time, I should acknowledge that for the most part, my research in different sites in the film, television, and dot-com sectors in India involved spending time with people who are, as Ortner points out based on her experiences in Hollywood, "really not much different from anthropologists and academics more generally."[50] After all, given that my research focus was on industry logics and practices as they related to Bollywood's emergence as a global media industry, a majority of my interactions were with "above the line" professionals.

I offer this brief account of my research experience partly to draw attention to the challenges involved in speaking with and representing subjects who are, as Vicki Mayer and others point out, "usually charged with representing us."[51] But my other objective is to make clear that what this book offers is a set of grounded but partial and situated perspectives on the transformation of the Bombay film industry into Bollywood. What Bollywood is, its political, economic, and cultural significance, its organization and structure, evolving production culture(s), the redefinition of film form and genres that accompanies and shapes industrial shifts and so on, is far from settled. Bollywood is an emergent cultural-industrial formation, and the challenge that I take up in this book is to craft a narrative of industrial transformation that is nevertheless attuned to and informed by other sites and dimensions of change.

Structure and Chapter Overviews

Chapter 1, "Bollywood Is Useful: Media Industries and the State in an Era of Reform," traces the sociocultural and political transformations in India that set the stage for the reimagination of the Bombay film industry as Bollywood. Building on George Yudice's argument that "there is an expedient relation between globalization and culture in the sense that there is a fit or a *suitability* between them," this chapter elaborates how the fit between globalization

and the cultural industries was worked out in the Indian context and specifically, posed as a problem of cleaning up and "corporatizing" the Bombay film
industry.[52] In particular, I focus on links between the state and the Indian
diaspora, redefinitions of citizenship and the boundaries of the "national
family," and Bollywood's mediation of these shifts. Through a close, thematic
reading of *Kabhi Khushi Kabhie Gham* (Happiness and Sorrow, 2001, Karan
Johar) and other diaspora-centric Bollywood films, I argue that this moment
of reform needs to be understood in relation to a range of other reforms
undertaken and negotiated by the state, and as part of the redefinition of the
nation-space in an era of globalization. The ongoing struggle over corporatization in Bollywood needs to be understood, this chapter suggests, as a
response to a wide-ranging spatial crisis involving the nation-state, the film
industry, and the city of Bombay in a period of rapid and profoundly uneven
political, economic, and cultural shifts. I show how the state's decision to reimagine its relations with the media industries and indeed, the very idea of
creating and defining Bollywood as a global media industry, was shaped by
a political discourse of cleaning/cleansing that played out at urban, regional,
national, and diasporic scales throughout the 1990s as India embarked on a
program of economic liberalization.

Chapter 2, "Staging Bollywood: Industrial Identity in an Era of Reform,"
begins by considering the ellipsis in the title of the KPMG report—*In the
interval . . . But ready for the next act*—as indexing a complicated and evolving terrain of media production, one marked as much by unpredictability
as by a sense of certainty regarding the "next act." I draw on my experiences and observations at FRAMES 2009 to complicate the official narrative in which the notion of an interval is understood as nothing more than
an interruption and, more crucially, that the "next act" was readily imaginable. Focusing attention on this moment of celebration opens up an opportunity to consider the entire decade—from 1998, when the government
granted "industry" status to Bombay cinema, until 2009—as a formative
interval. One of the major consequences of corporatization, I argue, is a
terrain marked on the one hand by small-scale (often family-owned) companies rearticulating their industrial identities and, on the other hand, large
corporations that have entered the film business only to find themselves
contending with the limits of corporate logics in the Bombay film world.
Drawing on panel discussions, various artifacts circulating at the convention, and trade-press coverage of the convention and this period of transition, this chapter outlines how Bollywood is being shaped by a productive,
if at times uneasy, coexistence of heterogeneous capitalist practices defined
as much by kinship networks and interpersonal relations as by modes of

speculation and practices of risk management that Hollywood has rendered globally recognizable.

Chapter 3, "'It's All about Knowing Your Audience': Marketing and Promotions in Bollywood," further develops the analysis of changing industry structures by focusing on the emergence of marketing and promotions as a key domain in Bollywood. Drawing on in-depth interviews with marketing executives and public relations agents in Bombay, I show how the phenomenal growth of the television and advertising industries during the 1990s and the related loss of a readily imagined "national audience" led to the emergence of marketing as a site of knowledge and decision-making power in Bollywood and, moreover, altered how the audience was imagined and constructed. Historicizing the relationship between the film and television industries, I argue that ongoing changes in the domain of film marketing are emblematic of broader reconfigurations of relations between capital, circuits of information, and forms of knowledge (in this instance, regarding the audience) in Bombay's media world. In a period defined by extraordinary technological, financial, and organizational flux, marketing and promotions emerged as practices that allowed the film industry to negotiate the transition to new circuits of capital that had redefined Bombay's media world throughout the 1990s and early 2000s.

However, television and marketing professionals working in Bombay were not in a position to shape Bollywood's relationship with overseas markets. Shifting attention to the emergence of dot-com companies during the late 1990s and early 2000s, chapter 4, "'Multiplex with Unlimited Seats': Dot-Coms and the Making of an Overseas Territory," analyzes how dot-com companies mediated Bollywood's imagination of an overseas audience. Building on the analysis of film-television relations in the previous chapter and tracing changes in the structure of film distribution and exhibition, I demonstrate how dot-com companies positioned themselves as "knowledge brokers" who could reconfigure a geographically vast yet vaguely understood overseas territory into a well-defined Non-Resident Indian (NRI) audience. Asserting their value in both aspirational (the Web as an index of globality) and strategic terms (the need to know NRIs), dot-com companies played a crucial role in the broader project of reshaping Bollywood's geography of operations by positioning the media industry as capable of imagining and institutionalizing an overseas audience.

While chapter 3 draws attention to issues of hype and speculation in an environment in which a proliferation of screens and platforms as well as new sources of capital have forced media producers to look beyond the box office as the primary site for imagining the audience and hence profitability, chapter 4 focuses on the dynamic relation between the expansion of capital into new territories and the work of rendering those new territories more imaginable. As we will see, what Bollywood got was a very limited "spatial fix" as dot-com companies interpreted and resolved the problem of space—of imagining the overseas territory—in terms of overseas audiences' cultural temporality with the nation. Furthermore, the story of Bollywood's relationship with overseas audiences is not only about Bombay-based professionals' imaginations of a multiplex with unlimited seats. Over the past two decades, Bollywood's cultural geography has been transformed by the efforts of diasporic media entrepreneurs in diverse locations worldwide. The next chapter thus shifts focus to map and analyze the role played by diasporic media professionals in rearticulating Bollywood's imagination of overseas territories.

Outlining the changing dynamics of migration, the politics of multiculturalism, and relations between "home" and "diaspora" since the mid-1990s, chapter 5, "'It's Not Your Dad's Bollywood': Diasporic Entrepreneurs and the Allure of Digital Media," begins by tracing changes in the South Asian American mediascape from grassroots- and community-managed media production, particularly the use of public access television, to the entry and dominance of India-based television channels like ZEE and Star TV, and finally the launch and failure of MTV-Desi, a niche television channel for South Asian American youth. I relate MTV-Desi in particular to efforts by advertising and marketing professionals to construct South Asian Americans as an untapped and lucrative consumer demographic over the past decade. While the intersections of South Asian cultural production and American public culture can be traced through the work of artists like DJ Rekha and subcultures in cities like New York, Chicago, and Los Angeles, media companies' interest in this hitherto marginalized community was sparked in part by the results of the 2000 U.S. census which revealed that the median household income for South Asian families was $64,000. In much the same way that advertisers and marketers worked to commodify Latinos during the 1990s, companies such as *Ethnik PR* and *Evershine Group* took on the task of constructing a Desi demographic. In relation to this marketing logic, I examine television channels' programming, marketing, and distribution strategies to illustrate how they remain caught up in a discourse of long-distance nationalism, and in the process fail to respond to the particularities of diasporic youth culture. This analysis of the limits of television as a medium for reconfiguring Bollywood's geographic reach, especially as it pertains to a vast, networked, and diverse youth culture, informs my analysis of digital media initiatives.

In the second part of this chapter, I describe the emergence of Saavn.com, a digital media company that has emerged as one of the most prominent nodes in the circulation of Bollywood films and film music as a way to understand the challenges faced by media producers and cultural critics in imagining and mobilizing diasporic audiences in an era of increasing global connectivity. I analyze the ways in which this digital media company has leveraged ties in India and the U.S. to respond to the transcultural nature of contemporary diasporic culture and, in the process, established new trajectories of circulation for Bollywood that are overlooked by professionals working primarily in Bombay. This chapter thus reflects on what it takes to conjure the diaspora as a viable scale of media production and circulation in a terrain defined not only by changing relations between Bombay and Los Angeles but perhaps more crucially, by informal and grassroots networks of media circulation and mobile social networks that commercial media ventures find nearly impossible to match in scale and scope.

In the concluding chapter, "Fandom and Other Transnational Futures," I begin by reflecting on how a focus on industrial change and ongoing shifts in Bollywood's presence in the world speaks to broader issues of relationships between geography, cultural production, and cultural identity. I then shift attention to the ways in which Bollywood's cultural geography has also been shaped by the work of media users who circulate and engage with Bollywood content in ways that transcend the traditional boundaries of the nation-state, linguistic barriers, and market segments imagined by industry professionals. Plugged into and in many instances defined by a world encircling pirate infrastructure, fan practices forge trajectories of media circulation that challenge industry discourses of illegality as well as scholarly paradigms for understanding global media cultures. Presenting an example of participatory culture surrounding Bollywood—a fan community that has cohered around the renowned music director A. R. Rahman—I outline the implications of focusing on participatory cultures for our understanding of the spatial logics and politics of media globalization.

1

Bollywood Is Useful

Media Industries and the State in an Era of Reform

Held in the "grand ballroom" of the five-star Renaissance Hotel in suburban Bombay, the inauguration of the FICCI-FRAMES 2009 convention was
a lavish affair that opened with Amit Mitra, the Secretary-General of FICCI,
inviting the Minister of State for Information & Broadcasting and External
Affairs, Anand Sharma, on to the stage to light a lamp—a widely practiced
ritual to begin an event on an auspicious note. As the ritual came to a close,
Mitra invited five others to join the minister on the stage: Sushma Singh, Secretary, Ministry of Information & Broadcasting; Yash Chopra, legendary film
producer and director, head of the powerful family-owned studio Yash Raj
Films, and chairman of the FICCI Entertainment Committee; Kunal Dasgupta, CEO of Sony Entertainment Network and co-chairman of the FICCI
Entertainment Committee; Amit Khanna, Chairman of Reliance Entertainment and chair of the FICCI Convergence Committee; and Donald Whiteside, Vice President and Director of Global Public Policy, Intel Corporation.
And as I mentioned in the previous chapter, a few minutes into his address,
Yash Chopra proceeded to invite Karan Johar, another influential producer-
director in Bollywood, to join him on stage.

The prominence granted to Anand Sharma and Sushma Singh from
the Ministry of Information & Broadcasting was not surprising given the
remarkable shifts in state policy toward the media industries in general
and the Bombay-based Hindi film industry in particular. Yash Chopra and
Karan Johar's presence seemed appropriate as well. After all, their films—
Dilwale Dulhania Le Jayenge (The Big-Hearted Will Take the Bride, Aditya
Chopra, 1995) and *Kabhi Khushi Kabhie Gham* (Happiness and Sorrow,
Karan Johar, 2001)—had played such a crucial role in reimagining relations
between India and the diaspora as well as establishing the overseas territory
as a lucrative market for Bollywood. Further, the importance accorded to
these two personalities also spoke to the influence that family businesses
and kinship-based networks of media production and circulation wielded
in Bollywood.

In sharp contrast to the exception that Chopra and Johar seemed to personify was Amit Khanna. A media entrepreneur with over two decades' experience in the film and television industries in Bombay, Khanna is currently chairman of Reliance Entertainment, a media conglomerate that is shaping Bollywood's transnational imprint in important ways. Khanna has also served as the chairman of the Convergence Committee within FICCI, a group that focuses on emerging media technologies and platforms. Seated beside Khanna was Donald Whiteside, an executive from Intel Corporation who was leading a U.S. delegation to the convention on behalf of the US India Business Council (USIBC). Finally, bringing these industry and government figures together was Amit Mitra from FICCI. Established in 1927, FICCI is a colonial-era institution that represents the interests of Indian businesses across a range of sectors. Since the mid-1990s FICCI has played a crucial role in mediating ties between the Indian government and the media industries and, most importantly, in assembling a Media and Entertainment sector with Bollywood at the center. Taken together, the people assembled on stage at the inauguration of the tenth anniversary of the FICCI-FRAMES convention represented the different sites and interests that had played pivotal roles in the production of Bollywood as a global media industry.

This chapter traces how these various relations between the state, the media industries, and institutions such as FICCI and the Confederation of Indian Industry (CII) were forged, and situates them within a broader set of sociocultural and political transformations that set the stage for the reconfiguration of the Bombay film industry as Bollywood. Building on George Yudice's observation that "there is an expedient relation between globalization and culture in the sense that there is a fit or a suitability between them," this chapter elaborates how the fit between globalization and the cultural industries was worked out in the Indian context and specifically, posed as a problem of cleaning up and corporatizing the Bombay film industry.[1] I begin with an analysis of links between the nation-state and the diaspora, redefinitions of citizenship, and Bombay cinema's mediation of these shifts to show that the state's efforts to manage the cultural industries is part of a larger process of managing a wide-ranging set of spatial crises engendered by processes of economic liberalization and globalization. As Leela Fernandes and others have shown, economic reforms enacted by the Indian state during the early 1990s resulted in a profoundly uneven restructuring of urban space, a process that was oriented primarily toward the needs and desires of a new and highly visible middle class.[2] Focusing on Bombay, Fernandes also argues that a politics of "spatial purification" and a range of movements to "cleanse spaces of the poor and working classes" accompanied new claims on urban space.³ Building on these insights, I show how changes in state policies toward the media and entertainment industries and indeed, the very idea of creating and defining Bollywood as a global media industry, was shaped by a broader political discourse of cleaning and cleansing (*safai*) that played out at urban, national, and diasporic scales throughout the 1990s and 2000s.

Reforming the National Family

In an essay titled "The Diaspora in Indian Culture," Amitav Ghosh writes of an "epic relationship" between India and the diaspora to emphasize the "tremendously historical and imaginative nature of diasporic belonging."⁴ To speak of the "Indian diaspora," then, is to take into account indentured laborers who left India to work as coolies on sugar plantations in countries such as Fiji and Guyana during the colonial era, immigrants in oil-rich Gulf nations, the more recent wave of high-tech migrants to locales such as the Silicon Valley in the United States, and so on.⁵ However, despite what is a long history of travel and migration, it is only since the late 1980s that expatriate Indians have begun attracting attention. In fact, for nearly four decades after independence, the Non-Resident Indian (NRI) was inscribed in the Indian imagination as someone who had betrayed the nation to seek better fortunes elsewhere. Positioned squarely within a narrative of brain drain, the NRI was, until recently, "not really Indian." As Sinha-Kerkhoff and Bal point out, unlike Gandhi, who had seen overseas Indians as integral to anticolonial struggles, Nehru believed that "expatriate Indians had forfeited their Indian citizenship and identity by moving abroad and did not need the support of their mother country."⁶ In the Nehruvian imagination, the "national family" was territorially bound. This was reflected very directly in official policy as well, as the following quote makes clear:

> It is the consistent policy of the government that persons of Indian origin who have taken foreign nationality should identify themselves with and integrate in the mainstream of social and political life of the country of their domicile. The government naturally remains alive to their interests and general welfare and encourages cultural contacts with them. As far as Indian citizens residing abroad are concerned, they are the responsibility of the government of India.⁷

It is important to note that there was considerable opposition to Nehru's views. Right-wing groups such as the Vishwa Hindu Parishad (Global Hindu Council), which was formed during the 1960s with the goal of organizing

Hindus on a global scale, characterized Nehru's policies toward expatriate Indians as "confused, erratic and apathetic."[8] As early as 1977, when the Janata Party held power in New Delhi for a brief period of two years, Atal Bihari Vajpayee, who was the Minister of External Affairs at the time, declared: "India would never disown overseas Indians, or fail to appreciate their loyalty to the motherland."[9] The ruling Janata Party attempted to reframe India's relationship with the diaspora through a number of formal and informal initiatives—sponsoring seminars on overseas Indians, exploring the viability of establishing a department that would deal exclusively with the affairs of overseas Indians, introducing new laws to allow overseas Indians to return to India even if they held citizenship elsewhere, and so on. None of this, however, made any significant impact until the late 1980s and early 1990s when India's gradual integration into the global market economy was set in motion. Several scholars have shown that the program of structural adjustment and economic liberalization that successive Indian governments undertook during the 1990s was not just a matter of reframing economic policies. These structural changes also opened up, as Aditya Nigam observes, "immense imaginative possibilities for the new elite imagination of a deterritorialised global nation."[10] He writes:

> In the vision of this "global nation," those who went away were no longer to be seen as traitors. They were the resources that the nation, now preparing to move into the brave new world, could profitably utilize. They had state-of-the-art skills, knowledge and capital to invest in the new areas that needed to be rapidly developed. Enter, therefore, the ubiquitous figure of the NRI—the privileged citizen of this global nation.[11]

While this transition in the cultural and political elites' imagination of a deterritorialized national family began during the 1980s with Prime Minister Rajiv Gandhi inviting diasporic entrepreneurs like Sam Pitroda to guide India's march into the twenty-first century by capitalizing on the "microchip and communications revolution," it was only during the late 1990s when the right-wing Bharatiya Janata Party (BJP) came to power that the state began forging ties with the diaspora in aggressive fashion.[12] Refashioning India's relationship with the diaspora, particularly with wealthy first-world expatriates in countries such as the United States and England, was a key element of the BJP's agenda for governance. In a document titled "Foreign Policy Agenda for the Future," this objective was clearly articulated: "The people of Indian origin living abroad are an asset, which the BJP would try to utilize to the fullest extent to foster relations of friendship and cooperation between the countries of their residence and India. The BJP will seriously examine the question of dual citizenship to NRIs."[13] In September 2000, the BJP government appointed a High Level Committee under the chairmanship of L. M. Singhvi, an MP who had served as High Commissioner to the U.K. and was regarded as someone familiar with issues relating to the Indian diaspora. The committee had a clear mandate: to conduct a "comprehensive study of the global Indian diaspora" and to "recommend measures for a constructive relationship with them."[14] Redefining the NRI as a Person of Indian Origin (PIO), the BJP government went on to declare a few years later:

> We believe that the vast community of NRIs and PIOs also constitute a part of the *Great Indian Family*. We should endeavour to continually strengthen their social, cultural, economic and emotional ties with their mother country. They are a rich reservoir of intellectual, managerial and entrepreneurial resources. The government should devise innovative schemes to facilitate the investment of these resources for India's all-round development (my emphasis).[15]

The BJP government also followed the Singhvi report's recommendation to organize an annual event that would celebrate the nation's relationship with its diaspora, and serve to strengthen cultural ties. In 2003, the Ministry of External Affairs and the Federation of Indian Chambers of Commerce and Industry (FICCI) jointly organized the first ever Pravasi Bharatiya Divas (The Day of the Diaspora). Held during the month of January, this event hoped "to bring the Indian family from all over the world together . . . and to acquaint the Indian people with the achievements of the Indian diaspora and to use them as a bridge to strengthen relationships between India and the host countries in this age of globalization."[16] Attracting individuals from over sixty different countries, the extravagant event was billed as "the largest ever gathering of the *global Indian family* (my emphasis)."[17] It was, as Bakirathi Mani and Latha Varadarajan note, "a striking example of the new historical, political, and cultural relationship between the Indian state and diasporic populations in the early twenty-first century . . . and crucial to the reimagination of the postcolonial Indian state and constitutive of India's place in a neoliberal global order."[18]

How does this transition in state-diaspora ties and the reimagination of the figure of the NRI as pivotal to India's fortunes in a global economy relate to what Ashish Rajadhyaksha terms the "Bollywoodization of Indian cinema"?[19] There are two interrelated developments that need to be elaborated: first, Bombay cinema's role in mediating changing relations between India and the diaspora; and second, the crisis in the Bombay film industry, particularly regarding financing, and the state's decision to intervene. Let me turn, then, to NRI-centric Hindi-language films and the ways in which Bombay-based producers and directors imagined the NRI figure and represented the "global Indian family."

"From Bihar to Manhattan": Bombay Cinema and the Global Indian Family

In June 2003 I received an invitation to attend the publicity event for Rajshri Productions's *Main Prem Ki Diwani Hoon* (I'm Crazy about Prem, dir. Sooraj Barjatya, 2003) in New York City. The email invitation, extended by a friend whose family lived next door to the Barjatyas in Bombay, explained that the event was part of Rajshri Productions's marketing and promotions strategy and was designed to give journalists and film critics in the United States a glimpse of the film before its worldwide release. Given Rajshri Productions' reputation as having reintroduced the "family film" in India with box-office hits such as *Maine Pyar Kiya* (I Fell in Love, 1989), *Hum Aapke Hain Kaun. . !* (What Do I Mean to You? 1995), and *Hum Saath Saath Hain* (We Are Together, 1997), these films' enduring popularity in India and among diasporic audiences, and Rajshri's position as one of the first production companies to have developed innovative strategies to market their films, I was excited at the opportunity to attend the event and perhaps even ask the marketing manager, Rajat Barjatya, a few questions.[20]

The event, attended by well over thirty journalists, began with a screening of the trailer of *Main Prem Ki Diwani Hoon* and three song sequences from the film. This was followed by a twenty-minute session during which Rajat Barjatya fielded a range of questions about the film's plot, the stars, and the music. Throughout this question and answer session, he reminded everyone about Rajshri Productions' commitment to making "wholesome films with melodious music that the entire family could watch." Toward the end, when it was clear that the journalists and other attendees had no other questions, Barjatya announced that there was one important idea he wished to convey. Speaking softly and affecting a solemn tone, he delivered his marketing pitch:

> Everyone knows that Rajshri has made family films that appeal to viewers in every strata of society across India—north, south, east, and west. Today, we wish to appeal to families all the way from Bihar to Manhattan. *From Bihar to Manhattan, Indian families everywhere* (my emphasis).

About half an hour later, I had an opportunity to meet Rajat Barjatya and ask him to explain what he meant by saying Rajshri Productions wished to appeal to families "from Bihar to Manhattan." "If you've seen films like *Dilwale Dulhania Le Jayenge (DDLJ)*, *Pardes*, and *Kabhi Khushi Kabhie Gham (K3G)* you know exactly what I mean," he began. "Indians in America exist in two worlds. They have spent many years here and they know what it means to live in America. But they also have an Indian side, and Bollywood connects them to India. Not only do they watch Bollywood films, they perform our songs at festivals and local functions. Deep down, they are Indian. Don't you think so?" Before I could reply, he continued. "And the family in Bihar that goes to see a film like *Kabhi Khushi Kabhie Gham* knows that there are Indian families in the U.K. or the U.S., and they see that these NRI families are also Indian, deep down. They're successful, they've made it big, but they're Indian at the end of the day. That's why these films work in Bihar too. And that's what I meant when I said from Bihar to Manhattan."

Dilwale Dulhania Le Jayenge (The Brave-Hearted Will Take the Bride, 1995, Aditya Chopra), *Pardes* (Foreign Land, 1997, Subhash Ghai), and *Kabhi Khushi Kabhie Gham* (Happiness and Sorrow, 2001, Karan Johar) are all films that resonated strongly with viewers in India and abroad and count among the most successful films of the 1990s and early 2000s. These films, among several others of the same period, explored the cultural space of Non-Resident Indians in countries such as the United States, U.K., and Australia, and as Rajat Barjatya observed, affirmed that the expatriate community remained "Indian, deep down." Bombay cinema's role in mediating the newfound centrality of the diaspora, particularly the "first-world" diaspora, to India's navigation of a global economy is all the more striking given that Tamil- or Telugu-language films that also circulate worldwide, for instance, did not address diasporic communities or wrestle with the issue of reterritorializing diasporic Indians.[21] So how did Hindi films articulate this sentiment of remaining "Indian, deep down"? Let me elaborate by turning to *Kabhi Khushi Kabhie Gham (K3G)*, a film that is particularly relevant here given that its narrative marks a crucial departure from earlier efforts to recognize and represent the expatriate Indian community.

K3G is a story about an affluent Indian family: Yashvardhan "Yash" Raichand (Amitabh Bachchan), his wife Nandini (Jaya Bachchan), and their two sons, Rahul (Shahrukh Khan), who is adopted, and Rohan (Hrithik Roshan). The family splits when Rahul falls in love with and marries Anjali (Kajol), a girl from the working-class neighborhood of Chandni Chowk in Delhi, instead of marrying the girl his father had chosen. Yashvardhan disowns Rahul, and Rahul and Anjali move to London accompanied by Anjali's younger sister Pooja (Kareena Kapoor) and Rahul's nanny (Farida Jalal). A few years later, Rahul's younger brother Rohan learns about these incidents and sets out to London, taking a solemn vow to reunite the family. In London, Rohan manages to make his way into Rahul's family under an assumed name and with Pooja's help, reconciles the divided family.

K3G is no different from NRI-themed films such as *Dilwale Dulhania Le Jayenge* (*DDLJ*) and *Pardes* in its heavy-handed depictions of a patriarchal family, the upholding of conservative gender norms, and conflicts surrounding the institution of marriage. Consider, for instance, the famous sequence in *DDLJ* in which the hero (Shahrukh Khan as Raj) and heroine (Kajol as Simran), having missed their train on a trip across Western Europe, end up spending the night in a small town, with Simran swilling a bottle of cognac before falling asleep. When Simran wakes up on Raj's bed wearing his clothes, panic-stricken and unable to recall what really happened, Raj holds her close and growls: "You think I am beyond values, but I am a Hindustani, and I know what a Hindustani girl's honor (*izzat*) is worth. Trust me, nothing happened last night." Vijay Mishra recounts this scene to argue that Hindi film consumption in the diaspora speaks to first-generation Indians desperately trying to sustain a value system and inculcate the same in their children in order to set them apart from mainstream society in countries like the United States and the U.K. "These differences," Mishra writes, "are generally about tradition, continuity, family, and often, the importance given to arranged marriages."[22] Focusing on the same sequence, Uberoi and Mankekar have also argued that *DDLJ*, in spite of locating the female protagonist outside the space of the nation, does not challenge gender norms and ends up reining in female sexuality and "disciplining desire."[23] In the film, Simran refuses to marry Raj until her father gives his consent.

In *K3G*, several scenes in the Raichand family home clearly establish Yashvardhan's position as the head of the household. Once the narrative moves to London, the role that married women are expected to play in an expatriate context is also detailed in no uncertain terms. In London, Anjali is clearly responsible for maintaining an "Indian" home, including ensuring that the son is well-schooled in Indian traditions. In addition to performing an elaborate Hindu prayer (*puja*) at the crack of dawn, she is ready to serve breakfast to her husband and son. As she mills around, she begins singing a patriotic Hindi film song, chastising her son for not being attached enough to India (*mere desh ki dharti—the land of my country*, from *Upkar*, 1967). The scene borders on the comical, but Anjali's riposte to her son's indifference to all things Indian is telling. Turning to her husband, she retorts: "He's already half-English (*angrez*), don't complain to me if he becomes completely English."[24]

Such a positioning of women as the primary custodians of "Indian" culture in the diaspora is neither new nor surprising. The repositioning of women in relation to changing configurations of public/private domains can be traced to representational shifts in Bombay cinema during the 1980s. Examining changes in Bombay cinema's representations of romance and the romantic couple, Sircar has argued that the shift in Bombay cinema's love-story genre during the 1980s, coinciding with the project of economic liberalization, marked a key change in the configuration of the "Indian woman." She observes that "paralleling the 'celebrations' of the identity of the New Woman there also appeared in the media a whole spate of features asserting the continuity of traditional institutions in the new time."[25]

Jyotika Virdi, writing about Bombay cinema during this period of transition in India, also focuses her attention on the "return of the romance." Examining films such as *Qayamat Se Qayamat Tak* (From Eternity to Eternity, 1988, Mansoor Khan) and *Dil* (Heart, 1990, Indra Kumar), she reads the transition to bourgeois individualism, challenges to parental and patriarchal authority, and a change in the sites of romance (college campuses emerging as key spaces, in sharp contrast to the use of nonspecific, often foreign locales in countless Hindi films prior to this period) as indicative of larger sociocultural shifts engendered by economic liberalization. As Virdi argues, even as these films satirized "capitalism and patriarchy's imbrication in a new phase of capitalist development in India," they soon gave way to a neoconservative assertion of the "Indian family" as the site to defend against transnational forces.[26] In films such as *Hum Aapke Hain Kaun* and *Dilwale Dulhania Le Jayenge*, constructions of the "Indian woman" remain a key realm of negotiation. Once again, women are expected to participate in the nation's progress, marked now by the nation's tentative entry into a transnational economy, while simultaneously preserving all that is unique and authentic about "Indian culture."[27] Further, as several ethnographic accounts of media consumption reveal, the "synecdochic relationship between the purity/sanctity of women and the purity/sanctity of the nation" that films such as *Dilwale Dulhania Le Jayenge*, *Pardes*, and *K3G* have set in circulation is not lost on first-generation Indian immigrants.[28]

This rehearsal and testing of values, ideals, and norms becomes even more pronounced with questions concerning marriage and the family. Films like *Dilwale Dulhania Le Jayenge* and *Pardes* sought to fold the diaspora into the nation by insisting on a return to India to resolve familial conflicts, where NRIs were asked to demonstrate their cultural competence to belong in the nation. In his critique of *DDLJ*, Mishra argues that Bollywood's representation of NRI life reflects a "center-periphery understanding of the homeland-diaspora nexus in which the diaspora becomes a site of permissible (but controlled) transgressions while the homeland is the crucible of timeless dharmik virtues."[29] In a similar vein, Jyotika Virdi observes that Bombay cinema's national family, "imagined . . . over the decades through binary oppositions—the feudal vs. the modern, country vs. city, east vs. west, rural vs. urban—now pits the national against the transnational."[30] In contrast, *K3G* inaugurated a new imagination of a transnational family in which the flow of cultural elements that lent authenticity was no longer a heavy-handed one-way flow from India to its expatriate Other. In exploring and legitimizing the cultural space of expatriate Indian families, *K3G* rendered the diaspora less of a transgressive Other and more as an acceptable variant within the fold of a "global Indian family."

The Nation Seeks Its Citizens

K3G's negotiation of India's relationship with the diaspora is, as Madhava Prasad observes, related to a growing sense within India of the "relocat[ion] of what we might call the seismic center of Indian national identity somewhere in Anglo-America."[31] Hrithik Roshan's character in *K3G*, Rohan, the quintessential transnational cosmopolitan who can navigate multiple cultural spaces with consummate ease, needs to be understood in relation to this. I would argue that Rohan is, in fact, an embodiment of a "super-Indian" whose *Indianness* transcends both that of the resident and non-resident Indian.

Rohan arrives in London to the strains of a remixed version of *Vande Mataram*—a nationalist song invoked possibly to remind viewers in the diaspora and within India of the irrevocable link between the homeland and the diaspora. While billboards and storefronts of international labels and chain stores frame the first five to ten seconds of his arrival, in subsequent frames women wearing saffron-white-green (the colors of the Indian flag) *dupattas* walk by Rohan, he is greeted by a group of Bharatanatyam dancers (the preeminent classical dance form that is highly popular in the diaspora) in the middle of busy traffic intersection, and sashays down a boardwalk flanked on both sides by a bevy of white, British women also sporting clothes colored saffron, green, and white. We then see Rohan in a cybercafé, looking up a directory listing for his brother's contact information. As the address is pulled up, and the song in the background changes to *Saare Jahan Se Accha, Hindustan Hamara* (Better than any place in the universe, our India), we see Anjali folding her hands in prayer in front of her parents-in-laws' framed picture. Not only is the diasporic family rendered

In *Kabhi Khushi Kabhie Gham* (*K3G*), a surprised and overjoyed Anjali (Kajol) embraces her son after he leads his classmates in a rendition of the Indian national anthem.

inextricable from the nation, it is also an explicit acknowledgment, both to viewers in India and the diaspora, of the diaspora's abiding desire to stay in touch with India. In a subsequent scene, we witness Rohan speaking with his parents (in India) on the phone. Sporting a tricolor T-shirt, he assures his parents that he is happy to have found accommodation with an Indian family instead of staying in a hotel: "They're very nice people papa. When I met them, I felt like I have known them for years, a laughing, happy, contented family, like we used to be."

This piece of dialogue could be read not just as a reference to the rift within the Raichand family, but also as an allusion to commonly held views of NRI families struggling to define a sense of cultural identity and as a comment that India, imagined as a transnational family, is unimaginable without the diaspora. While one could point to several other instances that hint at an impending rapprochement between India and the diaspora, it is Anjali and Rahul's son Krish's performance of the Indian national anthem at a school function that serves as the pivotal event which legitimizes and mitigates the "othered" status of the diaspora's version of *Indianness*, and reconstitutes the NRI as the ideal citizen-to-be of a "global Indian family."

Having learned about Krish Raichand's participation in a school function, and Anjali's disappointment at her son not being able to sing the same songs she sang when growing up in India, Rohan decides to intervene. As Anjali, Rahul, Pooja, and the rest of the audience wait to hear Krish and his classmates sing "Do Re Mi," he steps up to the microphone, says "this one is for you, mom," and leads his classmates in a rousing rendition of the Indian national anthem. A close-up shot of the visibly moved diasporic family cuts to a long shot of the kids singing, followed by pans and cuts to different parts of a surprised but respectful audience. Anjali is reduced to tears as she runs down the aisle to embrace her son, and the background music reverts to *Vande Mataram*, finally fading into *Saare Jahan se Accha, Hindustan Hamara.*

Such sequences function both as reassurance for a vast majority of first-generation immigrants that they can live in the U.K. or the United States, yet belong and claim cultural citizenship elsewhere, and as a paradigmatic moment of India embracing the diaspora and defining the NRI as one of its own. It does not matter that Anjali's son, a second-generation Brit-Asian who has never experienced life in India, sings the national anthem with a British accent, his mispronunciation toward the end is forgotten (the anthem is completed by Anjali), and his being "half-English" is not a concern any more. Every anxiety of negotiating a sense of *Indianness* is erased in those 52 seconds that the national anthem is sung. The diaspora is no longer different and threatening. In Rajat Barjatya's words, the diaspora is "Indian, deep down."

In one respect, then, Bombay cinema's mediation of relations between India and the diaspora can be understood as having set the stage for India to remap symbolic and material relationships with the diaspora. Such a reading is useful because it allows us to locate our analysis of these narratives within a broader historical conjuncture and to grapple with the implications of the state's efforts to redefine its relationship with the diasporic community and articulate a new idea of citizenship that is, as Rajadhyaksha puts it, "explicitly delinked from the political rights of citizenship."[32] In other words, this concerns the centrality of the NRI figure and why the NRI is now, in Prasad's words, a "more stable figure of Indian identity than anything that can be found indigenously."[33] To understand this, we need to first recognize the implications that India's decision to integrate itself into a global economy held for the imagination of the nation in time and space.

In the mid-1980s, when Prime Minister Rajiv Gandhi and his team of technocrats announced that India would have to capitalize on the communications revolution and participate in the emerging information economy in order to become a key player in the twenty-first century, they were also calling for a new imagination of the nation in relation to global modernity. As Nigam points out, the notion of participating in the new information and communications revolution in order to reach the twenty-first century is "not simply the sign of a movement from a point, say, 1999, to a point 2000, in the endless duration of time . . . arriving in the 21st century meant arriving into a utopian future."[34] It is also important to note the influence that political leaders and technocrats' life experiences had on their vision of progress and development. Figures like Rajiv Gandhi, who had studied and lived abroad, and Sam Pitroda, a Chicago-based entrepreneur who played a key role in effecting changes in telecommunications policies during the 1980s, had actually "spent a large part of their lives in lands where that future was actually the present."[35] This new vision of development articulated in the mid-1980s did not just mark a decisive break from older notions of self-reliance and an abiding belief in the necessity of public sector undertakings and protectionist policies for a postcolonial, developing nation. While the Nehruvian idea of a self-reliant nation fixed the Non-Resident Indian within a narrative of brain drain, this new vision of a nation that would soon be part of a global economy included the NRI as a crucial resource.[36]

In other words, in inhabiting the space and time of the future in countries like the United States and the U.K., the NRI did not only come to be seen as someone inhabiting India's present-to-be. As someone who inhabited the time-space of global modernity and was playing a part in shaping the global information economy in sites like Silicon Valley in the United States, the NRI emerged as the model citizen-consumer who could address and bridge the disjunctures and anxieties that lay at the heart of India's efforts to participate fully in a global economy and redefine citizenship in the language of consumption. As Mazzarella has argued through an analysis of advertising campaigns in post-liberalization India, "progress through pleasure" emerged as the new "aesthetic teleology" that supplanted a developmental imagination that was defined in terms of self-sacrifice and austerity.[37]

To grasp this shift in the terms of Bombay cinema's mediation of the national family and the figure of the citizen-consumer, consider the differences between Raj Kapoor's articulation of a cosmopolitan self in a newly independent nation in *Shri 420* (1955) and that of Hrithik Roshan in *K3G*. A quintessential 1950s social film, *Shri 420* laid bare the enormous difficulties of sustaining a vision of postcolonial development while a vast majority of the population was struggling to make ends meet. In the film, Raj (played by Raj Kapoor) migrates to the city of Bombay from the town of Allahabad, is drawn into a world of deceit and dishonesty, and eventually regains his innocence and his integrity (*imaan*). In a long speech delivered toward the end of the film, Raj admits his mistakes, points out the nation's problems, and asserts that the only "solution to poverty and unemployment is courage and hard work . . . the nation's development and people's unity." Following this populist commentary, we see Raj attired in the same tattered clothes he had on when he first migrated to Bombay, and back on the very same highway he had taken to travel to the city. He begins walking away from the city and his troubles, singing the famous song:

> Mera joota hai japani, ye patloon englistani (My shoes are Japanese; these trousers are from England)
> Sar pe lal topi rusi, phir bhi dil hai Hindustani (A red Russian cap on my head, yet, my heart is Indian)

Shri 420 is, without doubt, a celebration of a cosmopolitan Indian identity but also one that links citizenship to the ideal of sacrifice and the deferral of pleasure through consumption in the interest of the overall project of "development" and nation-building. It is this contract between citizenship and consumption that has been rewritten over the last three decades in India, and which finds expression in films such as K3G where avowedly "global" NRIs affirm their belonging in the national family and demonstrate that no matter what, their *dil* remains *Hindustani* (the heart remains Indian). To consider just one instance in K3G, by teaching his "British" nephew to sing the Indian national anthem in London, Rohan soothes the anxieties of a nation worried about the diaspora's insufficient ties to India. In doing so, he bridges the spatiotemporal gap between nation and diaspora and inaugurates a new imagination of a transnational Indian family where belonging is no longer cast in the either/or language of pleasure/duty, what Mazzarella describes as a "powerfully elaborated regime of bodily self-discipline that combined the austerities of Gandhian swaraj with those of Nehruvian socialism."[38] In this new imagination of a global Indian family, belonging is defined in terms of one's willingness and cultural competence to participate in India's integration into a global economy and the consumerist vision of the nation that undergirds this transition.

These are some of the imaginative shifts in relation to which we need to situate negotiations between the state and the diaspora, Bombay cinema's role in setting the stage for these negotiations, and the state's decision to grant "industry" status to the Hindi film industry. In fact, statements from Sushma Swaraj, the Minister of Information & Broadcasting in the BJP-led government during this period, point to the fact that the importance of the legitimization of diasporic versions of Indianness by cinema is not lost on the Indian state. In a speech delivered at the Pravasi Bharatiya Divas in 2003, Swaraj drew attention to the work done by the cultural industries and Bollywood in particular in raising "awareness, as never before, about India."[39] Citing the London-based Selfridges' month-long event that involved transforming the store into a Bollywood film set, the British Film Institute's Imagine Asia festival, and screenings of Bollywood films at various film festivals, Swaraj went on to argue that "culture" was now more than just a vital economic sector. In her view, the cultural industries had played a central role in redefining relations between India and the diaspora:

> This entertainment and media explosion has brought India closer to our diaspora. More important is the fact that the diaspora has also majorly contributed in fueling this growth. *Perhaps geographical divisions between Indians in India and the Indian diaspora is blurring if not disappearing altogether* [my emphasis]. And with the announcement made by the Hon'ble Prime Minister at yesterday's inaugural session, the dual citizenship will bring the diaspora closer to us not merely due to our cultural bonds but also by a legal system.[40]

However, shifts in notions of citizenship and rearticulations of the boundaries of the "national family" do not fully explain the state's decision in the late 1990s to rethink its relationship with the media and entertainment industries. The other dimension to state-media ties concerns the material and symbolic crises facing the film industry during the 1990s, and the emergence of a discourse of "cleaning up" (*safai*) that posited corporatization as the way forward.

From Bhais (Dons) to Bankers: Cleaning Up Bombay and Its Film Industry

On May 10, 1998, at a national conference on "Challenges before Indian Cinema" held in Bombay, Sushma Swaraj announced that the government had decided to accord "industry" status to the business of filmmaking in India.[41] The justification for this policy change that the BJP-led government offered centered on the issue of financing. As Swaraj asserted:

> If you are committed to good cinema, you will have to provide good finance. By according the status of industry, we have given pictures the much-needed eligibility to seek funds from legitimate places. Thus, a semblance of order is now possible in what has been a rather confused and convoluted state of affairs.[42]

The decision was framed as an attempt to rid the film business of "black money" (untaxed and unaccounted) as well as the involvement of the mafia/ underworld. That tax-sheltered money shaped the workings of the film business came as no surprise, given that the Bombay film world has for long been a site for the investment of unreported income. Further, beginning in the mid-1990s, a series of media reports had drawn public attention to the speculation, risk, and at times, violence that marked the world of film financing in Bombay. As Sucheta Dalal, a journalist who has covered Bombay's financial world extensively, wrote in 2001:

> As many as 20 films released recently are suspected to have been financed by the underworld don, Chhota Shakeel, who allegedly forced film stars into signing movies and rescheduling their shooting dates, he told PTI here. Since the arrest of Mr. Nazim Rizvi, producer of the unreleased film *Chori Chori Chupke Chupke* allegedly financed by Chhota Shakeel of the notorious Dawood Ibrahim gang, Crime Branch sleuths had got a lead and were now zeroing in on more "go-betweens" in the film industry, he said. "A few more arrests within a couple of days are expected."[43]

Such reports documented in considerable detail the involvement of organized crime in film production and distribution (particularly where overseas territories are concerned), and the complex relations between local politicians, the police, and money laundering operations involving Bombay's merchant communities. Further, with the murder of Gulshan Kumar, a prominent industry figure and owner of an influential music label (T-Series), in 1997 and the attempted killing of key personalities such as producer Rakesh Roshan in 2000, the film financing-crime nexus was firmly established in the public imagination, with the state and FICCI positioning tax-sheltered merchant capital and "underworld" money laundering practices within the same frame.[44]

Thus, among a series of financial and regulatory concessions that accompanied the shift in state policy—such as reduction in import duties on cinematographic film and equipment, exemption on export profits, and other tax incentives—the most significant one was a declaration made in October 2000. The Industrial Development Bank Act of 2000 made it possible for filmmakers to operate in "clean" and "legitimate" fashion.[45] Not surprisingly, policy shifts did not translate into actual changes in financing practices right away. While many in the film business greeted the government decision with enthusiasm, it soon became clear that "clean" funds came with their own strings attached. The Industrial Development Bank of India, for instance, would only invest in Hindi-language films that had a capital investment of over Rs. 5 crore (50 million) and stipulated that the borrower had to be a corporate entity with an established record.[46]

For their part, banks and financial institutions were unwilling to invest in a highly disorganized and unpredictable industry in which only a handful of well-established production companies could produce two or three films in any given year.[47] This hesitation was also partly due to the failure of a few high-profile attempts by film stars such as Amitabh Bachchan to launch publicly traded companies.[48] Further, interventions in financing were never simply a question of transparent accounting practices and sources of capital. This moment of reform also generated a discourse of "corporatization" as the way for the film industry to clean up, shed its image as a dysfunctional "national" cinema, and assume its place as a global player. In a report tracing events leading up to the arrest of Bharat Shah, a leading film financier and diamond merchant, the English-language news magazine *India Today* noted:

> Pundits are hopeful that the cleansing operation will eventually lead to more legitimate sources of funds and increasing corporatization. Shah's arrest has also sent a strong message down the ranks in Bollywood. Everyone—from directors to stars—will think twice before signing on with unknown entities and, hopefully, only the genuine makers will thrive. Says a leading star secretary, "*Safai ho raha hai, accha hai*" (it's being cleaned up, it's good).[49]

The deployment of the word *safai* is particularly telling and worth dwelling upon. Going along with government and industry discourse, *safai* does simply mean "cleaning up." But the word also evokes notions of "neatness," "purity," and "cleansing" that, in turn, signal the need to situate this moment of transition in state-media ties in relation to other contexts and developments: the deindustrialization of the city of Bombay beginning in the late 1970s and the gradual transformation of urban space; the shift to a service-oriented economy and reconfiguration of Bombay's location in the world economy; the rise to power of the nativist, right-wing Shiv Sena party in the state of Maharashtra whose leaders tapped into the resentments and frustrations that these changes had wrought; and a range of other wrenching transitions that the official renaming of Bombay as Mumbai indexes.[50] The desire to refashion the Bombay film industry into Bollywood needs to be understood, then, alongside other "clean" visions of the future of the city that were articulated, for instance, in the widely circulated and critiqued document, "Vision Mumbai: Transforming Mumbai into a World-Class City," developed by an organization called Bombay First in collaboration with the New York-based McKinsey Consulting.[51] In other words, the issue of redefining Bombay's *media space* was very much caught up in a broader spatial politics that involved the production of clean and purified spaces—from ridding parks and pavements of loiterers and hawkers to the construction of high-end malls, multiplex cinema halls, and gated residential communities.[52]

Where the film industry is concerned, these spatial conflicts and the production of an image of urban India that is no longer chaotic and filthy but rather, projects an image of success, competence, and cultural stability, were resolved on the screen well before processes of corporatization were set in motion. Mapping the emergence of a group of professionally trained interior designers in the media industries, Ranjani Mazumdar has argued that "in India after globalization, particularly in Bombay, the physical topography of public space has accelerated the stylization of the interior both in literal (through the redesigning of homes, offices, banks and cafes) and imaginative (through film) terms."[53] Mazumdar's analysis shows how the creation of a new "panoramic interior" in films such as *Hum Aapke Hain Kaun. . !*, *Kuch Kuch Hota Hai* (Karan Johar, 1997), and *Dil Chahta Hai* (The Heart Desires, Farhan Akhtar, 2001), spaces that "operate almost like pages out of an interior-design catalog," is intimately linked to the transformation of elite spaces, both private and public, over the past two decades and speaks to the desire to conjure up a "shining India."[54] However, cleaning up, be it by removing street hawkers or shady financiers, could never be a straightforward and uncontested affair, particularly given the limited reach and appeal of the idea of corporatization, as we will see in the next chapter. Furthermore, reorientation in state policy was not limited to cleaning up and creating opportunities for filmmakers to approach banks and other financial institutions. The larger goal was to create a media and entertainment sector with Bollywood at the center.

Repositioning Bollywood

Beginning in the late 1990s, the state began playing an active role in articulating a vision of Bollywood positioned at the center of a larger media and entertainment sector that would be aligned with the demands of global capital. At stake was nothing less than a complete overhaul of the institutional framework of the Bombay film industry, and one of the key moves involved bringing the film industry under the purview of the Federation of Indian Chambers of Commerce and Industry (FICCI). In addition to "facilitating the policy framework for the growth and development of the film industry,"

Poster at the FICCI-FRAMES convention signaling Bollywood's position within a transnational and multimedia terrain.

this committee also began organizing an annual convention (FRAMES) that brought the film industry into contact with prominent NRI venture capitalists, influential diasporic filmmakers such as Shekhar Kapur, NRI media producers and executives based in the United States (such as Ashok Amritraj of Hyde Park Entertainment), the IT and software sector in India and abroad, representatives from countries interested in coproduction treaties, executives from transnational media corporations such as Sony and Warner Bros., global consultancy firms, and financial institutions.[55]

By 2000 the annual FRAMES convention had emerged as one of the most important sites where the transition from Bombay cinema to Bollywood was staged. Further, since 1998 FICCI had also assumed responsibility for producing the official reports on the media and entertainment industries. In sharp contrast to the reports on film and television generated by the Ministry for Information and Broadcasting until the 1980s, FICCI commissioned multinational accounting and consultancy firms such as KPMG, Pricewaterhouse Coopers, and Arthur Anderson to produce glossy reports using statistics and terminology in ways that fit within global business paradigms. I shall focus on this aspect of language and performance in the next chapter. But for the moment, I want to draw attention to the fact that these reports redefined film as "filmed entertainment" and situated Bollywood as part of a larger "Media & Entertainment" industry that included television, print media, radio, music, outdoor media, animation and special effects, and gaming.

It is also not entirely surprising that the IT and software services sector was invoked as a model for imagining Bollywood as a global media industry, given that it was taking shape within the broader context of India's rise as an economic and political power on the world stage. For instance, the day after his production company Mukta Arts successfully went public and listed on the Bombay stock exchange, producer-director Subhash Ghai commented, "You've seen what India has done with IT. We'll make the same leap with Indian cinema."[56] And at the 2005 FRAMES convention, Narayana Murthy, CEO of one of the most well-known software companies, Infosys Technologies, offered a "5-point plan" outlining how the film industry could learn from and replicate the successes of the IT industry. Suggesting that the film industry could easily adopt business and management practices that had served the Indian IT industry very well and enabled companies like Infosys Technologies to benchmark themselves with global competitors, Murthy went on to reinforce the idea that "corporatization" was a necessary first step to going global:

> To have a global mindset, you need to produce where it is most cost-efficient, source capital from where it is the cheapest, and sell where it is the most profitable. When we (Infosys) set out, we knew that India had the talent and the markets were in the West. The Indian film industry is similar to the IT industry. The film industry is knowledge-based, where talent is crucial and creativity very high. The rules of globalization apply very well to the film industry and media.[57]

I do not wish to suggest that the idea of corporatization was normalized in a matter of months or even a couple of years, or that the "rules of globalization" were, or could be, clearly defined. Several stars, directors, producers, and other persons and groups in the film industry expressed reservations about the feasibility and indeed, even the necessity of corporatizing the film industry. However, in March 2003, following a disastrous year in which 124 films out of 132 reportedly flopped at the box office, when Ravi Shankar Prasad, Union Minister for Information & Broadcasting (I&B) at the time, inaugurated FRAMES by asking filmmakers to "introduce an element of corporate governance" and "respond to the demands of present competitive business," corporatization seemed just the tonic that the industry needed.[58]

Without a doubt, the long and complex history of state-cinema relations does bear on this moment of transition.[59] Ashish Rajadhyaksha focuses on these transitions and observes that "while cinema has been in existence as a national industry of sorts for the past 50 years, *Bollywood* has been around for only a decade now" (emphasis in original).[60] Revisiting the period between 1945 and 1951, when the Bombay film industry managed to establish itself as a "national" film industry in the absence of state support, he goes on to argue that the most recent attempt by the state to redefine its relationship with cinema is, quite simply, a response to the problem of defining "national culture" in globalized modernity.[61] Rajadhyaksha's argument is an important reminder of the state's previous attempts to define its relationship with the film industry and indeed, define cinema's role in postcolonial India.

As Madhava Prasad has documented, the film industry did entertain hopes that the government of postcolonial India would "recognize the potential that cinema held as a medium of mass education and would give it the same encouragement that was envisaged for other industries."[62] Drawing on observations made by a group of producers from Bombay, Calcutta, Madras, and Lahore who traveled to Europe and America in 1945 to study the film industries there, Prasad notes that their report, in addition to positioning cinema as a "partner in the about-to-be independent country's campaign to modernize and project a good image abroad," also detailed what the government could do to provide a "stable and progressive foundation" for the industry.[63] However, the Nehruvian state did not regard cinema as crucial to the project of modernization and development. While communications systems including the telegraph, telephone, radio, and later, television, were brought under the purview of the state and included as an area of both economic and political-cultural importance, cinema was seen as a distraction at best and at worst, a site of moral failure akin to gambling.[64]

Even as cinema was marginalized in the overall project of nation-building, the postcolonial state did acknowledge its usefulness as a vehicle for propaganda. In 1949, the S. K. Patil Film Enquiry Committee was appointed and charged with the task of reporting on the status of the film industry.[65] Critiquing the "shift from the studio system to independent entrepreneurship" and the involvement of black market money in the film business, this report also recommended that the state invest in film production, establish a film finance corporation, a film institute, and film archives.[66] Nearly a decade later, the central government set up a Film Finance Corporation (1960, FFC) and in 1964 it brought the FFC under the control of the Ministry of Information & Broadcasting and sought to provide low-interest loans to select projects. In 1970 the FFC was merged with the Indian Motion Picture Export Corporation (IMPEC) and renamed the National Film Development Corporation (NFDC). These changes, while welcomed by the film industry, did not lead to any substantial changes in state-industry relations. As Prasad notes, not only was the financial assistance provided insufficient, but in the absence of a "political alliance between the state and the industry . . . the economic intervention via the FFC was ineffectual."[67]

In fact, by the late 1970s it was clear that the film industry did not anticipate any significant changes in the state's ad hoc approach to cinema.[68] Reacting to an announcement of a commission to "hold extensive consultations with all sections and regions of the industry," an editorial in the leading film magazine *Filmfare* remarked:

> Our first reaction to this suggestion was that it would be redundant, the Film Enquiry Committee of 1951 and the Estimates Committee Report of Films, 1974, having already fully researched and explored the subject matter of an enquiry into the trade's ills and woes. The trade's problems are the same as they were in 1951, they have only become acuter . . . if at all such a commission is appointed, it will not do to confine its scope to the trade's current problems . . . above all, the commission will have to examine the Government's responsibility to cinema and the social responsibility of cinema.[69]

Given this history, the Indian government's overtures toward the film industry during the last few years and its support of a series of "reforms" directed at the film industry do appear remarkable and indicative of a major shift in the relationship between the state and the Bombay film industry. The state's investment in refashioning the Bombay film industry into Bollywood, worked out over the past decade in various settings and most visibly at venues such as the FICCI-FRAMES conventions, was perhaps best demonstrated by the "filmy" remarks made by the finance minister Yashwant Sinha. In his budget speech in 1999, Sinha made the government's intentions clear, saying: "Do not ask us *hum aapke hain kaun* (Who are we to you?) . . . let me assure you that it would be our endeavour to support the entertainment industry *Dil Se* (From the Heart)." In the following year, Sinha went on to remark: "I hope these concessions combined with what I have already done on the indirect tax side will reassure the entertainment industry that *Hum Saath Saath Hain* (We Are Together)." In 2001, Sinha invoked the title of another big-budget "family film" (*K3G*) and observed that it was "time to bring about a fiscal regime to usher in more *Khushi* (joy) and take away the *Gham* (sorrow)."[70]

Over the next few years, corporatization became a catch-all buzz word that alluded not only to new modes of film financing and the attenuation of the mafia's hold over the film industry, but a series of changes at every step of the filmmaking process, including preparing a bound script, developing and working with schedules, getting stars to sign and honor contracts instead of proceeding with verbal assurances, in-film branding through corporate tie-ups, aggressive marketing and promotions that reflected processes of market segmentation underway in India, the entry of large industrial houses, corporations, and television companies into the business of film production and distribution, and the emergence of multiplexes to replace single-screen cinema halls across urban India.[71] As a journalist reporting from FRAMES 2003 for the English-language national daily *The Hindu*, noted: "Bollywood has an itch and it has much to do with the perennial drone of corporatization as panacea for its ills. For the second day at Frames 2003, sections of the film industry continued to outline how far the tie-clad manager could venture into their private turf."[72] By the time I arrived in Bombay in the fall of 2005 for my first phase of field research, critics in the film industry who had dismissed corporatization as little more than a set of cosmetic changes seemed to have been silenced. As the widely circulated KPMG-authored consultancy report for FRAMES 2005, titled "Focus 2010: From Dreams to Reality," declared:

> The seeds of corporatization have been sown . . . the stakeholders, especially the new generation of producers, directors and performers are now much more receptive to international best practices to redefine the way of doing business. Better discipline has resulted in a slow turnaround in the industry, which recovered from an unsuccessful 2002 to record better profitability in the last two years. Aided by investments in technology and the right measure of governmental intervention, India could establish itself as an important global filmmaking hub outside of Hollywood.[73]

With a string of hits in 2005–06 that broke several box-office records, an increasing percentage of "clean" funds, a slew of commissioned reports from corporate consultants emphasizing the importance of "filmed entertainment" to the growth potential of the overall media and entertainment sector in India, and unprecedented levels of global visibility, memories of an industry plagued by losses and operating under the ominous shadow of the underworld had been banished.[74] The *safai*, it seemed, was paying off and the future, as it were, was close at hand.

One way to understand this moment of transition is in terms of the media and entertainment industries, and Bollywood in particular, having become useful to the state. Of course, the argument regarding usefulness had been made in terms of the media and entertainment industries having become a vital part of the Indian economy. For instance, every report produced by consultancy firms such as KPMG included tables and charts detailing how, given the right economic and regulatory policies, the "Indian M&E industry" (media and entertainment) would match, if not outperform, the overall growth of the Indian economy. But the usefulness of the media and entertainment industries was articulated in more than just this narrow economic sense.

Consider the way in which Bollywood was deployed as part of an "India Everywhere" campaign at the 2006 World Economic Forum in Davos, Switzerland. Organized under the aegis of the Confederation of Indian Industry (CII), the campaign was designed by the India Brand Equity Foundation, a public-private partnership between the Ministry of Commerce and the CII with the mandate of "building positive economic perceptions of India globally."[75] While billboards and advertisements declaring India to be the "fastest growing free market democracy in the world," gifts for attendees (including an mp3 player loaded with Indian popular and classical music), and lavish dinners cooked by top Indian chefs from London attracted attention, it was the Bollywood-themed parties that news media focused on the most. For instance, Aroon Purie, the editor of *India Today*, declared in a cover story that Bollywood had redefined India's image in Davos:

> Picture this. The most happening nightspot in Davos called the Cabana Bar, packed with Europeans dancing to the thumping beats of *Kajra Re* played by DJ Aqueel, drinking Kingfisher beer and wolfing down chicken tikkas. The crowd, mostly tourists and people working at the annual World Economic Forum, were enjoying the taste of modern India, dancing till the wee hours of the morning . . . the next night was more of the same, with Shiamak Davar and his modern dance troupe along with DJ Aqueel. This was the face of contemporary India that was being showcased to the high and mighty at the famed ski resort at the WEF's annual jamboree in Davos.[76]

Purie and other journalists who reported on the annual meeting of the WEF interpreted these Bollywood-themed soirees as a timely refashioning of India's image on the world stage. This performative dimension of Bollywood's usefulness as a cultural resource is crucial to take into account. As George Yudice points out, "a performative understanding of the expediency of culture," one that goes beyond the dictionary meaning of expediency as that which is "merely politic," allows us to focus attention on the "strategies implied in any invocation of culture, any invention of tradition, in relation to some purpose or goal."[77] Bollywood's presence in settings such as the World Economic Forum and the Pravasi Bharatiya Divas (Day of the Diaspora) was not just a reflection of the growing economic importance of the cultural industries. Rather, such events reveal that the transformation of the Bombay film industry into Bollywood was caught up in a larger process of the state realigning its understanding of "culture as resource" away from well-worn developmentalist paradigms toward meeting the demands of new circuits of capital.

Conclusion

This chapter has traced the sociocultural and political transformations that set the stage for the reimagination of the Bombay film industry as Bollywood, focusing on changing relations between the Indian state, the Indian diaspora, and the media industries. My goal in doing so was to locate this moment of transition in the media and entertainment industries within a wider historical and spatial terrain marked by a range of other reforms undertaken and negotiated by the state, and as part of the redefinition of the nation-space in an era of globalization. In arguing that a discourse of *safai* (cleaning/cleansing) defined state practices in a number of domains (urban space, diaspora relations) in a conjuncture marked by policies of economic liberalization, I want to emphasize the role played by the state in the production of a "clean," corporatized, and global media industry. The reconfiguration of Bombay's media space and the emergence of Bollywood is, in other words, part of a larger process of spatial restructuring in which the state participated.

However, as my account of the inaugural session of FICCI-FRAMES 2009 in the previous chapter signaled, the transformation of the Bombay film industry into Bollywood was not just a matter of balance sheets, clean financing, and globally recognized consultancy firms and their business jargon. In postindependence India, the production, distribution, and exhibition of Hindi-language films has been defined by a vast and intricate network of private financiers, hundreds of independent producers and distributors, powerful family-owned production companies, and exhibitors operating a range of cinema halls across the country. It hardly needs to be pointed out that the impact of changes in policy, new circuits of capital, and the growth of the television and advertising industries on existing conditions and structures are bound to be complex and uneven. It is also crucial to keep in mind that the transformation of the Bombay film industry into Bollywood has been unfolding in the context of broader changes in the media landscape, defined in particular by the phenomenal growth of the television and advertising industries throughout the 1990s. To consider just one example, the Indian government's attempts to reform Doordarshan, the state-controlled television network, in response to challenges posed by the rapid growth of commercial and transnational television during the 1990s could also be framed in terms of the state's need to reassert itself in the domain of cultural production. Indeed, Shanti Kumar's account of debates surrounding the *Prasar Bharati* bill (Prasar—to disseminate; Bharat—India) during the 1990s shows very clearly that Doordarshan's plans for expansion and discussions surrounding the proposed creation of an autonomous corporation for public broadcasting were also about the state dealing with anxieties stemming from the impact of economic liberalization and globalization.[78]

Even as we recognize that redefining policy and establishing control over the Bombay film industry reveals the extent to which the nation-state continues to play an important role in the production of a global media industry, we also need to move beyond state-centric analyses that tend to approach Bollywood as an undifferentiated and monolithic industry. Thus the next chapter focuses on the FICCI-FRAMES 2009 convention and in particular, the reformulation of industrial identities, as a way to examine the partial and contradictory nature of industrial transformation that a decade of cleaning up and corporatizing Bombay film industry has wrought.

2

Staging Bollywood

Industrial Identity in an Era of Reform

In many respects, the filmic exemplar for Bollywood in a phase of transition is Rommy Rolly, one of the central protagonists in *Luck by Chance* (2009), a film that takes an affectionate and at times critical look at the workings of the film industry in Bombay. Written and directed by Zoya Akhtar, daughter of established screenwriter Honey Irani and acclaimed lyricist and screenwriter Javed Akhtar, the film revolves around the struggles of two young actors who arrive in Bombay with hopes of making it big in the film industry. Taking us behind the scenes of a film being produced by Rommy Rolly, a well-established producer-director, Akhtar offers glimpses of various aspects of Bombay's film world: stardom and film journalism, disenchanted extras and choreographers, marginalized screenwriters, erratic production schedules, and so on. But above all, what the film captures is the way in which kinship and long-standing social relationships structure nearly every aspect of the film industry in Bombay. In fact, the answer to the question that Akhtar asks—how this industry of no contracts, no paperwork, inadequate technology, and limited equipment produces the largest number of films the world over, year after year—would likely be anything but "corporatization."[1] While one could point to several instances in the film that speak to the challenges and limits of corporatizing the Hindi film industry, scenes involving Rommy Rolly's attempts to secure financing for himself and for his brother-in-law's venture are particularly telling.

Banking on his reputation of having produced a number of hit films, Rolly approaches a corporation that has recently entered the film business in Bombay. In a nondescript office, seated across a table from two executives, Rolly and his brother-in-law Satish Chowdhary make their pitch. Encouraged by the positive response from one of the executives, Chowdhary begins speaking: "That's fantastic, thank you. And Rolly*ji* must have mentioned that John and Bipasha have been confirmed and dates. . . ." Cutting him short, the younger of the two executives responds, tapping his fingers on the script in front of him: "And we're happy. But our basic criteria is this property."

His colleague, having noticed the quizzical looks that Rolly and Chowd-hary are exchanging, explains: "You see, in Hollywood the script is referred to as property." Rolly's response—"out here, only property is referred to as property"—invites a smirk and another patronizing remark from the young executive: "You see, there content is king. We want to bring that culture to your industry. There needs to be a change in your mind-set." Unfazed, Rolly immediately responds that "change is indeed taking place" and that they had signed John Abraham and Bipasha Basu not only because they were promi-nent stars but more importantly, because the "script demanded it."

A few months later, with his own production in disarray owing to the hero (Zaffar Khan) of the film pulling out and other actors unwilling to work with him, Rolly finds himself back in a meeting with the corporate executives. "You had said 'content is king,' 'script is property,' 'you want to change the culture of this industry.' And now you ask me 'first tell me who is the hero!'" With the executives refusing to finance his film without a major star in place and deciding to back his brother-in-law's project instead, we then see a forlorn Rolly having tea with the heroine's mother and her friend, Dinyar Sadri, a shipping merchant with no ties to the film indus-try. As it transpires, Sadri is willing to finance the entire film on the condi-tion that once the agreement was signed, he would have nothing to do with the project. A visibly overjoyed Rolly then turns to the heroine's mother to address her concerns about casting a new actor at short notice. "New face," he declares with a flourish. "I have been thinking about this, and I now real-ize that Zaffar's exit was a blessing in disguise. This role demands a new face!" The newcomer from New Delhi gets the role, and the film goes on to become a superhit. Luck by chance.

Watching *Luck by Chance* in a Reliance Entertainment-owned multiplex in a suburb of Detroit, Michigan, a few weeks before traveling to Bombay to attend the FICCI-FRAMES 2009 convention, I had wondered about how the celebration of a decade of corporatization and globalization would be staged. As it turned out, the contradictions and disjunctures between the rhetoric and practice of corporatization, the ambivalence that a producer like Rommy Rolly expressed regarding ongoing changes, the persistence of estab-lished modes of filmmaking and anonymous (*benami*) financing, and the topsy-turvy culture of production in Bollywood that *Luck by Chance* alluded to were on display for all see at the convention. In this chapter, I draw on my experiences and observations at the FRAMES 2009 convention to examine how a decade of industrial change was staged. In particular, I consider the ellipsis in the title of the report that the consultancy firm KPMG released during the inaugural session of the convention—*In the Interval . . . But Ready for the Next Act*—as indexing a complicated and evolving terrain of media production, one marked as much by unpredictability as by a sense of certainty regarding the "next act."

Drawing on panel discussions, various artifacts circulating at the convention, and trade-press coverage of the convention and this period of transition, my goal here is to complicate the official narrative in which the notion of an interval is understood as constituting nothing more than an interruption and, more crucially, that the "next act" was readily imaginable. Focusing attention on this moment of celebration opens up an opportunity to consider the entire decade—from 1998, when the government granted industry status to filmmaking in Bombay, until 2009—as a formative interval. The interval, in other words, is not just an arbitrary break in a neat and linear narrative of progress toward a seamless integration into the logics of global capital. As Lalitha Gopalan has argued, where Indian cinema is concerned the interval "lies at the bedrock of our comprehension of the structuring of narrative expectation, development and closure . . . at times exceeding the intentions of the filmmakers whose rational choice of the interval may be one among several ways to read the film."[2] I build on this theorization of the interval to draw attention to novel responses and adaptations that shape an industry in transition. I show that the result of a decade of corporatization has been the emergence of a hybrid terrain of media production characterized by family businesses reformulating their industrial identities to meet the demands of new circuits of capital as well as a range of media corporations that have entered the film business only to find themselves contending with the limits of corporate logics in the Bombay film industry.

But understanding how the discourse of corporatization has played out in Bombay requires us to go well beyond the issue of emerging models and relations of film production, marketing, distribution, and exhibition. Thus, in tracing the ways in which a range of industry professionals speak of this period of transition, I also draw attention to the construction of industrial identity as a crucial and defining aspect of corporatization. John Caldwell, for instance, has shown us how industrial identity practices (branding, syndication, franchising, and so on) are related to specific institutional and economic logics.[3] In his view, our understanding of the concept of identity as "something more slippery and transitory" and involving performative dimensions can be fruitfully extended to see that the "media's approach to corporate identity can be similarly contingent, slippery, volatile, changing, tactical, and theatricalized."[4] Indeed, Rommy Rolly's performance in *Luck by Chance* typifies several established industry professionals' response to calls for corporatizing their businesses and production cultures—a tactical reformulation and performance of industrial identity that allows them to participate in new regimes of risk and speculation, while continuing to leverage and strengthen their ties within established social and financial networks in Bombay.

In focusing on this performative dimension of industry practice, this chapter also sets the discussion of corporatization and industrial transformation in relation to a broader discourse of derivativeness that has haunted the Bombay film industry and even more so, Bollywood. As Rajadhyaksha reminds us, Hollywood does after all remain "the overdetermined barometer of comparison" for media industries across Asia.[5] While this issue of derivativeness has been addressed from textual and aesthetic perspectives, we have yet to pay close attention to how this plays out in relation to industrial imaginaries and logics. I show here that the refashioning of the Bombay film industry as Bollywood has to do with a range of players in the industry—from corporate executives like UTV's CEO Ronnie Screwvala to Karan Johar, who manages a family business—carefully cultivating and maintaining a position of difference in the global media landscape (in relation to Hollywood in particular) even as they adopt new perspectives and practices.

This focus on industrial identity is warranted not only because it allows us to push beyond state-centric explanations of media transition or a narrow focus on economic impact. Exploring the strategies adopted by family businesses like Dharma Productions (Karan Johar) and Yash Raj Films (Yash Chopra) also opens up an opportunity to situate the operations of the media industries in Bombay within a broader history of the enduring presence and powerful role played by family businesses in Indian capitalism. The work of historians and anthropologists of market cultures and kinship-based capitalism also, therefore, informs my analysis here.[6] For instance, Ritu Birla has argued in her analysis of vernacular capitalism (Marwari merchant communities, for instance) in colonial India that there has always been "extensive negotiability between the symbolic values of kinship, lineage and community, and the material values of credit, trade and investment."[7] Birla's analysis of the ways in which indigenous capitalists negotiated various aspects of colonial law even as they "folded their bazaar idioms into new languages of capitalist development" during the late nineteenth and early twentieth centuries is particularly relevant when considering how family-run media companies in Bombay and indeed, other prominent media capitals like Hong Kong, have responded in creative ways to sociopolitical and economic changes at different historical conjunctures.[8] Framed in relation to these broader questions, this chapter shows that the picture of Bollywood that emerges at the end of a decade of corporatization is that of a media space being shaped by a productive, if at times uneasy, coexistence of heterogeneous capitalist practices defined as much by kinship networks and interpersonal relations as by modes of speculation and practices of risk management that Hollywood has rendered globally recognizable.

"Celebrating a Decade" at FRAMES 2009

The 2009 edition of the FICCI-FRAMES convention, as I have already mentioned, spanned three days (February 21–23) and was attended by media industry professionals and policymakers from around the world. Held in the five-star Renaissance Hotel in suburban Bombay, the main space of the convention was defined by an L-shaped hallway. This hallway was flanked on the one side by stalls and on the other side by rooms of varying sizes for panel sessions, workshops, and keynote speeches. Like other such industry-focused conventions, the stalls featured technology exhibits relating to design and special effects (companies like HP, Intel, and Adobe), media companies for whom the convention was a key site for raising brand awareness as well as a space for networking (Sony Entertainment Television, ZEE TV, Nokia, X-Box 360), and organizations that were trying to forge ties with the media industry in Bombay (UK Film Council, MIP TV). With a number of tables stocked with water, coffee, tea, and biscuits throughout the day, this hallway served as the primary space for interaction among attendees. These interactions, moreover, were mediated by television networks that were reporting on the convention in "real time" (that attendees could watch on television screens throughout the hotel) as well as a number of pamphlets and brochures that were distributed by representatives of various companies and film councils. For instance, UTV, one of the main sponsors of FRAMES 2009, had set up a stall at the entrance to the hallway where its business news correspondents conducted interviews with a range of high-profile industry professionals who were attending the convention. Taken together, the spatial layout, networking events, entertainment shows each evening, and "live" television and print coverage did serve, as Caldwell argues based on his observations at trade conventions in the United States, to "interpret and chart the meanings, the social significance, and the economic logic"[9] of the entire convention. FRAMES 2009 was, as this official interpretation would have it, about "celebrating a decade" of media globalization in India and in particular, Bollywood.

Among the many artifacts circulating at FRAMES 2009, there was one publication, called *Picklemag*, which was in the hands of virtually every attendee by the end of the first day. Featuring advertisements from major

UTVi, a 24-hour English language business and financial broadcast news channel providing "live" coverage of the FICCI-FRAMES convention.

companies and organizations that had a presence at the convention, this
magazine included stories about the improbable success of the Oscar Academy award-winning film *Slumdog Millionaire* (2008), interviews with prominent personalities attending the convention, spotlights on different sectors of
the media industry in India, a report on the UK Film Council, and an overview of the performance of BIG Pictures (Reliance Entertainment), one of
the largest and most well-funded companies operating in Bollywood. These
stories and features were no different from those produced by the trade-press
on a routine basis and as such, were not particularly remarkable. If anything,
they only served to confirm my initial assumption that FRAMES 2009, like
other such media industry conventions, would also serve as an "industrial
consensus forming gathering" where a range of bureaucrats and industry
professionals would, over a span of three days, generate a neat narrative of
Bollywood going global and becoming "corporatized."[10] Consider the first
few pages of *Picklemag* where Amit Mitra, the Secretary General of FICCI,
offered his reflections on a decade of corporatization.

Titled "Framing Indian Media's Progress," Mitra's opening article reminds
us of the instrumental role that FICCI has played since 1998 in "bringing
about several policy changes through consistent dialogue with the policymakers and stakeholders."[11] Situating changes in film production alongside

developments in cable and satellite television, the emergence of multiplex chains across urban India, and the entry of large media and nonmedia corporations into the film business, he outlines a predictable story of change. Further, according to Mitra, the first and foremost challenge revolved around the issue of film financing. Corporatization meant working with film companies to develop, at the very least, a balance sheet that banks and other investors could examine. By the same token, this process also involved getting banks to understand how to assess risk in the film business. As he recalled:

> Banks had no idea how to lend. FICCI worked closely with IDBI (Industrial Development Bank of India). We took the then Minister for Information & Broadcasting Sushma Swaraj to New York where 22 bankers from the world congregated. She discussed for three hours the feasibility of lending to the business of movies. They explained how they are lending and are also making money, how they diversify risk, how they balance portfolios where eight films are made—one succeeds and seven fail, and yet you make a buck. So, the technology of lending in a risk environment was shared.[12]

From this perspective, corporatization was about bringing the operations of the film industry—and in particular, notions of risk and modes of speculation that shaped the workings of the industry—into alignment with the demands of global capital. And in Mitra's view, this was beginning to happen. However, several panel discussions at FRAMES 2009 revealed that the transition from Bombay to Bollywood was, far from being seamless, a contested, uneven, and at times volatile reworking of the prevailing culture of capitalism in the Bombay film world.

One panel in particular—"The Business of Filmmaking in 2008: Agony or Ecstasy?"—disrupted the celebration and became a topic of conversation for the remainder of the convention. Held on the second day of the convention, this panel brought together filmmakers from established family businesses as well as executives from large media corporations that have entered different sectors of the film industry over the past decade. The question that each panelist had been asked to address was this: despite unprecedented levels of investment in production, distribution, and exhibition, why does the film industry continue to grapple with failure on such a large scale? The year 2008, the moderator noted, had been a particularly dismal one with less than ten films earning enough to classify as a "hit."

The first speaker, Goldie Behl, son of well-known producer and director (the late Ramesh Behl), said nothing that was new either to his fellow panelists or those in the audience. Reminding the audience that low-budget films that attempted "something different, something new" had done well that year, Behl trotted out a well-worn cliché about the difficulties of treading the fine line between commerce and art that defined filmmaking. As he saw it, "if the studios are playing a stock market game, then they are going to be in trouble." After pointing to a few areas that needed improvement such as script development and marketing, Behl ended his talk with a vapid, if reassuring, comment: "There will always be funds available for someone with a solid story to tell. I'm a second-generation kid in the industry, and I have seen many ups and downs."

Things took a much more exciting turn, however, when Vishesh Bhatt, son of producer Mukesh Bhatt and nephew of well-known director Mahesh Bhatt, was handed the microphone. Beginning with an account of his family-run company's films that had failed at the box office and the one hit they had delivered in 2008 (*Jannat*, Heaven), Bhatt's speech soon grew more pointed. While his comments on the unreliability of box-office figures and questionable reporting practices in the Hindi film industry drew knowing nods and a few "yeahs" and "hmms" from the audience, his next set of comments set the room abuzz. "We, in our company, foolishly believed that a good story was the only formula for success. But we also knew that marketing muscle only was not the way out and definitely not worth the risk," he began. Pausing for a moment and waving his hand, as if to draw our attention to the corporate executives on stage, he continued, "considering that we invest our own hard-won money." As his fellow panelists smiled nervously and nodded politely, Bhatt delivered the lines that made them visibly uncomfortable: "In the past we also failed, but we at least came clean of the blood that most corporate companies have on their hands . . . after unknowingly, initially, and later knowingly deceiving the public and bringing down the industry with exaggerated spending and then claiming bogus returns."

Three more speakers followed Bhatt—Sunil Kheterpal, a former banking industry executive now serving as the chief operating officer of BIG Pictures, Reliance Entertainment's film division; Vikas Bahl, a television and advertising industry executive who now oversees *Spotboy*, a division of UTV Motion Pictures; and Vishal Kapur, chief operating officer of FUN Cinemas, a prominent multiplex chain. Not surprisingly, they all avoided responding to Bhatt's claims. While Bahl sidestepped the question of film financing and speculation altogether by talking about the importance of developing good stories, both Kheterpal and Kapur delivered talks involving PowerPoint slides, graphs, and statistics that seemed designed to avoid precisely the kind of discussion that Bhatt apparently wanted to generate. Their presentations

Panelists at FICCI-FRAMES 2009 listening to Vishesh Bhatt deliver a scathing talk about the problems with large corporations entering Bollywood.

were decidedly "corporate," designed to assuage any nervousness about the state of the industry and of potential investors' doubts about entering a business space where risk management involves propitiating the right spirits as much as it is about conjuring a "superhit" for financiers. As Kheterpal, after explaining that access to funding to the tune of Rs. 2,000–2,500 crores at the beginning of 2008 had led to a number of rash decisions in the film industry, asserted: "Corrections are inevitable, we need to stick to core business, and further corporatization will make a difference."

In one respect, Goldie Behl's comment that "there will always be funds available for someone with a solid story to tell" does need to be taken seriously. His remark about being "a second-generation kid in the industry" speaks to the fact that the interpersonal networks in which he is ensconced provide him with both the cultural and financial capital needed to weather periods of economic uncertainty. On the other hand, Kheterpal's almost casual mention of the spectacular sum of Rs. 2,000–2,500 crores points to a key dimension of change in the Indian media landscape. To begin with, rapid expansion in print and television markets in India during the 1990s had led to the emergence of media conglomerates with a presence in the film industry as well. Groups such as Network 18, Essel, and Times that own and operate television channels, gaming companies, cable and satellite companies, and newspapers and magazines have, since the early 2000s, established film production and distribution divisions. With home video rights, television rights, remake rights, and merchandising contracts emerging as major revenue streams, moves toward conglomeration reflect growing competition and, crucially, the interest that foreign players have shown in the Indian media and entertainment sector. Coproduction and distribution deals signed by companies like Sony, Warner Brothers, Disney, and Fox have in turn increased capital flows in Bombay's media world.

Changes in access to capital have also been a function of increased private equity investments in the media and entertainment business. Influential players such as Merrill Lynch, Goldman Sachs, and Citigroup have made significant investments in different sectors of the film and television industries. In addition, the decade of 2000–2010 also witnessed a surge in Indian media companies with stakes in filmmaking making the move to list on the Indian stock exchange and, in a few cases, in Singapore and London as well. Finally, with regulatory changes making 100 percent FDI (foreign direct investment) possible, there is no doubt that 2000–07 was a period marked by dramatic changes in capital flows in Bombay's media world.[13]

There is no denying, however, the "occult" nature of this domain of finance capital. As Jean Comaroff and John Comaroff observe, contemporary

Table 2.1. A selected list of prominent Bollywood companies with foreign investors and/or strategic partnerships with foreign companies

Company	Foreign Investor/Strategic Partner
UTV	Walt Disney Company (I)
Yash Raj Films	Walt Disney (P)
Reliance Entertainment	George Soros (I), Dreamworks (I)
Shree Ashtavinayak Cine Vision	JP Morgan (I)
PVR Pictures	JP Morgan (I)
Ramesh Sippy Entertainment	Warner Brothers (P, I)
Studio 18	Paramount Pictures (I)
Percept Pictures	Lachlan Murdoch (I)
Sanjay Leela Bhansali Films	Sony Pictures (I)
Cinemata Entertainment	Ratnam Sudesh Iyer, Singapore (I)
Times Global Broadcasting	Reuters (Singapore) (I)

global finance is rooted "in two inscrutables: a faith in probability (itself a notoriously poor way of predicting the future from the past) and a monetary system that depends for its existence on 'confidence,' a chimera knowable, tautologically, only by its effects."[14] If anything, this realm of speculation involving global financial institutions, transnational media conglomerates, and the Bombay film industry is just as magical, unreal, and unpredictable as, say, the shadowy world of "black" money that linked Bombay's media world with other transnational circuits of capital.

Moreover, as we will see in the next chapter, modes of speculation in Bollywood are intimately linked to production rituals such as the *mahurat* (an auspicious date and time for launching new ventures) that invoke the divine even as they conjure economic performance at the box office. It is precisely this intimate relationship between global speculative capital and vernacular practices that we are reminded of in the film *Luck by Chance* as Zoya Akhtar cuts from the *mahurat* for Rommy Rolly's production to a Hindu astrologer's home where Rolly is involved in an altogether different practice of risk management. In the presence of various Hindu deities, Rolly adorns his fingers with rings set with different gemstones to help him deal with the pressures, vagaries, and risks of production in a rapidly changing media world.

Further, Vishesh Bhatt's outburst suggests that the fashioning of Bollywood as a global media industry, approached by the Indian state and institutions like FICCI as a problem of corporatization, was not merely about financing and accounting practices. Rather, it was also concerned with transforming the culture of production in the Bombay film world in such a way that the purportedly rational and globally recognizable languages of risk and modes of speculation would, gradually, supersede the predominantly kinship-based logics of trust and long-standing interpersonal relations that had shaped the workings of the film industry in Bombay for well over five decades. As Madhava Prasad has noted, "pre-capitalist ideologies in which relations based on loyalty, servitude, the honor of the *khandaan* (clan) and institutionalized Hindu religious practices" have for long structured social relationships as well as the production process in the Bombay film industry.[15] Not surprisingly, then, "diversification," "innovation," "optimizing margins," "leveraging IP," "brand differentiation," and "balanced portfolios" were the words and phrases that appeared frequently in the PowerPoint slides that Kheterpal and Kapur used for their presentation, signaling their distance and difference from people like Vishesh Bhatt, while also framing the challenges facing the film industry in a period of transition in terms of a struggle between two distinct and seemingly incommensurable cultures of capitalism.

Staging Difference

At the height of the economic boom in 2006–07, numerous news and trade stories framed this period of transition as one in which new corporate studios would change the workings of the Bombay film industry. Consider, for instance, this account in *Mint*, a leading English-language business and finance daily newspaper:

> *Over the next two years, India's film industry will actually start function-*
> *ing like one.* In this period, business groups and companies like Network
> 18, the Reliance-Anil Dhirubhai Ambani Group, UTV Motion Pictures,
> Percept Holdings, Carving Dreams Entertainment Ltd., and Eros Interna-
> tional have lined up between 120 and 140 projects at a total cost of around
> Rs. 4,000 crore. Each of these companies will produce between 10 and
> 30 films in the next two years. All of them will have a steady pipeline of
> releases. And most are signing actors, scriptwriters, and directors for more
> than one project, ensuring that they have the required bench strength to
> function pretty much like a motion picture assembly line. Or a Hollywood
> studio (my emphasis).[16]

In reporting on the organizational transition under way and Indian companies' emulation of the Hollywood model, stories like these also focused attention on the challenges now facing small-scale, family-run production companies. Glowing profiles of companies like UTV led by urbane and cosmopolitan media executives like Ronnie Screwvala—hailed by a journalist for *Newsweek* magazine as "Bollywood's Jack Warner" and whose company was "setting the modern standard of studio efficiency in Bollywood"—were set in stark contrast to the staid, old-fashioned, and feudal production companies managed by a father-son (rarely -daughter) team.[17] The safari suit-wearing Hindi film producer was no match for the suave corporate executive who, according to these news and trade-press stories, had little patience for established modes of production. Of course, small-scale production companies and family businesses were recognized as important players, given that their extensive social and financial networks had defined Hindi film production and distribution since the late 1940s and early 1950s. And while executives from companies like UTV and Reliance Entertainment came to be seen as embodying a set of traits and values befitting a media industry with global ambitions, exceptions were always made for influential players like Yash Chopra and Karan Johar. These prominent producer-directors were framed as exemplars of the family firm in the Bombay film industry and indeed, "Indian" capitalism more broadly. Moreover, they were seen as belonging to a very select group able to negotiate between the global and the vernacular.

But for the most part, the discourse of corporatization positioned film producers, distributors, and exhibitors in the Bombay film industry as outsiders in an emergent Bollywood formation and regarded them as *objects* of reform. Indeed, the assessment on the part of the trade- and business-press as well as consultancy reports during the late 1990s and early 2000s had been dire. As a *Business Week* report from 2002 declared: "Bollywood, as a business, is a mess."[18] Comparing the chaotic mode of production in the Bombay film industry, one marked by a lack of proper budgeting, little preproduction planning, half-baked scripts that were modified as the shoot progressed, and the entire project hinging on the whims and fancies of stars, to the streamlined, efficient, rational, and corporatized mode and culture of production that the likes of UTV and Reliance had supposedly ushered in, such stories framed the transformation of the Bombay film industry into Bollywood as a decisive break from the past.

This is reflected in these media corporations' websites as well. In fact, the most striking aspect of websites and other branding strategies of major corporations like UTV Motion Pictures is the emphasis they place on how well their missions are aligned with the FICCI-state narrative of change in the Bombay film industry. For companies like UTV and Shree Ashtavinayak Cine Vision, their industrial identity fit neatly in relation to the linear progression from Bombay cinema to Bollywood, defined in particular by the adoption of rational systems of management and the formalization of business practices in production, financing, and distribution. Consider the website for UTV Motion Pictures. Beneath the UTV logo and a banner advertising the latest film produced by the company is an introduction to the company that declares:

> Movies enjoy an almost 'basic need of survival' status in India. UTV Motion Pictures has worked consciously to ride on that phenomenon, pioneering not just newer films and story ideas, but also the very manner in which films are made in India. From novel plots and stories that one would think can never work in mainstream cinema, to pioneering the studio model in movie production, UTV has contributed to a positive change in the Indian motion picture industry.

This narrative, in which UTV takes credit for professionalizing the film production process and establishing new organizational forms in Bombay,

UTV's home page, in which the company is defined as a media conglomerate that has transformed prevailing organizational structures and cultures of production in the Bombay film industry.

is one that Shree Ashtavinayak Cine Vision, Percept Picture Company, and other corporate entrants also rely on to establish their presence in Bollywood Inc. In fact, Shree Ashtavinayak Cine Vision's claim is even bolder, with the company declaring itself to be "the pioneering corporate structure in the tinsel town."[19] Further, in keeping with the discourse of *safai* (cleaning/cleansing) that I discussed in the previous chapter as being crucial to the refashioning of Bombay's media space, these websites also place great emphasis on presenting companies as operating within a very different culture of capitalism, especially in relation to the issue of transparency. Both the UTV and Shree Ashtavinayak sites, for instance, include a prominent link ("Investors") leading to a page with details regarding the board of directors, quarterly results, annual reports, and shareholder details. Declaring that the company is "committed to maintaining the highest standards of corporate governance, financial transparency, and maximizing shareholder value," this section of the Shree Ashtavinayak website deploys the same formal vocabulary of business administration as various FICCI consultancy reports. Without a doubt, these elements of industrial identity are related to changing patterns of corporate governance and the emergence of a managerial system that is built on clear distinctions between different domains of the business entity. At the same time, this emphasis on company structure and managerial logics signals another key difference. Even as this corporate narrative emphasizes the importance of key executives (UTV's Ronnie Screwvala, for example) by mentioning their vast experience in media production in Bombay and their ties to prominent and well-established directors and stars in Bollywood, great care is taken not to allow any one person's identity to overshadow the corporation's professional outlook and approach to the business of media production and circulation.

This positioning of the corporate and professional cultures of production as utterly incongruent with the kinship-based workings of the Bombay film industry informed discussions at FRAMES 2009 as well. In fact, this was the argument that several panelists on another panel—"U.S.-India: Overcoming Obstacles to Doing Business in the Two Largest Global Film Markets"—had made the previous day. One panelist in particular, Anadil Hossain, a diasporic South Asian entrepreneur who facilitates Bollywood productions in the United States as well as Hollywood productions in India, framed it in stark terms:

> Bollywood has an incredible talent pool, resources, great actors and technicians. But where the whole process tends to fall apart a little is in production. The fact is that there is no transparency, no locked budget, and no accountability. It is open ended and loose, and no reporting back. That is something I miss when I work with Indian companies that come there. Over the years, I have tried to instill some of the systems . . . but one film at a time is not enough. I hope now with the slow corporatization, with UTV and all the studios that are coming up who are now adopting systems . . . in production, finance, distribution . . . some of that paperwork, contracts, budget, the way deals are being made, will have an effect on the industry here.

Hossain's interactions with producers, directors, stars, and a range of below-the-line professionals in Bollywood began in 2003 when she facilitated the production of the Yash Johar-produced *Kal Ho Na Ho* (Tomorrow May Not Be, dir. Nikhil Advani, 2003) in New York City. Hossain's company, Dillywood Inc., handled a range of responsibilities, including arranging accommodations for cast and crew members, securing permits for shooting in different parts of New York City, recruiting extras, and renting equipment. This led to several other assignments for Bollywood films involving American locations as well as a Hollywood film (Wes Anderson's *The Darjeeling Limited*, 2007) shot in India.

What Hossain and her fellow panelists offered was a straightforward and homogenizing narrative of progress in which the transition from a "precapitalist" mode of production to one that would be in tune with global capital was framed as being inevitable, if not entirely seamless. Needless to say, the notion that a specific mode of organization, built on logics of kinship and interpersonal ties, has remained stable and shaped the functioning of the Bombay film industry for over five decades is equally problematic. I shall focus on this aspect further in the next section where I examine family businesses' reconstruction of industrial identities. But for the moment, I want to signal that Vishesh Bhatt's outburst, during which he accused corporate executives of being irresponsible and even underhanded, needs to be understood in part as a response to this corporate narrative in which Hollywood would, in the fullness of time, come to define business logics, industrial practices, and production cultures in Bollywood.

Of course, Bhatt's remarks were also a performance of incommensurability, with the difference being that he mobilized a different strain of the same culturalist discourse. While the corporate narrative located the Bombay film industry in a "prolonged state of not-yetness," a familiar trope that has been deployed, as Madhava Prasad points out, by western critics as well as the Indian state, Bhatt positioned small-scale and family-owned companies like his own as part of a culture of production that was culturally distinct and, moreover, had the Indian public's interests at heart.[20] Not surprisingly, Bhatt was not the only one to make this rhetorical move. By the end of 2008, news and trade coverage of Bollywood had shifted to arguing that the studios, particularly those from Hollywood, were stumbling because they simply could not come to grips with the specificities of the culture of media production in Bombay. As Karan Johar put it in an article that catalogued a series of Hollywood studios' production fiascos in India: "I think the studios have adjustment issues, cultural issues and inadequate human resources. They understand the business, but how well do they understand the pulse of the audience?"[21]

That Johar and Bhatt took recourse to claims of cultural difference and authenticity should not come as a surprise. Invoking the figure of a culturally different and unique Indian "audience" had, after all, been standard operating practice for a range of media industry professionals in Bombay. As Mazzarella has shown, constructing the figure of "the Indian consumer" allowed advertising and marketing professionals to situate themselves as "experts on, and guardians of, local cultural difference" and, in the process, fortify their position vis-a-vis global clients.[22] In the Bollywood context too, this move on the part of producers and directors like Vishesh Bhatt and Karan Johar, as well as stars like Aamir Khan and Shahrukh Khan who manage their own small-scale production companies and also routinely invoke "local cultural difference," points to how this identity claim is tied to a broader economic and institutional imperative. Consider the following exchange.

Toward the end of the question and answer session of the panel titled "The Business of Filmmaking in 2008: Agony or Ecstasy?" a middle-aged, diminutive man seated in one of the last rows raised his hand and stood up.

Q: I am an independent businessman, and I have been in this business for many, many years now. I belong to the exhibition sector. We own theaters. And I read FICCI's PwC (Pricewaterhouse Coopers) report regularly. Once, I was called for an interview at Star Plus and a PwC rep was also there. He projected that in 2006, the industry was worth 43,700 crores and in 2009, 1 lakh crores—across entertainment and media. I said, please you talk only about entertainment because I know only film production, distribution and exhibition. Figures were showing 8,500 crores, and projection was some 12,000–13,000 crores. Even last year, 216 films were released. Only six were hits.

VISHESH BHATT (INTERRUPTING): A lot of people are trying to dodge the discussion, but I'm on your side.

Q: Once a picture is released on Friday, its fate is decided. So I asked the PwC man: how do you get those figures? Ultimately, he said please don't ask such questions. Then they gave me a ring. I said you tell me where you got those figures. They are misguiding.

Before he could finish, Amit Khanna, seated in the first row, interrupted. Khanna, Chairman of Reliance Entertainment, also serves as Chairman of the Convergence Committee of FICCI and has been one of the most influential industry figures to champion corporatization as the way forward for the Bombay film industry. Even before this question was posed, Khanna had expressed his disapproval of Vishesh Bhatt's outburst. Paying no heed to the moderator's request to let the audience member complete his question, Khanna intervened:

AMIT KHANNA: I am responding on behalf of FICCI. It's very simple. No figures are fudged. You probably don't know how to read the report. These are not numbers that are pulled out of a hat. There is a lot of research that goes into this, and there is a methodology. There were 3.6 billion admits in India last year. So we average out the costs.

Consumers paid that much money at box office. So that is real money. Reports are not throwing numbers. If you are talking about 12,000 crores as revenue for the film industry, you have to take into account the money that the music industry, home entertainment business, overseas returns, mobile operators—money that they all paid the film industry. So these numbers are not cooked up, let me assure you.

Recall Rommy Rolly's quip in *Luck by Chance* during his meeting with corporate executives—*yahaan property ko hi property kehte hain* (here, we only refer to property as property). Consider also an anecdote that Amit Mitra, the Secretary General of FICCI, narrates in his reflection on the struggle to get banks and other financial institutions in India to understand the risks involved in funding films:

> The example given to me was how the Punjab National Bank had lent to Dev Anand some money for a movie. The movie flopped and Dev Anand sent a truckload of celluloid back to the Punjab National Bank saying this was the only property he had and returned it.[23]

Here are stories that speak to one of the most crucial dimensions of change that being part of Bollywood demanded—the ability to speak a new language of risk and participate in new modes of speculation. Reports produced by management consultancy firms each year for the FRAMES convention, branding and other identity practices, and the FRAMES conventions themselves have served as spaces and occasions in which new modes and idioms of risk and speculation are specified and rehearsed, and since 2000 have emerged as crucial to the legitimization of a vision of Bollywood as a global media industry. But there is no guarantee, as the exchange above shows, that such performances are left uncontested. Indeed, it would be safe to assume that everyone in this conference room was keenly aware of the disjuncture between corporate identity claims and actual practices.[24] Even as Khanna finished speaking, another person in the audience piped up: "And we know how reliable PwC figures are!" A few weeks before the FRAMES convention, it had come to light that Pricewaterhouse Coopers had been complicit in a major infotech company's (Satyam) fraudulent accounting practices. Amid much laughter from the audience, the moderator brought the panel to a close, saying: "In FICCI's defense, this year's report was produced by KPMG, not Pricewaterhouse Coopers!"

Amit Khanna's stern response—*the numbers are not cooked up . . . you probably don't know how to read the report*—may not have been enough to silence the independent businessman or Vishesh Bhatt, both of whom posed questions critical of both consultancy reports and the spectacular accumulation that they claimed to document. But it was a telling indication as to how crucial the formal language of business administration had become for participating in the modes of speculation that new sources of capital demanded. I would argue, then, that the panel session on film financing and indeed the FICCI-FRAMES 2009 convention as a whole revealed that the transition from Bombay to Bollywood was, at its core, about the shift to a new mode of speculation. What the discussions at the convention and statements by figures like Vishesh Bhatt and Karan Johar elided, however, were the ways in which small-scale and family-owned companies have adapted, maneuvered, and successfully negotiated this transition. By the same token, corporate executives' performances and the identity strategies they deployed through websites and other platforms masked the extent to which the rational business models and managerial practices that they espoused were, in fact, tempered and modified by powerful and well-established social networks in the Bombay film industry. In other words, the reality on the ground was far more complicated than straightforward corporate/kinship or global/local dichotomies underpinned by a narrative of incommensurability could suggest.

Managing Difference

We could begin by observing that small-scale and family-run companies, given their capacity to leverage long-standing social relationships, have continued to shape production dynamics and the organizational form of Bollywood. As a number of scholars have documented, the development of the social network comprising producers, financiers, directors, and actors in Bollywood can be traced back to the late 1930s and 1940s.[25] The 1951 *Report of the Film Enquiry Committee*, which provides considerable detail on the operations and structure of the film industry during the interwar period, notes that the industry was defined by a large number of independent producers.[26] By the time World War II had ended and India gained independence in 1947, there were as many as 125 "new producers" releasing 228 films out of a total of 283 films, a sharp rise from a total of 42 independent producers operating in 1940.[27] Comparing the situation in Bombay to Hollywood at the time, this report goes on to blame these independent producers, many of whom left the business after a few attempts, for the problems afflicting the film industry.

This problem of independent producers with access to capital from a range of sources is often cited by government reports as well as the trade-press as a key reason for the emergence of a chaotic production culture in which personal trust was highly valued and determined deal making. This explanation also focuses on the prominence of independent producers as the main reason for the demise of the studios that were established during the 1920s and 1930s. But as Brian Shoesmith has argued, there were a number of other forces and factors that led to the gradual marginalization of studios in central and north India.[28] Besides, it is worth keeping in mind that production relations and the structure of studios that emerged during the 1930s and 1940s in south India varied a great deal in comparison with those that emerged in Bombay. But for the purposes of my analysis here, it is important to note that the studios and other production companies that dominated the Hindi-language film industry operated on what Barnouw and Krishnaswamy call the "one-big-family" principle with tight family control over ownership and key managerial positions. In other words, even during the so-called "studio era," film production was defined by kinship ties and close-knit social networks.[29] And what is particularly striking in the case of the Bombay film industry is the reproduction and sustenance of these relationships and networks over successive generations to the extent that the families and close friends of producers, directors, and stars from the 1950s continue to dominate the film industry today.

Where the transition from Bombay cinema to Bollywood is concerned, the influence of kin networks has meant the evolution of an organizational form in which a small group of established producers and a number of independent producers, both operating small-scale companies, dominate a fragmented production sector. A recent study by Mark Lorenzen and Florian Taube notes that "all the top 30 earning Bollywood films in 2003–05 were produced by a total of 20 production companies," with "retained earnings, private loans by family, rich friends or associates, and agreements with distributors still the preferred modes of finance for more than two-thirds of Bollywood film projects in 2006."[30] In fact, as the table detailing the top 5 earning Bollywood films from 2000 to 2009 reveals (Appendix 2), a majority of the most successful films have been made by established producers operating companies that are more often than not, family-owned and/or managed by a small circle of trusted friends and family members (only 8 of the top 100 earning films were produced by large media corporations).[31]

Consider the trajectory of Yash Raj Films, a celebrated, privately held family-run production company that was founded by Yash Chopra in 1970. It built on its successes during the mid-1990s to establish itself as a vertically integrated company in Bollywood with interests in television and music as well. Yash Chopra began his film career as an assistant to his brother B. R. Chopra, directing such films as *Dhool Ka Phool* (1959, Blossom of Dust) and *Dharmputra* (1961, Dutiful Son) under the production banner of B. R. Films before launching Yash Raj Films and going on to produce and direct his own films throughout the 1980s and 1990s. Although a notable selection of his successful 1970s films (e.g., *Deewar*, TheWall, 1975, *Trishul*, Trident, 1978) were not produced by Yash Raj Films, the company's own narrative of its history seamlessly considers these part of Yash Raj Films' legacy. Until 2000, Yash Raj Films produced 19 films, one every few years, with Yash Chopra directing more than half of these. The company's reputation was not made, however, until the remarkable box office success of *Dilwale Dulhania Le Jayenge* (1995), the directorial debut for Yash Chopra's son, Aditya Chopra. The blockbuster reinforced Yash Raj Films's commitment to lavish romantic musicals and heralded significant structural changes in the company. From 2000 to 2009, the company produced 27 films, with Yash Chopra credited as the director of only one. Beginning in the mid-1990s, Yash Chopra stepped back from his directing duties and the father-son team took on production and managerial positions in a rapidly expanding and vertically integrated company.

In 1995, Yash Chopra teamed up with a management executive Sanjeev Kohli (who would go on to become Yash Raj Films' CEO) to create music-based television shows, forming the Metavision Company in the process. Although they discontinued this venture, the Chopras began producing television shows again over a decade later (in 2010, the television production division of Yash Raj Films produced five scripted programs for Sony Entertainment Television). Starting in 2004, the company also started releasing the music albums associated with its films and the label eventually began producing smaller releases of a select number of nonfilm music artists. Overall, the most notable feature of Yash Raj Films's activities since about 2000 surround Yash and Aditya Chopra's efforts to style the company as "India's leading Entertainment Conglomerate" through promoting it as "veritably a 'Studio' in every sense." As the company's website proclaims, this involved building a "state-of-the-art, fully integrated film studio" that included three sound stages and a range of amenities that match international standards.

While expansion into music, television, and production/postproduction processes were crucial to positioning the company in relation to the larger refashioning of Bollywood as a transnational media industry that was more than Bombay cinema, the most important structural changes were in the domain of film distribution. There is no doubt that Yash Raj Films had established a formidable distribution infrastructure well before the moment of corporatization. Beginning in the mid-1990s, the company began distributing its films and those of other companies in certain regions in India and internationally for theatrical and home video audiences. As the 2000s progressed, Yash Raj Films began exclusively managing its home video and international theatrical releases, as well as orchestrating its domestic releases in a manner that distinguished it from other small-scale, family-run companies in the Bombay film industry. Yash Raj Films currently has distribution offices in eleven major Indian cities as well as an office each in the United Kingdom, the United States, and the United Arab Emirates.[32]

To be sure, companies like Yash Raj Films or Rajshri Media, another family-run company that has reimagined its scale of operations over the past decade, appear to be exceptions. However, their trajectories do suggest that small-scale and family-run production companies were not completely averse to the notion of "going corporate" or forging relations with large media corporations. Even as the producer-director-star network ensured that media corporations' capacity to refigure the domain of film production would be limited, finance and distribution were another matter. Since 2000 small-scale and independent production companies have entered into distribution arrangements with a handful of large media corporations, which has translated both into a measure of stability and the opportunity to envision overseas territories (see Appendix 2).[33] In Lorenzen and Taube's account of ongoing organizational changes in Bollywood, it is in the domain of distribution that media corporations have managed to challenge existing industry practices.[34] The top ten earning films during the 2000 to 2009 period were distributed not only by established family companies like Yash Raj Films and Rajshri Media but increasingly by corporate entities including UTV Motion Pictures, Eros Entertainment, Reliance Entertainment, and Shree Ashtavinayak Cine Vision. Further, as Adrian Athique and Douglas Hill note in their analysis of the multiplex economy in urban India, these shifts in distribution are intimately linked to dramatic changes in the domain of exhibition.[35] Identifying and analyzing a number of factors that contributed to the "multiplex boom," they go on to note that five companies—PVR Cinemas, Adlabs Films Ltd., Shringar Cinemas Ltd., INOX Leisure Ltd., and FUN Cinemas—that "share some key characteristics, operational practices and business outlooks in opposition to the traditional working model of film exhibition in India" have come to operate over two-thirds of India's multiplexes.[36]

Of course, it goes without saying that this is an emergent and rapidly evolving terrain. And we do need to keep in mind that these details regarding production and distribution arrangements only tell part of the story. One way to gain a better understanding of what is undoubtedly a complex set of accommodations and alliances is by examining how small-scale family businesses have refashioned their industrial identities in response to the vision of Bollywood that the Indian state and FICCI wanted to celebrate. Karan Johar's Dharma Productions is a particularly good example of this group of companies, and the narrative that the company's website offers speaks precisely to the calibration of industrial identity for a new phase of capital.

Designed by an IT company that developed web solutions for Yash Raj Films, UTV, Reliance Entertainment, and other prominent media companies, the Dharma Productions home page includes standard elements such as details of films produced by the company as well as information about upcoming productions, a list of key awards that Karan Johar-produced films have won, and promotional materials including screensavers, wallpapers, and mobile phone ringtones that fans can download. To understand how Karan Johar repositioned his family-run company in Bollywood, we need to navigate to the "Our Profile" section of the website. Featuring a picture of Karan Johar's father Yash Johar, whose career in the Bombay film industry began in the early 1950s, the profile begins by listing a series of well-known films that Yash Johar produced. Reminding us that he established Dharma Productions Private Limited in 1976, the profile situates the company as one that has been a key player in the Bombay film industry for over three decades. Three decades of production history are glossed over, however, as the narrative then leaps from the 1970s to the moment of corporatization during the late 1990s:

> Dharma Productions Pvt. Limited's reputation as a *clean, honest* company grew with each of these films and helped build a tremendous amount of goodwill within the fraternity. From then on Yash Johar formed a proprietary concern under the name of Dharma Productions in 1997. What followed next was cinematic history from Dharma Productions (my emphasis).

The emphasis on Dharma Productions being a "clean" and "honest" company suggests that the articulation of industrial identity became an imperative only during the late 1990s and specifically in relation to the film financing scandals and the discourse of *safai* (cleaning up/cleansing) that I discussed in the previous chapter. Having made the transition into the late 1990s, the rest of the three-page profile focuses entirely on Karan Johar's career beginning with his directorial debut (*Kuch Kuch Hota Hai*, Heartbeats, 1998). And it is through Karan Johar's trajectory in Bollywood that Dharma Productions's identity as a family-run yet thoroughly professional and globally oriented company is constructed.

A page from the website of Dharma Productions, a family-owned company. The narrative offered here and in other sections of the website positions Karan Johar within long-standing social networks in the Bombay film industry.

Kuch Kuch Hota Hai was no fluke, we are told, as Karan Johar went on to script, produce, and direct *Kabhi Khushi Kabhie Gham* (*K3G*, 2001), a film that broke several box-office records and "featured a line-up of Indian megastars across generations." *K3G* was nothing short of a "casting coup" as the film brought together "industry stalwarts Amitabh Bachchan and Jaya Bachchan, contemporary megastars Shahrukh Khan and Kajol, and current heartthrobs Hrithik Roshan and Kareena Kapoor." Accompanied by a picture that shows Karan Johar sitting beside his father on the sets of a film, listening attentively, this narrative firmly embeds the young producer-director within the industry's social network.

Of course, the capacity to tap into long-standing social and kinship relations is only one dimension and predictor of success. The profile also works to establish Karan Johar's directorial and writing skills by tracking the many awards and accolades that both *Kuch Kuch Hota Hai* and *K3G* won at film festivals in India and, perhaps even more significantly, across Europe and in prestigious settings such as the Cannes Film Festival. This move beyond the "national" is framed not only in terms of Dharma Productions films' diaspora-centric narratives and screenings at international film festivals but also, crucially, in relation to distribution. *K3G*, the profile points out, "was released all over the world with 635 prints and holds the distinction of being the highest grossing Indian film in the UK and the USA."

Here is a "second-generation industry kid," the profile suggests, who is leading the way for Bollywood to envision a transnational audience. Even as Karan Johar is positioned as the individual now in charge of Dharma Productions and moreover as one who has the skills as well as the social and cultural capital in the film industry to produce films with the most sought-after actors, there is a recognition that this might not be sufficient in a changing media landscape. The profile then draws our attention to Karan Johar's managerial acumen and willingness to professionalize his family-run company: "In order to take Dharma Productions into the future, Karan Johar embarked on producing films for independent directors under his banner." Tracing Karan Johar's successes as a producer who backed films such as *Dostana* (Friendship, dir. Tarun Mansukhani, 2008), which sparked debates about homosexuality in India, Dharma Productions is defined as a company that is "unafraid to raise issues that are less discussed" and that strives to "push the envelope thematically."

Overall, what the website reveals is the construction of a hybrid industrial identity, one that strives to strike a balance between presenting a professional and corporatized image while maintaining its position as a company led by an individual (Karan Johar) who occupies an important position within Bollywood's powerful social network. It emphasizes, in other words, the ability to move back and forth between the corporate world and one in which interpersonal relations continue to be valued just as much as (if not more than) written agreements and contracts. Dharma Productions's shift from being a family-run production banner ensconced within mercantile circuits of capital in Bombay, in which a father-son team produced and directed a film every two or three years, to becoming a corporatized production company in which the charismatic Karan Johar makes every decision yet has expanded his company's operations to produce a range of films involving a number of writers and directors, illustrates one key trajectory that small-scale companies have taken since 2000 (see Appendix 1 for profiles of other key Bollywood companies and their development since this time). The profile thus gives us a sense not only of Dharma Productions' industrial identity but also how this hybrid identity and flexible structure have enabled a family-run, small-scale company to stake a claim in Bollywood.

Mapping this phase of transition gets all the more complex when we move beyond large-scale corporations like UTV and family businesses like Dharma Productions to consider production companies like The Factory.

Established by Ram Gopal Varma with initial financial backing from K Sera Sera, a company started by Non-Resident Indians, the production company was initially called Varma Corporation Limited (VCL). In February 2003, K Sera Sera entered into an agreement with VCL to produce films. Later that same year, K Sera Sera signed an agreement with Sahara India, a major conglomerate, as well as Priya Village Roadshow (PVR), a company that has played a key role in reconfiguring the exhibition sector across urban India.[37] While the deal with Sahara India ensured a steady financing stream and the opportunity for additional revenues by broadcasting films on Sahara's television channel (Sahara One), the agreement with PVR targeted marketing and distribution. Building on a series of hit films including *Satya* (Truth, 1998), *Company* (2000), and *Bhoot* (Ghost, 2003), Varma had by this time rebranded his company as The Factory and established himself as a versatile and edgy filmmaker whose films also succeeded at the box office.

Observing that Ram Gopal Varma's identity and mode of production is as much a part of Bollywood as that represented by Karan Johar or Aditya Chopra, Ravi Vasudevan goes on to argue that The Factory "appears to have opened up a different network of industrial access than those controlled by film-making dynasties, their families, business partners, hangers-on and protégés."[38] Thus the ways in which companies managed by "second-generation industry kids" like Karan Johar, Aditya Chopra, Vishesh Bhatt, and Goldie Behl are positioned in Bollywood or, for that matter, influential firms like The Factory or Pritish Nandy Communications, suggest neither corporate dominance nor resistance on the part of small-scale companies and family businesses. The picture of Bollywood that emerges at the end of a decade of corporatization is that of a space of media production whose contours are being shaped by interactions among a range of players negotiating the transition to a new phase of capital and new modes of speculation.

Conclusion

Building on the analysis of changing relations among the Indian state, the media industries, and the Indian diaspora in the previous chapter, I have focused attention here on the tenth anniversary of the FICCI-FRAMES convention as a way to examine the impact that a decade of corporatization has had on the Bombay film industry. As it turned out, the panel discussions at FRAMES 2009 revealed a far more complex and hybrid media landscape than the official narrative of the emergence of a corporatized

Bollywood that FICCI tried to weave. Over a span of three days, it gradually became clear that the refashioning of the Bombay film industry as Bollywood hinged on a set of unequal and deeply ambivalent interactions across three interlinked fields: the Indian state and its tentative embrace of the cultural industries; Hollywood hegemony, particularly as it defines what constitutes the "global" for institutions like FICCI, powerful corporate consultancies, and that of course, continues to shapes the Bombay film industry's response; and a range of family businesses, small-scale production companies, and large media corporations grappling with changing conditions and emerging structures of production, marketing, distribution, and exhibition.

I have suggested that focusing on these interactions is crucial for at least two reasons. First, it forces us not to reduce the complexities of media transition by focusing too narrowly on the state-cinema relationship. In contrast to state-centric analyses that flatten out different domains and layers that constitute Bollywood, I have attempted to show that the transition from Bombay cinema to Bollywood is not a straightforward evolutionary movement from one distinct organizational system and culture of production to another. Rather, it is best understood as a process that is ongoing, uneven, and as we have seen, volatile at times. Much as the Indian state, institutions like FICCI, and corporate consultancies imagine a Hollywood-like future for Bollywood, it remains clear that such projections cannot wish away deep-rooted social relations and cultural infrastructures that mediate transitions across the production, financing, distribution, and exhibition sectors.

Furthermore, approaching this decade as a formative interval allows us to push back against official narratives that posit a neat integration of Bollywood within globally dominant modes of capitalist media production and circulation. Paying greater attention to industry dynamics reveals, instead, how established practices—be they globally recognizable corporate logics or the seemingly "local" realities of production relations in Bombay—are being gradually reassessed and remodeled to meet the demands of changing economic and sociopolitical conditions. It would be easy to discuss Yash Raj Films or Dharma Productions as exemplars of "Indian" family businesses, and equally easy to regard companies like UTV and Studio 18 as representing the new, corporate Bollywood. But all these companies and the professionals that work in them are embedded in the same transnational media space that is now Bollywood. The same forces of capital, technology, and state policy shape their practices. There is no cultural essence, then, that defines the workings of family businesses in Bollywood. By the same token, companies like UTV are not simply corporate players that resemble and operate like Hollywood studios. Rather, what we are seeing is the productive, if at times uneasy, coexistence of varied capitalist practices. It is against this background of a media industry-in-transition that the next chapter draws attention to the emergence of marketing and promotions as a key domain where the shifting relations between capital, speculation, and industrial identity are further worked out.

3

"It's All about Knowing Your Audience"

Marketing and Promotions in Bollywood

In April 2004 the *Times of India* began publishing a comic strip featuring two characters named *Hum* and *Tum*. As soon became clear to readers across the country, the comic strips were part of a marketing campaign for a film produced and distributed by Yash Raj Films (*Hum Tum*, 2004, You and Me, dir. Kunal Kohli). The marketing team at Yash Raj Films had, in what seemed unusual at the time, been involved in the filmmaking process from a very early stage and decided to build a campaign around the film's protagonist, Karan Kapoor (Saif Ali Khan), who plays the role of a cartoonist in the film.[1] As the comic strip became a topic of conversation, the marketing team invited audiences in India and abroad to develop their own strips using *Hum* and *Tum* and submit them to Yash Raj Films. The winning strips, it was announced, would be integrated into the film. In addition to the comic strips, *Hum* and *Tum* also featured prominently in television promotions for the film. Woven into an otherwise standard promotion of various song sequences from the film on music channels (such as MTV-India and Channel [V]) and general entertainment channels (such as Star Plus and ZEE), the cartoons leant a measure of novelty to film marketing, a practice that had never occupied a prominent position in the Bombay film industry. And on May 27, 2004, a day before the worldwide release of the film, Saif Ali Khan appeared as Karan Kapoor on Sony Entertainment Television's popular television program *Jassi Jaisi Koi Nahin* (There Is No One Like Jassi), the Indian adaptation of the Colombian telenovela, *Yo Soy Betty La Fea*. A year later, in the fall of 2005, every film journalist, marketing executive, and public relations agent I spoke with in Bombay referenced *Hum Tum* as a key moment for the film industry. Marketing, as one trade story put it, was the new mantra in Bollywood with Yash Raj Films, in its corporatized incarnation, leading the way.[2]

"Until *Hum Tum*, we were doing vanilla stuff," declared Tarun Tripathi, the marketing manager at Yash Raj Films, when I met him in the offices of Yash Raj Films in northwest Bombay. What did "vanilla" mean? "You know,

Screen capture from Yash Raj Films's promotional website for the film *Hum Tum*.

you simply look at what is available and do something with it. Like with MTV, *ek big picture banate hain, ek love line banate hain aur jitne bhi shows hain, usmein hum apne stars ko dalte hain aur publicity mil jayega* [let's do *Big Picture*, one *Loveline*, and in all the other shows that exist let's place our stars and that will generate publicity]. You don't use your mind to figure out how to exploit a medium in a specific way. *Hum Tum* was when we said ok, enough of all this." *Big Picture* and *Loveline* were popular shows on MTV-India that had, since the late 1990s, regularly featured film stars and served as promotional platforms for upcoming films. Pointing to a string of other successful films produced and/or distributed by Yash Raj Films, Tripathi went on to offer his take on the changing place of marketing and promotions and more broadly, shifts in conceptions of the audience in Bollywood:

> Karan Johar created one of the biggest hits of Bollywood with a tagline that said, "It's all about loving your parents." You know, *K3G*. But you need to realize that Karan Johar knows very well that it's also all about knowing your audience. When you have to talk about branding and promotions, you need to be able to speak the language of market research. It is no longer enough to say *arre sir, badiya picture hai, gaane bahut acche hain, foreign locations hain, hit hogi pakka, hum keh rahe hain.* [It's a terrific film,

the songs are really good, there are foreign locations, it'll definitely be a hit, take my word for it]. It doesn't work anymore to say you *feel* the film will do well. You have to be able to talk about target audiences, key attributes of the film, what your positioning is, and so on. Which is why people like myself, a marketing man with an MBA from IIM-Lucknow (Indian Institute of Management), are at Yashraj Films. And let me tell you, the marketing department here has quickly become an important part of the company.

Tripathi's justification of his role in one of the most prominent companies in the industry, and his argument that established modes of film promotion and marketing were no longer viable, was not just self-promotion. Without exception, all the journalists, television executives, public relations agents, and marketing executives at film production companies that I spoke with emphasized that marketing was now a site and practice that was professionalized and highly valued in the film industry. With producers and distributors willing to allocate over 15 to 20 percent of their budgets to marketing and promotions, a change that was noted and commented on extensively in the trade-press, there was no doubt that this was a crucial shift.

Until the mid-1990s, the production and circulation of paratexts for Hindi-language films was a largely uncomplicated affair overseen by a publicist responding to directions from the producer and director of the film. As the media and entertainment landscape in India was transformed during the 1990s and early 2000s, authoring hype became a far more complex affair. Promoting and marketing a Bollywood film acquired new dimensions: tailoring promotional videos for various television channels, crafting innovative making-of features, negotiating spots for film stars on different television programs, designing websites for each film, coordinating online chat sessions involving transnational fan communities, contests and games for various mobile phone platforms, and so on. These changes were reflected in the credit sequence of Bollywood films as well. While the censor board certificate remained in place, it no longer cut to the usual sequence of titles and names of cast and crew members. Virtually every film now included details of partnerships or tie-ins with television channels, radio stations, dot-com and mobile phone companies, and an array of fashion labels and other commodities. Further, the figure of the "publicist" or "publicity coordinator" was now accompanied, if not replaced, by names of advertising and marketing companies such as Imagesmiths, Madison Mates, and Leo Burnett. Authoring hype was no longer the province of the producer and the director. It was clear that a new group of marketing and public relations professionals had come to occupy a prominent role in shaping the production and circulation of paratexts.

These changes in creative and industrial practice were all the more striking given the marginal position that marketing has historically occupied in the Hindi film industry. In her account of conceptions of the "audience" in the Bombay film industry, Tejaswini Ganti notes that a discourse of "hits" and "flops," that is, evaluating and speculating about the box-office outcome of films, is the "primary way that Hindi filmmakers relate[d] to their audiences . . . and commercial success or failure is interpreted by filmmakers as an accurate barometer of social attitudes, norms, and sensibilities, thus providing the basis for knowledge about audiences."[3] Ganti also notes that the "scientific" language of market research that drives business decisions and production practices in the television, advertising, print, and consumer goods sectors in India was rarely invoked by those in the film industry. However, from the perspective of the marketing and public relations professionals I spoke with, "class/mass," "city/interior," "family," "ladies," and so on—classifications of the audience derived from the carving of distribution territories, evaluations of these territories' revenue-earning potential, and filmmakers' assumptions about viewers' cultural capital—no longer seemed sufficient. As this new group of marketing and public relations professionals brokered deals with newspapers, purchased spots on various television channels, negotiated sponsorships with brands, entered into merchandising agreements, and sought the attention of audiences through ringtones and MMS clips,[4] the "audience" was reimagined as a construct that had purchase in a number of different sites of mediation and could no longer be defined and understood solely in relation to a film's performance at the box office.

This chapter examines how this shift came about by mapping the development of marketing and promotions as a new site of knowledge and decision-making power in Bollywood. Outlining the emergence of a distinct zone of creative and business practice—in-house marketing teams, freelance public relations agents, small-scale public relations firms, and film marketing divisions within prominent advertising agencies such as Lintas, Leo Burnett, and Ogilvy & Mather—I argue that ongoing changes in the domain of marketing and promotions are emblematic of broader reconfigurations of relations between capital, circuits of information, and forms of knowledge (in this instance, regarding the audience) in Bombay's media world. Further, I examine this transition by locating film marketing and promotions within a broader history of links between film and television. Tracing this relationship—from the early 1980s, when the state-controlled television network, Doordarshan, opened its doors to sponsored programming, to the entry and establishment of transnational television companies such as Star, ZEE, and Sony during the 1990s—reveals how the film industry responded to new circuits of capital and discursive practices (television ratings points, for example) that transformed Bombay's media world.

It would be a mistake, however, to conceptualize these changes as leading to a thoroughgoing break, of established practices giving way to new ones. In fact, Tripathi's account, in which he invokes both an established director like Karan Johar and MBA-style film marketing, signals not so much new marketing practices replacing older modes as the imperative to negotiate a media ecology defined by multiple, at times competing, notions of value. As we will see, marketing and public relations professionals became central to the process of authoring hype in large part because they were able to facilitate interactions and exchanges among professionals in film, television, and advertising despite the fact that these industries were defined by what appeared to be incommensurable regimes of value and modes of knowing the audience.

Reimagining the Audience: A Tale of Two *Mahurats*

Let me begin with *Kaante* (Thorns, dir. Sanjay Gupta, 2002), a project that trade narratives positioned as a test site for a range of stakeholders to envision Bollywood as a space of cultural production that would resemble Hollywood not only in terms of production values and processes, but most crucially, in terms of marketing strategy. *Kaante* was coproduced by Sanjay Gupta (also the director of the film), Pritish Nandy Communications (a television production company that entered the business of film production in 1999), Raju Patel, an NRI with over two decades' experience as a producer in Hollywood, and Lawrence Mortoff, a Hollywood producer. Gupta's story outline, an Indianized version of Quentin Tarantino's *Reservoir Dogs*, was converted into a script and the film itself was shot in Los Angeles with an all-American crew and actors from India reportedly working twelve-hour shifts and adhering to completion bonds. Billed as the Hindi film industry's first "truly international" film and a "pioneering effort to integrate the Indian film industry with the rest of the world," *Kaante* went on to do well at the box office in India and abroad, and was even listed in the Top Ten charts in the U.K. and the United States.[5]

While clean financing, discipline, and efficiency were all cited as reasons for *Kaante's* success, the film's marketing and promotional strategy also received a lot of attention.[6] "Forget the online trailer, the TV promos, the deal with Thums Up, the L.A. connection and everything else. All this was played up, yes. And it helped. But I would say that *Kaante* made everyone sit up and take notice because of the *mahurat*," explained Omar Qureshi, head of the entertainment division of indiatimes.com. Qureshi then proceeded to open the website that indiatimes.com had created for *Kaante*, and showed me a section titled "launch" where trade and press coverage of the *mahurat*—which refers to an auspicious date and time to commence any new venture—had been compiled. It was clear that the launch of *Kaante* had been a significant departure from the norm.[7]

The *mahurat* is an important production ritual organized by a film producer to announce a new project. In Bombay and other film-producing centers such as Hyderabad and Chennai, *mahurats* are usually held several months before actual production of the film has begun and in many cases, are lavish affairs held at five-star hotels. At a typical *mahurat*, following the announcement of the project by the producer and short speeches by the film's stars and other prominent film personalities present at the occasion, the film's main actors perform a scene that is filmed. As Ganti explains, "the customary nature of the event is emphasized by the fact that the scene is written especially for the occasion and the shot footage is never incorporated into the final film. The goal is to impart the essence of the film since at this stage the film is usually a germ of an idea—a script has not even begun to be written."[8] The *mahurat* also marks the first stage of publicity for a film, and is often used by producers to raise finances through the sale of distribution rights. Ganti provides a thick description of one such *mahurat* in order to demonstrate how kinship serves as the most important "principle of organization and hierarchy within the industry" and that it "functions as cultural capital, symbolic capital, and a form of risk-management or insurance within the industry."[9]

The long-term associations and friendships between directors, producers, stars, and distributors, well-known to anyone who follows the careers of stars in the industry, certainly present formidable barriers to entry for outsiders. But Ganti's analysis also makes it clear that every aspect of the film business—including the crucial activity of tracking a film's revenues, determining its box-office success or failure, and developing an understanding of the "audience"—relies on a web of personal contacts and relationships developed over a long period of time. Such informal and largely unorganized networks of information flows are hardly surprising, as Prasad and Ganti's accounts of the dominance of merchant capital and the distributor-financier nexus in the industry suggest. As we have seen in the previous chapter, this is an industry in which the production sector has, since the 1960s, consisted of a handful of powerful producers and a large number of (mostly unaccounted for) independent producers. Production has been, as Prasad notes, "subservient to distributors' capital which is advanced to producers, the production then belonging to the financier."[10]

These practices, not unlike those Curtin documents in the Chinese film industry, meant that not everyone had equal access to certain circuits of information flow (regarding box-office returns, for instance).[11] Social relations forged and cultivated over a long period of time, especially ones that have successfully negotiated successes and failures at the box office, have tended to define the operations of the Bombay film industry. In one sense, then, the *mahurat* is first and foremost an industry ritual that serves as an occasion for a range of industry professionals to reaffirm their ties to one another. It is what John Caldwell would characterize as a "semi-embedded deep text/ritual" that maintains, renews, and in some cases forges new relationships both among those involved in media production (producer-director-star-distributor) and between the production community and the trade-press (editors of trade publications and a number of print, TV, and dot-com media journalists).[12]

So why did the *mahurat* for the film *Kaante* attract attention? To begin with, as one film journalist noted, "[T]here was no cracking of the auspicious coconut, no lights, no camera, and no one shouting out the command . . . !"[13] At the *mahurat*, held at a five-star hotel in Bombay, after introductions by actor Sanjay Dutt and writer Anurag Kashyap, the six principal stars of the film assembled on a dais and proceeded to give the spectators an idea of the film by reading out sections from the script. A two-minute promotional trailer and a Q&A session for the journalists followed this script-reading session. "It had," another journalist exclaimed, "all the touches of a Hollywood film in the making."[14] Further, trade and press reports of this *mahurat* noted that the event was attended not only by stars and other personalities from the film industry, but also by fund managers and investment bankers.[15]

This *mahurat* can certainly be read as an early response to calls for corporatization, as an acknowledgment of the need to adopt practices befitting an industry seeking to go global. Journalistic accounts of the event reveal that this was precisely how the event was understood by the film industry, with one prominent film director commenting that "such displays would change nothing. . . . Bollywood is not about black ties and dinner jackets."[16] But I would argue that focusing on the Hollywood-like rituals of script reading and the screening of a trailer only serves to deflect attention from one of the most important changes that this particular industry ritual anticipated: the emergence of a network of social relationships defined not only in terms of kinship and long-term personal ties, but also through new circuits of capital. The *mahurat*, production, and marketing of *Kaante* signaled that the web of relationships that defined the social world of filmmaking in Bombay had expanded to include people and groups for whom the culturalist discourses of the film industry, particularly when it came to the question of imagining and mobilizing the figure of the "audience," were simply untenable. Needless to say, I am not suggesting that these new circuits of capital have erased or completely supplanted kinship networks.[17] And as I outlined in the previous chapter, family businesses and kin relations continue to play crucial roles in Bollywood's emergent production relations. Let us, however, consider some of the key changes that have taken place since 2000.

According to industry reports, financial institutions such as the Industrial Development Bank of India have sanctioned Rs. 1.8 billion for movie projects, of which Rs. 900 million have already been distributed. Bank of India has financed Rs. 250 million for five movies, and since April 2004 the Export-Import Bank of India has financed Rs. 580 million for nine movies, including Rs. 400 million to Yash Raj Films for big-budget hits such as *Veer Zaara* (Yash Chopra, 2004), *Hum Tum* (Kunal Kohli, 2004), and *Bunty Aur Babli* (Shaad Ali, 2005).[18] Another significant source of funds has been the entry of large corporations into the film business, the most prominent being the establishment of Reliance Entertainment, which is now involved in film production, processing, exhibition, and distribution. Since 2005 the television industry has also made forays into film production and distribution. Well-established groups such as the ZEE Network, Sahara Group, Balaji Telefilms, UTV, STAR, and SONY have all set up film divisions, bringing their production values and processes to bear on filmmaking. In a brief span of five to six years, these integrated media companies have also developed innovative strategies for marketing and distributing film content through their television channels. Further, by the year 2002, when *Kaante* was released, there were as many as 35 promotional agencies and 4 in-film advertising firms in Bombay, with large advertising agencies like Leo Burnett, O&M, and Lintas setting up divisions to deal exclusively with film accounts.[19] According to trade reports, the average marketing expenditure, excluding product placements and brand promotions, had increased from Rs. 5.2 million in 2001 to Rs. 8.8 million in 2004, with companies like UTV earmarking anywhere from 15 percent to 40 percent of a film's budget for marketing and promotions.[20]

Of course, such accounts of industry transactions, produced and circulated on a daily and weekly basis by the trade-press in Bombay, do need to be understood in relation to the broader emergence of industrial reflexivity in media industries across the world, which has been central to the overall project of imagining Bollywood as well. As Nitin Govil argues, "[N]umbers offer a possible solution to perceptions of the Indian industries' deficit of reflexivity. . . . [I[t was the lack of accurate statistics that led to local and global dismissals of the casual nature of the Indian film industries."[21] But these trade narratives also invite us to consider how shifts in capital flows are leading to changes in industry logics and practices. In this case, it is critical to recognize that these new modes of financing did not just bring "clean" money into the business of filmmaking.

Production companies like Pritish Nandy Communications, for instance, brought with them notions of risk management and an apparatus of media production, including a conception of the "audience," that were markedly different in an industry accustomed to a discourse of hits and flops. The audience was imagined not only by those involved in the typical production-distribution-exhibition cycle of a film—the producers, directors, stars, and distributors—and determined, in the final instance, in terms of how many people worldwide watched the film in a cinema hall. It was not only a matter of speculation by distributors who, as Pritish Nandy remarked at a marketing seminar, "possessed an uncanny ability to smell what kind of film would work in which territory."[22] To be sure, well-established assumptions regarding audiences were invoked. As Kumar Gaurav, one of the stars in *Kaante*, reasoned when asked by a journalist why the film did not do as well as predicted: "It did not do well because it catered to a rather urban crowd, not the *aam junta* [masses]."[23]

However, the figure of the "audience" was also mobilized in interactions between Sanjay Gupta, the film's director, and Saleem Mobhani, co-founder of the dot.com company (indiafm.com) that handled web promotions for the film; between Pritish Nandy, founder-CEO of Pritish Nandy Communications, and Sanjay Bhutiani, an advertising executive from Leo Burnett Entertainment; between Sanjay Bhutiani's team and marketing executives at Thums Up, a cola company that offered Rs. 70 million for in-film placements; and finally, in negotiations between television companies and advertising agencies, defined by the ratings points that the numerous television promotions generated. The *Kaante* case thus made it clear that the "audience" need no longer be defined and understood primarily in relation to the performance of the film at the box office. It was reimagined as a construct that had purchase in a number of different sites of mediation, the most prominent and important one being television.

The importance of television to the reimagination of the audience becomes even clearer when we recognize that the *mahurat* has been transformed from being a primarily industry-oriented ritual to one that also functions as a publicly disclosed media text that circulates via television programs and an online network of entertainment dot.coms, fan-produced blogs, and various social networking sites. Indeed, this is a shift that is not lost on the film industry, as Zoya Akhtar's take on the *mahurat* in *Luck by Chance* (2009) so clearly reveals. Of course, a *mahurat* scene in a film that offers glimpses of the Bombay film industry's cultures of production is no surprise. The main ritual element—filming a scene involving the hero and heroine of the Rommy Rolly-production—unfolds on a lavish set built for the occasion and in the presence of the director, producer, a range of production crew members, friends and family of the stars, and media journalists.

However, what is particularly striking about this representation of the *mahurat* is its acknowledgment of how television has come to mediate and, in the process, redefine the scope and scale of this production ritual. Tellingly, it is through the television set in a struggling actress's (Sona) one-room apartment that we first hear about the *mahurat* for *Dil Ki Aag*. As Sona settles down in front of her television, an anchor on a television channel called Glam 24 invites us to the *mahurat*, informing us that the new heroine (Nikki) was none other than the daughter of 1970s superstar Nikki Walia and that the hero, as always with Rommy Rolly productions, would be Zaffar Khan. At the end of the minute-long *mahurat* scene, the hero and heroine walk down the stairs to join the producer and director, ready to offer sound bites to a group of journalists from various television channels.

The *mahurat* scene in *Luck by Chance*, a telling indication of the extent to which television has come to mediate the film industry's imagination of the audience.

The *mahurat* scene in *Luck by Chance*, continued.

The *mahurat* scene in *Luck by Chance*, continued.

At one level, this is like any other film *mahurat*—a brief yet elaborately staged performance that asks potential investors to imagine a "superhit." It is, as Anna Tsing observes about speculation and contemporary global finance, a performance that is simultaneously economic and dramatic: "In speculative enterprises, profit must be imagined before it can be extracted; the possibility of economic performance must be conjured like a spirit to draw an audience of potential investors. The more spectacular the conjuring, the more possible an investment frenzy. Drama itself can be worth summoning forth . . . dramatic performance is the prerequisite of economic performance."[24] But at another level, Zoya Akhtar's staging of Rommy Rolly's production *mahurat* speaks to the redefinition of the *mahurat* from being primarily an intra-industry ritual to becoming the first promotional text directed at audiences in a rapidly expanding paratextual universe that includes film songs, making-of documentaries, director commentaries and other DVD extras, television talk shows, web-based and mobile phone contests, and so on. It also suggests that the audience, conjured in and through television and not just by the producer-distributor-star nexus, is now imagined through a different set of enumerative logics (television ratings points, web metrics, and other market research techniques), a marked departure from established practices in the Bombay film industry.

Let us also note the importance of recasting the audience as a measurable and knowable construct that could be used to generate additional revenues for these new players in the film business. Television corporations like STAR, Sony, and Zee, media subsidiaries of large corporations such as Tata (Tata Infomedia) and Reliance Industries (Reliance Big Entertainment), and companies like Kaleidoscope Entertainment set up by venture capitalists with experience in the IT sector, operated with business logics that required them to justify their investments. At one level, then, the push for more professionalized modes of film marketing and the emphasis on market research can be understood simply as a function of these new players' need to justify their entry into a business fraught with risk. At the same time, we cannot discount the symbolic value that marketing and promotions leant to the project of fashioning Bollywood Inc. Venture capitalists, prominent NRIs, and executives from transnational advertising agencies and television corporations certainly appreciated *mahurats* and other marketing/promotional tactics that would not seem out of place in Los Angeles.

Further, even if the economic transactions that this new kind of *mahurat* would animate were not readily apparent, producers, directors, distributors, exhibitors, and others associated with the film industry were acutely aware of the importance of Hollywood-style film marketing to the overall project of conjuring Bollywood. In addition to the annual FICCI-FRAMES convention, different groups in Bombay have organized "marketing seminars" to address how film, television, and the advertising and consumer goods sectors could work together and develop successful promotional strategies across media platforms. The most prominent among these have been the "Value Creation" seminars organized by the Advertising Club of Bombay, and the "Entertainment, Media, and Marketing Forum" organized by the Film Producers' Guild of India. While a range of topics were addressed at these seminars and forums, the overarching goal, as explained by Rajesh Pant, CEO of Percept Advertising, was to make the film industry aware that "well-packaged entertainment sells despite all odds."[25] Exhorting the film industry to observe and learn from Hollywood marketing practices, several speakers at these events argued that there was a "clear need for Indian films to take their marketing business more seriously if they want to increase their foot-print and kitty."[26] As we will see in the next chapter, it is precisely this aspect of marketing and promotions that dot-com professionals leveraged to great effect as they forged relationships with various people and groups in Bollywood.

In arguing that the audience was reimagined by industry professionals as a measurable, knowable, and controllable category that could be imagined outside the context of the box office, I am not suggesting that an audience commodity for film-based television programming never existed. In fact, the Hindi film industry's relationship with television, and thereby the advertising industry, can be traced back to the early 1980s. However, it was only in the early 2000s that the "empirical," professional, and globally accepted language of market research became a part of the discursive conventions for thinking about audiences where the Bombay film industry was concerned. This shift did not, of course, happen overnight. Beginning in the mid-1990s, the phenomenal growth of the television and advertising industries was already forcing filmmakers to rethink their assumptions about audiences. Furthermore, the film industry's links with new circuits of capital and modes of speculation—set in place by transnational television companies during the 1990s—were shaped by the ways in which state-controlled television forged links with the Bombay film industry during the 1980s.

The Doordarshan Years

When the state-regulated television network Doordarshan opened its doors to sponsored programming in 1983, signaling a departure from an earlier model of public service broadcasting with the express goal of utilizing television for "development," some of the earliest and most popular shows were film-based. As one prominent report from the Ministry of Information & Broadcasting, titled "An Indian Personality for Television," noted, "feature films and film-related programmes occupied the largest single chunk of telecast time (21.1%)."[27] The Saturday evening Hindi-language film, the film songs show *Chitrahaar*, and *Showtheme*, which used popular film songs and scenes to speak to a different theme each week, always garnered high viewer ratings. By 1984–85, these shows had established an immensely lucrative "national audience" for Doordarshan.[28] As Manju Singh, the producer and host of *Showtheme*, explained:

> We wanted to show clips from memorable films in a thematic way and it became a huge hit. We also connected themes to artists and these artists were getting TV exposure for the first time. For example, when *Hero* was released, we got Jackie Shroff to do a show on crime. At the time, people didn't get to see much film-related material on TV. So for Doordarshan, *Showtheme* was great—they paid a fixed amount to us, and we would pay a part of that to producers for film material. The amount was fixed, irrespective of what movie it was or which star it was. But then, most producers and distributors were happy. Many of them felt that the show brought back the film's saleability—a second release, maybe in smaller towns. And within Doordarshan, people were very happy and appreciative. For them, *Showtheme* was the perfect mix of entertainment and information.

Showtheme was produced by Creative Unit, a Bombay-based advertising agency, in collaboration with Network 7, a television production company owned and managed by Manju Singh. The advertising agency was responsible for bringing in film stars and obtaining permissions for the use of film clips from producers and distributors. While trade and press reports indicate that for the most part filmmakers and stars did consider *Chitrahaar* and *Showtheme* as a form of publicity, it is also clear that the film industry's involvement with such shows was limited to providing content.[29]

In fact, filmmakers were unhappy with the rates fixed by Doordarshan and continually lobbied bureaucrats at the network to increase payments for film clips and songs, pointing to the exorbitant sums that the network was charging advertisers for film-based shows.[30] These negotiations and, more broadly, the mandate to produce "quality" programming even led Doordarshan officials to explore the possibility of financing directors with the goal of making "socially relevant" films for television. Forging links with the film industry was, as newspaper and trade-press articles reveal, a central concern for Doordarshan during the early 1980s.[31] But overall, the film industry had little influence in shaping this new television audience commodity. It is also clear that at no point during the 1980s did the ratings discourse, which established the dominance and revenue-generating potential of film-based programming, become part of filmmakers' frameworks for imagining their audiences. As Ganti's research shows, even into the mid-1990s market research was largely absent in the film industry. Indeed, the film industry's view of the "audience" as a "collectivity that needs to be protected, to be led, and to be educated" coincided neatly with the "development" and infotainment-oriented programming of state-regulated Doordarshan.[32]

In addition to providing content for film-based television programming, during this period the film industry also became a major source of creative and professional talent for the production of sitcoms, dramas, and other sponsored television programs. Casting aside apprehensions that television would lure audiences away from the cinema theaters, prominent producers and directors like G. P. Sippy, B. R. Chopra, and Ramanand Sagar began producing television programs.[33] The spurt in television production during this time set in place a new "trajectory of creative migration" for actors, writers, and technicians, many of whom were graduates of the Film and Television Institute of India (FTII) struggling to break into the film industry.[34] And with major advertising agencies like Lintas and Trikaya-Grey establishing television production divisions and emerging as brokers between Doordarshan and production talent in the Bombay film industry, links between film, television, and advertising were firmly established. This three-way relationship, controlled in near-absolute fashion by Doordarshan during the 1980s, was dramatically altered by the entry and growth of cable and satellite television beginning in 1991–92.

Bollywoodizing MTV-India

Beginning in May 1991, when STAR TV started broadcasting over Asia from Hong Kong, audiences in India had access to a much broader range of programming that was radically different from "the censored news, regulated documentaries, patriotic songs, and nationalist sitcoms on the state-sponsored network."[35] While there were just four channels initially (Star Plus, Star Sports, BBC News, and MTV), by the late 1990s almost every transnational satellite television corporation had entered the Indian market. In addition, by the mid-1990s a number of commercial networks such as SUN and Eenadu had established themselves by catering to a large and lucrative regional-language market. This proliferation of television channels in India was part of a larger program of economic liberalization and deregulation that allowed multinational corporations access to various sectors of the Indian economy. Thus, the expansion of the television industry was paralleled and supported by an equally explosive growth of the consumer goods and advertising industries.[36]

These new television channels attracted audiences with a range of new programs, but they too discovered the appeal that film-based programming held with viewers, and thereby the potential for advertising revenues. ZEE, Star Plus, and other channels introduced a number of innovative shows based on film music, like *Antakshari, Sa Re Ga Ma,* and *Videocon Flashback,* weekly countdown shows like *BPL Oye* and *Philips Top Ten,* and shows that reviewed popular films and evaluated their box-office performance. Further, channels like MTV-India realized that they could not operate in India by offering Euro-American music-themed programming and by 1998–99 turned to Hindi films and film music. As Cullity notes, "this music was brought in, particularly to prime-time slots, and MTV's music videos became 70 percent Hindi music videos. Hindi film clips, popular song and dance numbers taken from hit films, made for stupendous, autonomous, self-standing videos, and this in itself effectively Indianized (and localized) MTV."[37]

While questions of hybridity and localization, which have been the focus of both popular and scholarly accounts, are certainly critical, the important thing to note here for the purposes of mapping links between the film and television industries is that music channels' turn to film content was meant as much for the film industry as it was for expanding their audience base beyond upper-class, English-speaking urban audiences. From the perspective of film producers and distributors, MTV-India in its early incarnation was seen as catering to a negligible fraction of the "national" audience. In fact, the film industry was far more concerned with the growth of the home video market and the proliferation of cable channels that aired pirated versions of new films within days of their release. Filmmakers routinely cited the penetration of cable television as the primary reason for the decline in box-office revenues.[38] During this time, television was perceived more as a challenge to existing distribution arrangements than as a new promotional platform. It is this perception that channels like MTV-India set out to change. But until I met and spoke with industry professionals who had been part of this early phase of satellite television in India, I did not fully recognize how crucial this period had been in shaping relations between the film and television industries. Let me elaborate by turning to my conversations with former MTV-India executives.

"Dovetailing Cool with Bollywood"

"So tell me, what did Shashanka say?" asked Jiggy George, as soon as we entered his office at Turner Networks. George had worked as the Marketing Manager at MTV-India and been a key member of the team in charge of the channel's transition during the late 1990s. In explaining that I was interested in his reflections on MTV's "Indianization" phase, I also mentioned that I had met people like Rajesh Devraj and Shashanka Ghosh who had been instrumental in shaping programming strategy as well as brand identity at Channel [V], MTV-India's rival. "He said people working at music channels were worse than ostriches. They didn't bury their heads in the sand, they had their heads up their own butts," I recounted. Laughing out loud, George agreed: "Sounds about right. I remember that in the beginning, no one in the film industry even thought about MTV. And for its part, MTV was quite condescending and not Indian at all in any sense. Hindi film music was not cool for MTV. And it took a while for us to recognize that the top artists for Indian youth were Kishore Kumar, Mukesh, Daler . . . not Guns N' Roses and Slash!" In fact, MTV-India went off the air for two years and returned in 1996 with a redesigned brand identity and, most crucially, with recognition of the importance of Hindi film music and "localized" programming to its fortunes in the Indian market. Suggesting that the makeover was not exactly an easy process, George went on to explain that the decision to start with the "look" of the channel, especially the on-air promos, turned out to be the right one and crucial in terms of reaching out to directors and producers in the Bombay film industry who were skeptical, if not dismissive, of music television. Bringing up examples of popular on-air promos, George reflected on this period of transition:

> Looking back now, did we do that for the trade? It wasn't only for the consumer . . . it was done to let everyone in the trade know that we were a cool destination, and most importantly, that we liked Bollywood. Most of the promos—*chai wallah, maalish wallah*, with *eena meena deeka* playing in the background—it was more than to just connect with youth. From the trade perspective, it helped create an image that we are cool in an Indian way. Things like that began connecting with people in the film industry. We made a conscious effort to change the way the channel looked. Because from a TV perspective, there is a youth demographic. But if advertisers don't get you, you're not going to get anywhere. Yes, I would argue that all our promos were for the trade—the film business and the advertisers. Reasoning internally was this—if Bollywood is the currency and if it

runs across all channels, how do we distinguish ourselves? So the promos, imagery, marketing, the catch phrases, lines, VJs . . . the whole mix. It was a way to *dovetail cool with Bollywood* (my emphasis).

During the mid-to-late 1990s, the search for "cool" was *the* marketing challenge worldwide and the Indian media marketplace was no exception.[39] And for MTV-India, aligning itself with what was considered "cool" by a majority of Indian youth clearly meant rethinking its position on Hindi film music as well as an emergent Indian pop music scene. Beginning in 1997–98 with a clear mandate to forge ties with the film industry, MTV-India executives began initiating conversations with a range of producers and directors in the Hindi film industry. According to George and other music channel executives I spoke with, it took well over two years before the film industry began responding to television executives' overtures.[40] Vikram Sathaye, who worked closely with George during this period, also pointed out that until this time the film industry saw no reason to forge links with television channels:

If you were a Yash Chopra, why would you need a music channel's 10 million viewers? You would go to a general entertainment channel, but even then . . . all that would happen was the channels would get a few songs from a film like *DDLJ* or *Kuch Kuch Hota Hai*, the songs would be part of a few countdown shows and placed on rotation on MTV. No effort. We would ask Yash Chopra for the songs and he would say *theek hai* (alright), you're a TV channel, here are the songs. And at the time, no one was aware of how payments would work. So it was all very informal. But music companies played a role—if I was Sony or T-Series, it was in my interest to promote the songs. Yash Raj had sold the rights to these companies. So we came to recognize the fact that if we were to drive programming and get people to watch our channel with Bollywood content, then we would have to go talk to producers and directors. We would have to say, we'll do this exclusive for you, give us an interview with, say, Akshay Kumar. Or can Akshay Kumar do a special show with Cyrus Broacha, let's say.

To be sure, film producers were keenly aware of the popularity of film music-based shows, Top Ten countdowns in particular, and television companies' struggles with ratings and attempts to define audience shares. Within a few months of the launch of countdown shows on television channels, including Doordarshan (*Superhit Muqabla*), ZEE TV (*Philips Top Ten*), and MTV-India (*BPL Oye*), arguments broke out about the techniques used to rank the songs. While Doordarshan relied on a viewers' poll, ZEE TV and MTV-India turned to sales figures supplied by the Indian Music Companies' Association.[41] At stake were the ratings points that each television channel could claim, and thereby the advertising rates they could set. And companies like Yash Raj Films did begin exploring television as a new medium for publicizing and promoting films.[42] In addition to airing songs and scenes from the film, promotional efforts also included stars appearing on popular shows like MTV's *Big Picture* and *Loveline* to talk about their experiences working on the film. Conversations initiated by television executives like Jiggy George and Vikram Sathaye were beginning to make a difference.

Popular and scholarly accounts explain this transition either by pointing to the enduring popularity of film music and its inevitable presence on television, or by noting that the sale of music and satellite rights became a major new source of revenue for filmmakers. This is the argument Rajadhyaksha develops in his analysis of the relative importance of the box office for Bollywood:

> In economic terms, "haute" fashion explains most clearly the transition that Bollywood negotiates as it moves the cinema away from the box office, hitherto its staple source of income, into a series of new production structures in transnational geographic and financial locations which offer cultural crossovers (movie sells fashion sells brand endorsement sells star sells movie sells music sells . . .), strategic tie-ups, merchandising, publicity avenues (new television channels), as well as new electronic distribution alternatives. This explanation locates the cinema's move in tandem with the global trend towards B-to-B sectors (businesses servicing other businesses as against dealing with the end-consumer), or, in the current instance, in films transgressing their earlier distribution "territories" and earning much more through selling *rights* than *tickets*.[43]

However, the foregoing account of Doordarshan and the film industry's ties with transnational television channels like MTV-India suggests that film-TV relations encompassed more than just the issue of negotiating rights or television emerging as an important new release window. Rajadhyaksha is right in arguing that one way to understand the shift away from the box office is to approach it from the perspective of "businesses servicing other businesses as against dealing with the end-consumer."[44] But his explanation tells us little about relations between various media institutions in Bombay and how new groups of industry professionals (in marketing and public relations) positioned themselves and negotiated their value in the industry. What kinds of stories did they have to tell about their place in Bollywood? To mark the shift from selling *tickets* to selling *rights* is an important first step. It is crucial, however, to then note that the notion of "selling rights" also signals a shift in the imaginations of audiences and territories. This in turn raises the question of how film industry professionals began responding to modes of conjuring audiences—television ratings points, market research, brand valuations, and so on—that underpinned the operations of the television and advertising industries and that also informed the worldviews of MBA-trained professionals like Tarun Tripathi at Yash Raj Films.

Knowing the Audience, MBA-Style

In his analysis of the different kinds of narrative that professionals in the film and television industries in Los Angeles deploy to "make sense of their specific work worlds and their creative or managerial task at hand," John Caldwell draws attention to "genesis myths" as a genre that is typical of stories told by above-the-line creative personnel.[45] These stories, he writes, "function less as celebrations of work (suffering at the production task and vocational survival) than as celebrations of an originating moment and artistic pedigree."[46] The stories I heard from Tarun Tripathi and other marketing and public relations professionals in Bombay certainly fit this category. Consider, for example, this response from Tripathi when I asked him how his position in the film industry had changed: "When I came to work at Yash Raj, the industry was not thinking about how to connect with other media. It was a black hole. The industry was not organized, was not prepared to speak the same language. But as things changed, people began seeing how valuable it was to have someone with my background."

Reeling off a list of films for which he spearheaded the marketing campaign, Tripathi positioned himself as a professional whose work had forced Yash Raj Films, and indeed the entire film industry, to acknowledge the importance of overhauling film marketing practices. Tripathi's answer was echoed by others who had entered the business of film marketing and promotions during the late 1990s and early 2000s. Consider this explanation offered by Archana Sadanand, who manages one of the most prominent film-promotion agencies in Bollywood (*Imagesmiths*), when I asked her how she had gained a foothold in the industry:

> In the last 5–6 years, no one quite knew what publicity meant. Even now, a lot of producers have this one-man publicity team who goes to the trade papers and some prominent magazines and newspapers. And there are

independent PR people—I don't think they've ever sat down, watched a film and thought about what kind of an audience the movie will appeal to, the kind of promotions we need to develop and all that. They would just talk to the producers, ask for some pictures, and that's it. Our first problem was in dealing with producers who were used to individual PROs. My team is entirely female, and some of the older producers were hesitant and still had some stereotypes—what can these women do, kind of attitude. There was a lot of bad mouthing that happened—oh these girls, just out of college, what do they know. But once we did our first film—*Taal*, with Subhash Ghai—then people started talking about us well and now we are well-known in the industry.

While these "narratives of self-affirmation" are interesting in and of themselves, embedded in them are also stories of a media environment in transition, a new ethos even, wherein established modes of imagining audiences are no longer deemed viable. In other words, they point to the revaluation of film marketing and promotions as a distinct zone of creative and business practice, one that was no longer on the margins of the film industry, and moreover as a practice that demanded specialized knowledge (an MBA degree, for instance). Tripathi and Sadanand's narratives suggest that this ongoing transition also demanded changes in the ways in which producers, directors, and stars talked about their films. Tripathi's response, when I asked him about filmmakers' interactions with marketing and account executives in television companies and advertising agencies, speaks to this shift:

When you're a content provider, you need to ask yourself why will MTV promote your film? You have to convince MTV, or a brand like Coke or Pepsi, that your content will draw audiences or consumers as the case may be. That people will watch MTV for your content. When you have to talk about promotions to a television channel, or to a corporate sponsor, you have to be able to talk about the attributes of your film—your target audiences, key features of the film, what your positioning is, what kinds of audiences you expect to attract, and so on. You have to address your pitch to others. Like I said, it's not enough to just tell them you *feel* that your film will work. You need to be able to speak the language of market research. And you need people who have the right training and background.

Not only did this new group of professionals establish themselves as key players in the world of film marketing and promotions, but they also played an important role in translating between two very different conceptions of the "audience." Recounting the marketing campaign for Subhash Ghai's *Taal* (Rhythm, 1999), Sadanand explained her company's role in very similar terms:

> When we came in, we started to look at films as products. We said look, you need to have some plan in place depending on your target audience. Go to Channel [V] for the youth segment; go to *Dainik Jagran* for the Hindi belt. So that's how we got started on building a campaign around a film. With *Taal*, we were new so we were taking directions from Sub-hash Ghai on what he wanted. But we also went beyond simply sending out regular updates. We also helped him with his company's IPO. We went to mainstream papers and said, you don't cover these aspects of the film industry. *Taal* was one of the first films to be insured. Ghai wanted his company to go public. We went to all the major websites and newspapers, not just the film magazines, and provided them with information.

In conversations with producers, directors, and stars, public relations agents like Archana Sadanand and marketing executives like Tarun Tripathi introduced market research and the language of psychographics as indispensable tools for operating in a media environment in which transnational television corporations and advertising agencies had reconfigured the "national family" into a number of enumerable audience segments. This fixation on mapping the many parts of the "national family" had grown more intense during the late 1990s with television channels and the consumer goods sector competing for the attention of the middle class. As Mazzarella has shown, "study after study of the habits and dispositions" of the burgeoning middle class charted an "ever-expanding series of manifestations of 'the Indian consumer,' each with their own subcategories: 'the Indian teenager,' 'the new Indian woman,' and so on."[47]

I would argue that in addition to bringing stars and filmmakers into more direct contact with producers and executives in the television and advertising industries, the development of television as a major new promotional medium also drew film industry professionals into the ratings discourse that underpinned the television and advertising industries. Further, as Parul Gossain, a public relations agent who has worked for film stars and managed film promotions since 2001, explained, producers and others in the industry also realized that working with television corporations, advertising agencies, and corporate sponsors called for a reconceptualization of the "relationship game" that had characterized the world of film marketing and/or promotions.

Earlier producers had a rather crude way of marketing. Their method was to have a PRO who would take journalists out to drink, feed them, give them some photos and material and tell them, *yeh chhap dena* (publish this). The story would be a synopsis of the film, and some stills. He wouldn't say *ki film ka image yeh hai* (this is the image of the film), this is how we'd like you to break up stories. Today when you sit with a producer, you get to see the film in preproduction stage, rough cuts. Then you sit down with the producer and think about the overall message of the film. Think about the phases of promotion—is it only interviews, what kinds of audiences you want to reach beyond the film audience, how you go beyond a film magazine or the *Bombay Times*, and so on. Think of different ways to create recall. You make deals with TV channels and say ok, we'll give you this much exclusive footage. Earlier, producers did have some ideas that worked, but not anymore. Before, the publicity system was different. Journalists were close friends—it was a relationship game. Today it is about who gets you more eyeballs, or better eyeballs. And that means knowing your numbers.

Public relations agents like Parul Gossain and marketing executives like Tripathi thus emphasized the need for market research to manage a film's promotion across multiple media platforms, and argued that a promotional strategy developed on the basis of gathering information on audience tastes, desires, and purchasing power was an absolute necessity in the prevailing media environment. Television corporations and advertising agencies did, of course, have to play their part in legitimizing this new mode of conjuring audiences for the film industry. Given the number of television channels competing for film-related content and consumer brands seeking product placement opportunities, particularly from established producers and directors, marketing professionals also had to demonstrate how promotional tactics would translate into better publicity and ultimately, audiences in theaters. At the same time, stories detailing interactions between film, television, and advertising sectors also suggest that the value of market research-based constructions of the audience does not derive from claims about objectivity and empirical rigor. Rather, it resides in the very nature of the audience as a construct that is central to the larger issue of defining value in the media industries. The "audience" is, much like the calendar images that Kajri Jain analyses, "traversed by various forms of value."[48] In her analysis of the production and circulation of calendar images in India, Kajri Jain argues that the power of the images resides "in their role as switching points between different frames of value, not all of which are strictly economic."[49] Jain's insight is particularly useful in approaching the question of the audience. Let me elaborate by drawing on observations and experiences in two different sites—a television corporation (MTV-India), and a film promotions division of an advertising agency (Madison Mates).

* * *

"Now It's Different"

Following conversations with former MTV-India executives who had worked through the channel's "Indianization," I had an opportunity to spend some time in the MTV-India office and talk to a group of people involved in film-based programming. I was particularly interested in developing an understanding of how professionals at MTV-India interacted with those in the film industry on a day-to-day basis. "We cannot sit back and expect producers to come to us with their films, even though as MTV we have a certain brand image," began Anjali Malhotra, who had worked on several film-marketing campaigns. "Stand up for a second and take a look around this office," she then said. "No, seriously, take a quick look," she insisted, when I hesitated. "No more Guns N' Roses, it's about Yash Raj and Shahrukh Khan now," she said, swiveling in her chair to look around an office in which almost every poster was related to a Bollywood film and every cubicle had assorted Bollywood film merchandise.

Echoing Jiggy George's reflections on MTV-India's efforts to forge relations with the film industry, Malhotra stressed that MTV did have something new to offer to Bollywood that other television channels did not. "MTV is all about the on-air environment," she explained. "We don't treat Bollywood like *Doordarshan* did—something boring, something sacred. Our interviews and shows were very interesting, and the way we packaged our stuff was very different from any other channel." MTV-India's efforts at "dovetailing cool with Bollywood" were driven no doubt by concerns about generating profits in an extremely competitive television market. As Malhotra acknowledged at a later point in the conversation, the channel's decision to "Indianize" and begin reaching out to a much broader cross-section of viewers across the country was motivated by the imperative to expand its portfolio of advertisers. This meant, according to Malhotra, taking seriously the life-worlds of viewers "not just in urban India but also in cities like Lucknow and Kanpur and SEC B and SEC C segments of the market within metros like Bombay and Delhi" (SEC—socioeconomic class).

Explaining that MTV-India routinely conducts surveys across the city of Bombay and occasionally in other cities in India to demonstrate the advantages of promoting a film exclusively on MTV, she went on to say: "At the end of the day, we need to explain to a producer or director why working with MTV will improve the chances of a film's success. No television channel can afford to not do this." Malhotra explained the process further with the help of two PowerPoint presentations designed toward the end of 2004 to showcase the benefits of promoting a film on MTV. The first presentation that she opened on her computer was titled "Bollywood Rocks with MTV," and sought to position MTV in relation to fifteen other television channels in India. Comparing metrics for MTV with other music-focused television channels (Zee Music, ETC, B4U Music, etc.), channels dedicated to airing Hindi films (Zee Cinema, Star Gold, B4 Movies, and the like) and general entertainment channels (Star Plus, Sony, Zee TV, and so on), these slides claimed that more MTV viewers watched films in theaters than any other channel. Pointing out that six out of the ten top-earning Bollywood films of 2004 were "exclusively tied up with MTV," this presentation also claimed that high-profile films that did not make significant profits also chose to work with MTV-India.

The second PowerPoint presentation that Malhotra proceeded to open focused on *Hum Tum* (dir. Kunal Kohli, Yash Raj Films, 2004), with the goal of "assessing the effect of promotions run on MTV on viewers' decision to see the movie *Hum Tum*." Developed in collaboration with the IMRB (International Market Research Bureau) and relying on standard market research parlance, this presentation claimed that a maximum number of respondents recalled seeing promotional spots on TV, that MTV "does best among young, male, SEC A respondents," and that 64 percent of respondents who said they recalled seeing a *Hum Tum* promotion on MTV also said "seeing ads/ promos on MTV made them feel like seeing *Hum Tum*." Offering to give me copies of the slides, Malhotra remarked: "I'm not sure these sorts of presentations would have been effective or made much sense to film industry people a few years ago. Now it's different."

* * *

"You Cannot Piss Off Anyone"

"Things have definitely changed in the past few years," began Shashwat Bhatt, a BBA-wielding (Bachelor's in Business Administration) marketing executive at Madison Mates, one of the leading advertising and marketing companies in Bombay, when I asked him to reflect on his interactions with film industry professionals. I had met Bhatt on the sets of a film for which his company had brokered a sponsorship deal with a major fashion magazine produced in Bombay. The editor of the magazine had invited me to attend this meeting where representatives from the fashion magazine (the editor, art director, and marketing manager), the art director of the film, and Bhatt intended to discuss various aspects of the "brand-film synergy." In a Film City (Goregaon) studio lot (Floor #11) where carpenters, electricians, and other wage laborers were busy building the office space for the film, all of us huddled around a table atop which the art director had built a model of the office space.

Moving her cup of tea, ashtray, pack of cigarettes, and a few pens and pencils to a larger worktable that had assorted design and drawing instruments, the art director took a few minutes to outline her vision of the office space. The description of the office layout that she provided became the basis for a discussion about what kinds of "placements" would work best for the fashion magazine—actual issues of the magazine strewn around, framed magazine covers, a large 4x6 foot logo of the magazine on the wall opposite the elevators in the building, coffee mugs with the magazine logo, ID tags featuring the name of the magazine, and even a URL pointing to a contest (online and on the mobile phone platform) that was part of a broader marketing campaign. After about half an hour of negotiating various "placement" details and arriving at an agreement about "deliverables" (when the team from the fashion magazine would deliver framed covers, when they would get to see a detailed mock-up of the set, and so on), we were on our way back to the magazine's office. Throughout, Bhatt had said very little. "I'm just the facilitator, you creative folks work it out," he had said at the beginning of the meeting.

"Do you think the director of the film cares about which magazine is part of the film?" asked the editor, as soon as we were back in the cab we had hired. "It's his first big film, and all he cares about is whether it's a hit or not. And all these deals are about the producer making his money whether the film does well or not. It's just that this agency approached us and we said yes because we know it's a big banner film." I was surprised by this reaction, having just emerged from a meeting in which everyone had been highly enthusiastic, and the film's art director had opened the conversation saying she had just heard from the director of the film and that he was thrilled to have the fashion magazine on board. "And it's not just that," the magazine's art director interrupted: "Our magazine won't be the only product in the office. The brands that each star endorses will also be a part of the space. Also, if they decide that everyone at the magazine drinks Coke, then Coke will be a major

Model of a film set that was being built in a studio in Film City, Bombay.

sponsor." As we drove out of Film City, the marketing manager, who had not said much during the meeting, put the discussion to rest. "You all are looking at it from the wrong angle," she began, turning to face the three of us in the backseat of the taxi. "Look, there is no guarantee that the film will be a hit. I agree. But one thing is for sure—every television promo will have to include at least a few shots of the office space in the film, which will have our name. And that matters. I can use those TRPs (television ratings points) too when I have to justify why we spent so much money making a deal with this film." The editor and the art director had to agree. "Yeah, you're right," the art director acknowledged, going on to say: "And you know what, it's worth building a relationship with this producer."

A few days later, I met Bhatt at a Café Coffee Day outlet in Andheri West, down the road from a major multiplex and a few blocks from the offices of Yash Raj Films and other prominent film and television companies. "That meeting is a great example of how things are changing," he began, before providing an explanation of what happens when a producer or director approaches Madison Mates for assistance with branding and product placements:

> Once we have an agreement from a brand, say a brand wants to invest Rs. 30 lakhs (3 million) in a film, we then ask the producer to tell us the exact scenes in which the brand will be integrated. We put that on paper and lock in a triparty agreement, which includes the producer, the agency, and the brand. We ensure that at no point in time is the brand mistreated . . . we have various clauses for that. We also handle payments and it is in three phases usually—once you lock in an agreement, you pay 50 percent as advance, and then the shoot happens. We show the brand the edits, where and how the brand has been placed. And if the brand is satisfied, we then deliver the next 25 percent to the producer. If changes are needed, we negotiate. And the final 25 percent comes in when the film is released. It's all very structured. Some people, of course, don't work with scripts. In those cases, we try to work things out between brands and directors or producers.

These contracts and agreements, always flexible enough to accommodate long-established practices in the film industry, were also supplemented with purportedly empirical research reports that sought to establish how a specific case of product placement benefited both the film and the brand. Even before we met, Bhatt had suggested I take a look at brief research summaries that MBA-trained professionals at Madison Mates generated on a regular

ANALYSIS, RESEARCH AND RESULTS:

- The film released 700 prints in India in Hindi and about 60 prints in dubbed South-Indian versions and did an overall business of 175 cr. This got him an all inclusive audience universe of 2.91 crore people over a period of 4 weeks.

- The film will release DVD's of the following no: 70000, which will take the communication further to 2.1 lakh people over one year.

- The film will be released on Star Plus who has the telecast right of the film, and on a pessimistic estimate, a blockbuster like this will deliver a minimum 5 TRP's, which will translate into audiences.

- Bournvita has never used a star endorsement, through the film; the brand got the Star endorsement at no cost.

- A dipstick done by the agency in Mumbai amongst 125 kids pre and post the release of the film, indicated improvements across key measures:
  1. An increase in brand favourability by 15%
  2. Intention to use the brand increased by 9%

- The AMOUNT PAID of the in-film opportunity, yielded to Bourn vita the following multiple benefits:
  1. Creatively incorporated scenes at key situations in the filmEndorsement from the superhero character Kristi (Hrithik Roshan)
  2. Extensive reach through the various vehicles on which Krrish will showcase
  3. Opportunity cost

Excerpt from a case study developed by Madison Mates on product placement in the film *Krrish* (2006). Such case studies form an important part of PR and marketing companies' construction of their own industrial identities.

basis. Here, for example, is an excerpt from a research summary that outlines the results of integrating Bournvita, a children's drink, in the film *Krrish* (Rakesh Roshan, 2006).[50]

Echoing explanations offered by Malhotra at MTV-India and other marketing/PR professionals, Bhatt too asserted that an increasing number of film industry professionals, particularly those in corporatized companies such as UTV, were now willing to speak the language that such reports relied on. People at companies like UTV and even at small-scale production companies, Bhatt argued, were now much more aware of brands and knew how to think about associating specific brands with films. He also went on to admit that agreements, contracts, and market research-driven practices did not always work in an industry in which powerful independent producers and directors continued to wield considerable influence. The business he was involved in, he explained, remained "relationship driven, but nowadays in a slightly different way":

> Earlier, it felt like producers were doing brands a favor by including one or two products. Like *DDLJ* and Strohs Beer. You would have the producer saying "yeh ho jayega" (*it will be done*), no contract or anything. Now that aspect has changed. But, it is still a relationship basis. That is what determines whether you are going to get the next contract. So you're servicing the producer as much as the film itself. We work with *Red Chillies, Dharma Productions, Shree Ashtavinayak* . . . you cannot piss off anyone.

* * *

Malhotra's account of MTV-India's relations with the film industry, mediated by everything from market research-driven PowerPoint presentations to notions of "dovetailing cool with Bollywood," and Bhatt's reflections on how an agency like Madison Mates designs and manages deals between filmmakers and a range of commodities, are particularly revealing. Even as they draw attention to some of the challenges involved in brokering ties between industries that operate with different economic logics and definitions of value, they also make it clear that this seeming incommensurability was never an insurmountable barrier. Kajri Jain's insights into the circulation of commodities that move across different "constellations of value" are useful in order to understand negotiations between different media sectors in Bombay. Jain suggests that it is not very productive to approach commodities like a bazaar calendar image "simply as a 'text' or sign to be 'read.'" Instead, she argues, it is far more useful to approach it as "a circulating or animated object, which, as the common element between different constellations of value, draws them into a relationship where it becomes possible for value to switch tracks, to jump from one economy to another, drawing their subjects into each other's networks."[51] Focusing attention on moments of exchange such as the one that Bhatt orchestrated, or the PowerPoint driven meetings that Malhotra spoke about, foregrounds how multiple and often competing notions of value have come to define Bombay's media world over the past decade. I would argue, then, that approaching the audience in terms of its circulation across the film, television, and advertising industries allows us to comprehend film marketing and promotions as practices that enabled the film industry to respond to the demands of a different kind of speculative capital and negotiate new regimes of value. And it is precisely by foregrounding their ability to navigate and forge links across seemingly incongruent terrains that marketing and public relations professionals positioned themselves as central to the process of authoring hype in Bollywood.

Conclusion

Focusing on links between the film and television industries, I have shown how an emerging group of marketing and public relations professionals introduced producers, directors, and stars in the film industry to new ways of imagining the audience. This shift was not only a matter of rethinking budgets and allocating a greater percentage of the production budget for promotions and marketing. I have shown that marketing and promotions came to function as a site of knowledge regarding audiences that was strikingly different compared to the practice of relying on distributors and exhibitors to assess audience tastes and gauge the fortunes of a film. At a structural level, increasingly expensive marketing and the language of market research does act as an organizational safeguard—as a technique of risk management for both family-run companies reinventing themselves as professional and corporatized entities, and companies such as UTV and Pritish Nandy Communications that have entered the film business over the past decade. But in practice, the "audiences" that marketing executives and public relations professionals spoke about were as much abstractions as categories such as "ladies" and "family" deployed in the Hindi film industry. At one level, there is no difference between a producer saying "it's a terrific film, the songs are really good, there are foreign locations, it'll definitely be a hit, take my word for it," and a marketing case study—such as the one that Madison Mates produced for the film *Krrish*—that predicts success on the basis of a survey conducted by intercepting people at malls in cities like Bombay. MTV-India's PowerPoint presentations and Madison Mates's case studies are, to be sure, acts of conjuring audiences and part of a larger set of discursive practices that underpin the television and advertising industries. It's not really about knowing the audience, then, so much as refiguring modes of constructing and circulating knowledge about audiences in a rapidly changing media environment. In one respect, film marketing is an extension of the *mahurat* and can be seen as a dramatic performance unfolding across multiple media platforms, designed to assuage filmmakers' anxieties while at the same time enabling them to leverage new sources of revenue.

It is crucial, however, to understand this shift involving the audience and the practice of marketing and promotion as part of a broader rearticulation of modes of speculation and forms of knowledge in the media industries in Bombay. In a period defined by extraordinary technological, financial, and organizational flux, marketing and promotions emerged as practices that allowed the film industry to negotiate the transition to new circuits of capital that had redefined Bombay's media world throughout the 1990s and early 2000s. It was also, as we have seen, key to the overall project of imagining Bollywood as a global media industry. It is in relation to the normalization of marketing and promotions as distinctive features of Bollywood and broader changes in the distribution and exhibition sectors that we need to examine dot-com companies' position as knowledge brokers who could construct for the film industry what the Bombay-based television, advertising, and marketing industries could not: an overseas territory. It is to this set of negotiations that I turn in the next chapter.

4

"Multiplex with Unlimited Seats"

Dot-Coms and the Making of an Overseas Territory

"So tell me, you left India for work or for higher studies?" asked Saleem Mobhani, cofounder of the highly popular and successful Bollywood website indiafm.com, a division of *Hungama.com* and recently rebranded as Bollywoodhungama.com. We were in a conference room in the office of Hungama.com, one of the few media and entertainment portals in India to have survived the dot-com crash. "Higher studies. I left in '99," I replied and before I could say more, he interrupted: "If you've been in the U.S., you know that it was students and expats sitting on the cutting edge of the boom, people like you, who created several Bollywood websites during the mid-90s. They were the leaders at the time." I nodded and said I knew about groups like rec.arts.movies.local.indian and the prebrowser days of Bollywood fan culture on the Internet. "But we've come a long way since then," Mobhani continued, pulling his chair closer to the table and leaning in. "We have become the most credible Bollywood property online, and even trade people now get their information from indiafm.com. So let me tell you how it all started."

"The first promotion which happened on the Internet was for the film *Kaante*," he began. "It was a very interesting case where Sanjay Gupta, master publicist that he is, shot a one-and-half minute promotional trailer, which he put up to distributors for funding. And by that time—this was in mid-2000—indiafm had made its presence felt in reaching out to the overseas audience. Satellite TV was not easy to consume, it was still expensive, and the spread was not all pervasive. So he made us a proposition—he would release the trailer globally on indiafm.com." As Mobhani recalled, Sanjay Gupta set a date—June 6, 2000—for the trailer to be made public on indiafm.com and would only be available through this one website for a week. Giving me no opportunity to ask questions, Mobhani continued: "No TV, no print, nothing. And what resulted was just amazing." According to Mobhani, publicity surrounding the release of the *Kaante* promotional trailer worked so well that on the very first day, 600,000 people tried to access the video, resulting in indiafm.com's servers crashing. Settling back into his chair, Mobhani went on to finish his story:

> What Sanjay Gupta did was go to the distributors with this information. He said look, this is generating so much interest from around the world that Indiafm's site is not able to keep up, their site is crashing. More than a million people have logged on to the site. Now you tell me the price for the film. He got the entire movie funded before it went on the floors. And he came to me and said, "Brother, because of you I got 25 percent more. I could tell people I had an overseas audience for *Kaante*."

During the rest of the conversation, Mobhani went on to plot a neat, linear trajectory of Bollywood's relationship with dot-com companies that began with this highly publicized launch of the *Kaante* trailer, went through a brief period of uncertainty owing to the spectacular and highly concentrated boom-and-bust of the dot-com economy during 2000–2001, and by the fall of 2005, when I met Mobhani and other dot-com professionals, had become an integral part of the Bombay media world. In his view, as Bollywood began attracting attention in a number of overseas markets, film industry professionals realized that "they could do much more with the Internet."

By 2005–06, the Internet had certainly become a vital component of every film's career, with marketing executives and public relations agents ensuring that every film had a dedicated website and a tie-in with a dot-com company. And producers and directors at prominent film production and distribution companies like Yash Raj Films, Eros Entertainment, Reliance Entertainment, UTV Motion Pictures, and Rajshri Productions shared Mobhani's view as they explored various online marketing and distribution initiatives to reach overseas audiences. For instance, Rajshri Productions, an influential family-run company that has produced and distributed films and television programs since 1947, launched its own broadband website in November 2006. Explaining that the site was designed primarily with the Non-Resident Indian community in mind, Rajat Barjatya, marketing manager at Rajshri Productions, emphasized that the broadband website would serve as a crucial distribution platform for the film industry and would also make it possible for Bombay-based companies to combat piracy and begin reaching out to a large but fragmented audience of non-Indians across Southeast Asia, Eastern Europe, and Africa. The Web, he declared, would be a "multiplex with unlimited seats."[1]

indiafm.com promoting established Bollywood companies' online presence. Such initiatives were crucial for dot-com companies to forge relations with established players in the film industry (*70MM*, vol. 3, issue 2; 2004).

On the one hand, the slogan—multiplex with unlimited seats—which could well have come from a dot-com executive like Saleem Mobhani, certainly reflects the desires of producers, directors, stars, and others in Bollywood keen on reimagining their geographic reach. On the other hand, the term "multiplex" connotes not so much openness to the world but rather, a well-defined and decidedly upscale audience demographic. It indexes not only a shift in conceptions of cinematic publics as the single-screen cinema hall continues to be marginalized across urban India but also, as Amit Rai argues in his account of the emergence of the "malltiplex," new kinds of social stratification and modes of surveillance.[2] In this broader context, this chapter analyzes the role that dot-com companies played in mediating the relationship between Bollywood and overseas audiences. What did it mean for the film industry to "do much more with the Internet" and for a director to claim, on the basis of page hits and click-throughs, that his film had an "overseas audience"? How did professionals in the film and digital media sectors forge relationships, and how did these relationships reconfigure the Bombay film industry's geographic reach?

Situating the emergence of the dot-com sector in India in relation to the growing importance of film marketing and shifts in the practice of film distribution and exhibition, I show how dot-com companies imagined and represented themselves as uniquely positioned to reconfigure a geographically vast yet poorly defined overseas territory into an overseas audience and specifically, a "Non-Resident Indian" audience demographic. Speaking a language of web-metrics and capitalizing on the growing interest in marketing and promotions, dot-com companies began generating knowledge about overseas audiences' engagement with Bollywood that was hitherto unavailable to filmmakers and stars operating primarily from Bombay. More crucially, dot-com professionals were able to forge connections and establish themselves within existing social networks in Bombay's media world. I argue that in doing so, dot-com companies emerged as powerful knowledge brokers who shaped the imaginations and practices of film industry professionals for whom envisioning an overseas territory had come to constitute an increasingly important dimension of going global.

Mapping and analyzing this relationship between the film industry and digital media companies foregrounds a broader theoretical issue at stake here. Drawing on David Harvey's argument that phases of transition in business cycles and capital flows call for and result in a "spatial fix," Michael Curtin outlines how a "logic of accumulation" shapes the operations of contemporary media industries. Even if a film or television corporation is established with the goal of catering to national cultures, Curtin writes, "it must over time redeploy its creative resources and reshape its terrain of operations if it is to survive competition and enhance profitability."[3] This chapter focuses on dot-com companies as a way to trace the reshaping of Bollywood's terrain of operations and in doing so, draws attention to the dynamic relation between the expansion of capital into new territories and the work of rendering those new territories more imaginable. As we will see, what Bollywood got was, in fact, a very limited spatiotemporal fix as dot-com companies interpreted and resolved the problem of space—of imagining the overseas territory—in the exceedingly narrow terms of overseas audiences' cultural temporality with the nation.

Diasporic Foundations

In order to map this relationship between dot-com companies and the film industry, we will first need to situate the emergence of companies like indiafm.com and indiatimes.com in relation to the development of the Internet economy and, more broadly, the experience of cyberculture in India. Ravi Sundaram's analysis of the arrival of computer networking in India and the

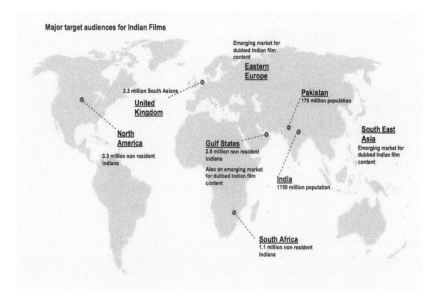

Major target audiences for Indian Films

Shree Ashtavinayak Cine Vision's vision of Bollywood's global reach is another example of the growing significance of the overseas territory.

role played by diasporic Indians during the late 1980s–early 1990s is particularly useful here.[4] Sundaram argues that the Internet needs to be understood in relation to a new nationalist imaginary that defined development as a problem of communication. This new vision of development marked a radical departure from what is characterized as the Nehruvian vision of modernization and national development that defined state policy toward science and technology for over three decades from 1947 until the early 1980s. Under Nehru's leadership, the Indian state embarked on an ambitious program of modernization driven by centralized planning, state ownership of heavy industries, massive investments in industrial development, and an accompanying emphasis on establishing institutes for higher education in science, technology, and engineering. Sundaram observes that during the 1970s, this elite and exclusivist vision of national development was "grafted to a highly centralized and repressive state" headed by Nehru's daughter, Indira Gandhi.[5] By the 1980s, with the "nationalist architecture" seriously in crisis, a new approach was ushered in by Prime Minister Rajiv Gandhi and his team of technocrats led by the charismatic diasporic entrepreneur, Sam Pitroda. Sundaram traces these shifts in the political landscape to make the case that "state discourse after 1984 posed a virtual space where issues of development would be resolved," one in which the personal computer, the network, and information became iconic of a new vision of progress toward the twenty-first century. Sundaram writes:

> The way forward was computerization, networking, and a new visual regime based on a national television network . . . the "national" was reaffirmed but through a new discourse which complicated the notion of borders and sovereignty that were so central to the old visual regime.[6]

It is in relation to this transition in the political elite's vision of development that we need to understand the evolution of computer networks during the 1980s, policy changes concerning telecommunications and the Internet during the 1990s, and the development of the Internet economy during the early years of the twenty-first century. A brief overview of the development of computer networks in India would be useful before we move on to consider how the Indian American "techie" diaspora influenced the dot-com economy in India.

The first nationwide computer network in India was developed by the National Informatics Center (NIC), a United Nations Development Program (UNDP) funded center that became functional in 1977 and was charged with introducing and promoting the computerization of government services.[7] Called NICNET, the satellite-linked network was inaugurated in 1984–85 and connected administrative and governmental bodies at the district, state, and central levels. By the late 1980s, NICNET, headquartered in New Delhi, emerged not only as a vast and powerful network but also, as Sundaram points out, introduced a "simulated space which would accelerate that which was lacking in the old" imaginary of development.[8] The development of NICNET was accompanied by other initiatives such as the establishment of the National Centre for Software Technology in 1986 in Bombay and the Education and Research Network (ERNET) that connected all the Indian Institutes of Technology and a cluster of other centers of higher education such as the Regional Engineering Colleges and the Indian Institute of Science.[9] In addition to these two networks, the rapidly growing IT industry was supported by high-speed data communication facilities set up by Software Technology Parks of India (STPIs) in cities like Bangalore, Pune, and Hyderabad. These networks, however, were not open for public use and only served the needs of the government, academic, and IT sectors. Public access to the Internet began only in 1995, when Videsh Sanchar Nigam Limited (VSNL), a state-controlled telephone company under the purview of the Department of Telecommunications (DoT), began offering Internet services through dial-up connections. By the mid-1990s, these state-sponsored networks provided email and Web access to approximately 120,000 users across the country.[10]

While VSNL controlled the gateways for international connectivity and remained the sole service provider for Internet access in India until 1998, the government and the Department of Telecommunications were under constant pressure from other state-regulated bodies like the NIC, industry leaders in the software sector, and even political leaders like the Chief Minister of Andhra Pradesh, Chandrababu Naidu.[11] Following a highly publicized ninety-minute discussion held as part of an "IT India" convention in 1996, during which VSNL was criticized for poor services, tariff structure, and practices designed to extend its monopoly, the government set up a committee to examine various aspects of privatization of Internet services. The recommendations of the Jalan Committee were announced in November 1997 and by November 1998, the BJP-led government announced that licenses for private sector Internet Service Providers (ISPs) would be issued and that private ISPs would be allowed to bring in foreign equity up to 49 percent.[12] In another policy decision made in 1999, the government cleared guidelines for setting up private gateways for connectivity, thus breaking up VSNL's monopoly on international gateway connectivity as well.[13] These policy changes paved the way for the entry of private ISPs such as Satyam Infoway, Dishnet, and Bharti-BT (British Telecom), and led to a gradual increase in the number of Internet users in India.

Sundaram contends that this phase of cyberculture in India, defined by state-controlled networks such as NICNET and VSNL, engendered a neo-nationalist and elite "cyberpublic" comprised of citizens who routinely embarked on journeys beyond the national "Border." He suggests that this process of deterritorialization marks an important phase in the redefinition of the nationalist imaginary—journeys through cyberspace were not only an opportunity for thousands of Indians to encounter the West, but also to rethink the spatial and temporal boundaries of the nation. Situating this shift in imagination in relation to macrostructural changes during the early 1990s in favor of free market economic reforms and the subsequent reconfiguration of the framework for governance and national development, Sundaram also points out that this elite cyberpublic had two sides to it. On the one hand, elite Indians were in a position to "travel" beyond the old "nationalist grid" that was defined in terms of physical territory. At the same time, "Indian" cyberculture was also being defined by the "creation of a naturalized space of 'India' on the Web, initiated largely by Indians in the diaspora."[14] Thus, in this new nationalist imagination, the Non-Resident Indian was no longer obliged to return "home"—s/he could be at home in cyberspace.

While Sundaram's analysis helps us understand how virtual journeys complicated the borders of national identity and notions of citizenship, it does not shed light on the creation of the dot-com economy as a distinct arena of cyberculture in India. The fact is that even six years after the entry of private ISPs and substantial reductions in the cost of Internet access, the number of Internet users in India remained low. As of March 2004, even after the introduction of broadband services, only 3.6 percent of the population was classified as being active Internet users and usage remained limited to an "urban core" of the educated middle and upper-middle class.[15] However, low rates of penetration and usage did not seem to matter at all when it came to the creation of thousands of India-specific websites and the establishment of major dot-com companies in India during this same time period. In fact, by the end of 2001 the size of the Internet economy in India was estimated to be $22 billion. To grasp the paradoxical nature of this development, consider this excerpt from a magazine feature written in May 2000, aptly titled "Is Anyone Not Setting Up a Dotcom?"

> This country has about 1 million Internet subscribers, perhaps 3 million net-enabled users in all. If they were all in Bombay, that isn't even every fifth person. And yet, every billboard in Bombay is taken by a dotcom. India this, Info that, My Search Engine, Your Personal Email, Woman Power, Man Power, Kiddie Power . . . it boggles the mind . . . the magazines the boys at the signal push at me, the newspaper my *vada pav* comes wrapped in; they are all full of this alone. All the signs point to the Internet and the World Wide Web, the brand new virtual world where lives and fortunes will be remade.[16]

This news feature, among hundreds of others published during 2000–2001, pointed to the yawning gap between the promise of cyberspace and the everyday realities of "third-world" India where a majority of the population had no access to the Internet. But to emphasize digital divides in India is to miss the significance of the development of the commercial web as a link between "home" and "diaspora." The development of the commercial web in India, in other words, had a distinctly diasporic bias.

The NRI Web

The role played by American NRIs in shaping the discourse of globalization in India, and more specifically, articulating the successes of the IT sector to the adoption of neoliberal economic policies by successive Indian governments during the 1990s, has been well documented. Paula Chakravarty, for instance, has examined how "Indian cyber-elites . . . overturn[ed] the previous correlation between science and the state and replace[d] it with a seemingly radical new turn to science and the market."[17] Historicizing the role of cultural and political elites in shaping state policy toward science and technology, she traces the influence of Non-Resident Indians in the high-tech sector to the mid-1980s when figures like Sam Pitroda arrived in India to serve in the Rajiv Gandhi administration.

A Chicago-based telecom engineer, Pitroda was responsible for establishing the Centre for Development of Telematics (C-DOT) and, as Pitroda himself writes, giving young Indians "the sense that they were contributing to nation-building."[18] In a column published in September 2000 during the frenzy of the dot-com boom, Pitroda reminded the readership of Silicon India, a magazine published in the United States, that "the current multi-billion dollar Indian high-tech industry began with some early moderniz-ing experiments that set the pace for growth."[19] In another column written in April 2000, Pitroda explained how the program of liberalization and the gradual legitimization of an antistate, market-led model of development during the 1990s in India helped the high-tech sector to grow in ways that had not been possible during the 1980s. Echoing ideas expressed by industry leaders in India and abroad, Pitroda went on to argue:

> The level of success achieved by Indians in Silicon Valley is inspiring the nation. The success of these Indians sends out the message that we are not losers; it has restored self-confidence in the nation. One may not accept a lot of the ideologies of the Bharatiya Janata Party but I personally love one: they want to restore the nation's pride and self-confidence. The second most important thing achieved by the Indians' success here is their new-found ability to guide development of the country—and, in many cases, also fund it.[20]

Furthermore, NRIs' desire to "guide development of the country" had tre-mendous support not only from leaders in the Information Technology (IT) industry in India such as Infosys CEO N. R. Narayanamurthy, but also from political leaders in IT-friendly states like Chandrababu Naidu in Andhra Pradesh and S. M. Krishna in Karnataka, and at the national level, the IT minister Pramod Mahajan and Prime Minister Atal Bihari Vajpayee. Addressing delegates at "Bangalore IT.Com '98," Vajpayee, for instance, pledged his government's support to the IT industry and remarked, "I would like all my countrymen to know that IT is *India's Tomorrow* (my empha-sis)."[21] As further evidence of the government's willingness to understand and respond to the IT sector's needs, the IT minister Pramod Mahajan led a task force to Silicon Valley to "gain fresh insights into mapping India's increasingly infotech-linked future," and to invite tech entrepreneurs and venture capitalists to establish stronger economic and cultural ties with their "homeland."[22] Thus, by the late 1990s not only were transnational connections between the government, the IT industry in India, and the Indian American "techie" community in Silicon Valley well-established, but the idea that success in IT and the new dot-com economy would enable India to assert its influence at a global level defined the political and cultural imaginary of both India and the diaspora.[23] Where the development of the dot-com sector in India was concerned, these transnational linkages and imaginaries played out in three important ways.

One of the most striking features of the development of the dot-com sector in India is that it has, from the very beginning, been closely associated with NRIs in Silicon Valley. It is difficult to exaggerate the extent to which Indian "cyberheroes" like Sabeer Bhatia (creator of Hotmail.com) and Vinod Khosla (cofounder of Sun Microsystems), and networks of Indian IT professionals such as The Indus Entrepreneurs (TiE), referred to as the "Indian Internet mafia," captured the imaginations of dot-com entrepreneurs in India.[24] Not only did major newspapers and business magazines write extensively about NRI successes in Silicon Valley, never failing to mention that "40% of all start-ups have an Indian founder," these cyberheroes' influence was felt most directly at major conventions such as India Internet World. The first India Internet World show was held in August 1998 in New Delhi at Pragati Maidan ("progress grounds"), a site that hosts a range of trade exhibitions, and attracted over 40,000 Web designers, software developers, and a number of "Internet evangelists, futurists and consultants."[25] While the first edition in 1998 featured speakers from major IT companies around the world, in 1999 every session was led by prominent NRIs who recounted their experiences building successful Internet companies in Silicon Valley and proceeded to model themselves as consultants to aspiring dot-com entrepreneurs in India.[26]

Second, these NRIs facilitated access to venture capital, cutting-edge technical expertise, and the latest managerial know-how for dot-com professionals in India. Dossani and Kenney have documented how changes in financial regulations in 1995 led to the entry of foreign venture capital funds into India for the first time.[27] Further, as Carol Upadhya notes, "much of the capital in these funds came from NRIs, especially wealthy NRI tech entrepreneurs who did well during the boom years in the U.S. and were flush with cash."[28] This initial wave of NRI funding also led to the creation of venture capital firms within India, and initiatives such as "India Venture 2000" by the global consulting firm McKinsey and Co.[29] These transnational flows and alliances were of critical importance for fledgling dot-com companies based in India because their association with industry leaders in the United States gave them the credibility and symbolic capital that in turn, led to more contacts and sources of funding in countries like the United States. Furthermore, between 1999 and 2001 several prominent NRI venture capitalists and entrepreneurs were directly involved in incubating Internet businesses and India-specific websites both in India and abroad.[30]

A third important variable that lent the "Indian" dot-com sector a diasporic bias was the business model that defined valuations, cash flows, and venture capital funding on the basis of a "user commodity" constructed using a set of metrics including page views and the number of unique visitors to a website. The highly publicized acquisition of Indiaworld.co.in by Satyam Infoway (Sify, based in India) is illustrative of how this exceedingly narrow notion of a "user commodity" shaped the business logics and identities of "Indian" dot-com companies. On November 29, 1999 the CEO of Sify announced a $500 million acquisition of Indiaworld.co.in.[31] Not only did this help Sify gain $600 million in market value, improve its profile in the NASDAQ listings, and consolidate its position as a powerful Internet corporation, it also made the NRI community the most sought after "user commodity" for other dot-com companies that were seeking funding. Even as speculation raged in business circles about Indiaworld being overvalued, with many raising the question of how "NRI eyeballs" would actually translate into dollars, it was clear that Sify's investors (at the time, 41 percent of Sify was owned by foreign investors) were attracted by Indiaworld's position as a leading NRI-focused portal that included twenty-two India-related "channels." As Rajesh Jain, CEO of Indiaworld explained, "Indiaworld has secured a unique position with overseas Indians. On an average, it generates 13 million page-views per month. And that was the basis for the valuation and the price paid for it."[32] Continuing problems with connectivity and low rates of credit card usage in India were also cited as key reasons for dot-com companies to focus their efforts on NRIs.

Sify's acquisition of Indiaworld was followed by a dramatic period of growth. According to a NASSCOM report (National Association of Software and Services Companies), by April 2000 three new India-centric websites were being launched everyday and close to 23,000 domain names with Indian addresses had been registered.[33] This boom lasted just over a year. By May 2001, *Business World*, the "magazine of the new economy," reported that only six dot-com companies could report profits and fifteen others appeared to be "on the path to profitability."[34] Among these survivors were

two prominent India-based companies—rediff.com and indiatimes.com—
that went on to define themselves as portals targeting Indians worldwide,
especially those residing in the United States. As Mallapragada has shown,
through a series of financial and strategic alliances, companies like rediff.
com were quick to define themselves as "Indian American."[35] In March 2001
rediff.com acquired a U.S.-based portal, thinkindia.com, and shortly there-
after, launched its U.S. edition. In August that year, rediff.com went on to
acquire two more U.S.-based companies—a long-distance telecom company
that enabled NRIs to call India (Valuecom Communications Corporation),
and *India Abroad*, one of the oldest and most profitable Indian American publications.[36] As rediff.com's CEO and Chairman Ajit Balakrishnan
explained,

> It is our mission to make rediff.com the online portal of choice for Indians
> worldwide. We will do this by helping all Indians living outside India to
> connect with their community, both in India and in the countries in which
> they live.[37]

Competing with rediff.com for NRI eyeballs, executives at indiatimes.
com also went on to frame their website as a portal for "global Indians."
On August 15, 2001, indiatimes.com proclaimed its goal of reaching out to
American NRIs in full-page advertisements in India's leading newspapers,
with the slogan: "Quit USA, Enter India." As Rajesh Sawhney, CEO of Times
Internet at the time, declared: "We are an Indian portal for Indians worldwide. That's our biggest USP (unique selling proposition)."[38] This diasporic
bias of the dot-com sector and specifically, the construction of the American
NRI community as the prized user commodity of the Internet, was a crucial
factor in enabling companies such as indiafm.com to imagine and represent
themselves as uniquely positioned to reconfigure the vaguely understood
overseas territory of diasporic Indians into a well-defined "NRI audience."
However, this also meant that this narrowly construed audience had come to
stand in for a heterogeneous and uneven terrain of circulation and consumption of Bollywood films.

To illustrate how indiafm.com was framed as a company that could forge
an "NRI audience," let me turn to my interview with its cofounder, Saleem
Mobhani. Toward the end of an hour-long conversation, Mobhani opened a
folder and pulled out a press kit. "Here, let me show you a couple of things,"
he urged and handed me a brochure which explained how indiafm.com had,
since its launch in 1997, emerged as the "only site trusted by the Entertainment Industry and consumers."

About us

What is IndiaFM ?
IndiaFM is the No. 1 Bollywood Portal. Since its launch on August 15th 1997, it has become a fountainhead for Bollywood lovers all over the world. It has maintained its leadership position and is the only site trusted by the Entertainment Industry and consumers.

International Rankings	
Rediff	172
Indiatimes	273
Sify	922
NDTV	1934
Hindustan Times	2088
IndiaFM	3082
Baazee	3309
Indiainfo	3530
Samachar	4206
Indian Express	5928
Expressindia	6562
Sulekha	6038
Indya	14545
B4U	49751
Aaj Tak	63167
India Today	97848
Filmfare	102078
123India	15248
Stardust	154531

IndiaFM, a vertical has more visitors, than many horizontal portals out of India. Rankings as per www.alexa.com updated as of March 2005.

Time spent on IndiaFM	
0 - 5min	21.3%
5 - 15min	38.3%
15 - 30min	22.7%
30min - 1hr	10.5%
1hr+	7.2%

The average time a visitor spends at IndiaFM is 18.9 minutes per visit.

Every month... over
10.1 million unique visitors
127 countries **107 million** page views
Drawing **4.2+Terabyte** bandwidth per month
849 sites linking to IndiaFM
including MSN & Yahoo!

IndiaFM weekly Bollywood Newsletter has over 1 million validated subscribers. No other Bollywood portal has as wide a reach internationally as IndiaFM.

Income Classification	
Less than 25,000$	23.4%
25,000-74,999$	43.8%
75,000-150,000$	26.6%
More than 150,000$	6.2%

Occupation	
Professional/ Managerial/ Technical	51.7%
Male/Female	66.9/33.1%

Distribution of Surfers	
US	49.2%
India	21.4%
UK	6.2%
Middle East	5.9%
EU rest	9.9%
Far East (Asia Pacific)	7%
Others	0.4%

Overseas territories constitute 77% of the total visitors. IndiaFM has presence in 127 countries worldwide.

Age Classification	
Less than 13	3 %
13 to 18	11 %
19 to 24	32 %
25 to 35	45 %
Above 35	9 %

An excerpt from the indiafm.com press kit, a set of carefully produced documents that sought to establish the company's credibility in Bollywood.

On the very first page, titled "HUM: About Us," we are presented with this information: "Every month . . . over 10.1 million unique visitors . . . 127 countries . . . 107 million page views . . . drawing 4.2 Terrabyte bandwidth per month . . . 849 sites linking to IndiaFM including MSN and Yahoo!" A box placed below this text reads: "IndiaFM weekly Bollywood Newsletter has over 1 million validated subscribers. No other Bollywood portal has as wide a reach internationally as IndiaFM." And in another box adjacent to this, a "distribution of surfers" indicates that 49.2 percent of indiafm.com's traffic comes from the United States. Pointing to the text beneath the various percentages, which summarized that "overall, overseas territories constitute 77 percent of the total visitors to indiafm.com," Mobhani asserted:

> More than 70% of the traffic base is outside India and the key market is North America, followed by E.U. about 10%, U.K. about 7%, Middle East about 6%, and the Far East about 7%. If you look at the span, as a global map of sorts, practically every place in the world there are Indians, Indiafm is accessed. Every month, more than 6 million wallpapers are downloaded by fans around the world. 3 million odd screensavers are downloaded and consumed every month. In fact, you'll find that Indiafm will be the logo most often seen on an NRI's desktop if it has a Bollywood wallpaper. That's the extent of our reach, and that's why we have become the industry leader.

At one level, press kits are a part of any media company's publicity efforts and such declarations by industry executives do not necessarily offer any deep insights. In fact, Mobhani's statement does sound like a "corporate sript" that he delivers on a regular basis at different venues. It is instructive to note, however, that this scenario was played out in interviews I conducted with professionals in other prominent dot-com companies such as Indiatimes and Rediff, with every executive and content producer asserting that 'NRI eyeballs' were what mattered the most. Omar Qureshi, who headed the team of journalists, web designers, and software engineers at Indiatimes' movies division, offered his own spin:

> When a producer comes to Indiatimes, what does he expect? From the producer's perspective, audiences within India get all their Bollywood news through print, radio, and television. So if you lived in India, especially when Internet usage hadn't taken off, when you had crappy connections or you had to sit in a dingy cybercafé, naturally you wouldn't go online to read about a Bollywood film or the latest scandal. Things might

be changing now, but the fact is, NRIs were the ones who were visiting our site the most and this holds true today also.

These perhaps ingenuous claims from dot-com industry professionals raise the question as to why it took several years for film industry professionals to forge ties with dot-com companies. For we must note that the emergence of commercial Bollywood-focused websites can be traced back to 1996 when *Filmfare*, one of the oldest and most reputed fanzines, was launched online.[39] Owned by the Bennett Coleman Company Ltd. (BCCL) and part of a family of prestigious publications including the *Times of India* and the *Economic Times*, filmfare.com was designed by a company named Pure Tech India Ltd. and hosted on an Internet server in Vancouver, Canada. For nearly three years, until movies.indiatimes.com was launched as a "channel" on the indiatimes.com portal and established as an independent division within BCCL's new media initiative, Times Internet Ltd., filmfare.com remained one of the most popular Indian webzines. The only other India-based commercial website that competed with filmfare.com during this early phase was indiafm.com. Launched on August 15, 1997, indiafm.com quickly rose to prominence as a one-stop portal for Bollywood content, including film and music reviews, film music, chat sessions, and audio interviews with stars, games, and contests, and a range of news from Bollywood updated on a daily basis.

In spite of these websites' success in attracting "NRI eyeballs," and the growing interest shown by prominent film stars who participated in online chat sessions with fans from around the world, the film industry did not regard the Internet as an important new medium that would influence their business in any way. Success stories revolving around the promotion of films like *Kaante* (Sanjay Gupta, 2002) or Aamir Khan's highly publicized tie-in with indiatimes.com to promote the Oscar-nominated film *Lagaan* (Land Tax, dir. Ashutosh Gowariker, 2001), made little impact. In fact, the dot-com boom during 1999–2000 only made matters worse for companies like Indiafm. As Mobhani explained, "some websites set up during the boom began offering money to film producers for content for their site and suddenly there was a perception in the film industry that this is another revenue stream. Instead of thinking about the Web as a medium for promotion and publicity, the film industry began expecting us to pay them for the content they were giving us." During this phase, filmmakers and stars in Bollywood continued to regard print (*Bombay Times*, for example) and television (STAR Plus, ZEE, and the like) as the most important sites for marketing and promotions and dot-com companies were burdened with the challenge of convincing the film industry that the Internet would affect their fortunes.

This situation can certainly be understood as one in which new media companies were grappling with the challenge of creating and delivering content that would attract enough consumers to make their businesses viable. Aware of how transnational television corporations like Star, ZEE, and Sony had successfully developed a range of film-based programming during the mid-1990s, dot-com professionals like Mobhani sought to understand how they could deliver Bollywood content to audiences around the world in ways that exploited the "multimedia" and "interactive" nature of the Internet. On the one hand, this challenge was hardly unique to dot-com companies in India.[40] However, in addition to struggling with the problem of repurposing Bollywood content for the Internet, dot-com companies in India and abroad were also burdened with the challenge of convincing filmmakers and stars in Bollywood that the Internet could improve their fortunes. As Archana Sadanand, who oversees a prominent public relations company, Imagesmiths, observed:

> A few years back, say 2001–2002, not many producers were interested in the Web. Billboards, print, and TV channels would be more than enough. People like Subhash Ghai, who encouraged us to use the Web to promote *Taal*, were exceptions. Most people in the industry didn't take the Internet seriously. Initially, they were skeptical about spending money for online promotions. These days, when we come up with a campaign for a film, we automatically include the Web, we send a press kit to dot-coms just as we send it to *Bombay Times* or *Dainik Jagran*. Now things are different.

By late 2005, things were indeed different. In fact, within two years of the dot-com crash and the subsequent stabilization of the dot-com sector during 2002–2003, companies like indiafm.com and indiatimes.com had emerged as important nodes in the circuit of marketing and promotions and were shaping Bollywood's imagination of overseas audiences.[41] The diasporic bias that defined the development of the dot-com sector in India, then, was only one of the factors that shaped Bollywood's relationship with dot-com companies. This relationship would also hinge on how well dot-com companies could position themselves as key marketing vehicles for the overseas market and more broadly, as knowledge brokers who could help Bollywood stars and filmmakers imagine and understand the "NRI audience." And dot-com companies' ability to establish themselves in Bollywood would in turn depend on how well they capitalized on two key developments—the growing importance of marketing and market research in the film industry, and changes in the realm of film distribution, particularly where the overseas territory was concerned.

"Do You Know Your NRI?"

Indiafm.com serves as a particularly compelling case to examine how dot-com executives participated in and shaped discussions of Bollywood's "corporatization" and in doing so, carved out a space for digital media companies in Bombay. It is important to recognize at the very outset that indiafm.com's identity as a marketing company was never in question. Since January 2000, when it was acquired by hungama.com, it has been positioned as an "entertainment marketing" company that could assist Bollywood with in-film branding, cosponsorship, movie promotions, and designing a movie website. Saleem Mobhani and others at indiafm.com recognized that in the long run, their success in forging ties with Bollywood would depend on how well they could establish the idea that Bollywood's ability to "go global" rested on the industry's willingness to match Hollywood in every domain, including the use of innovative new media strategies to promote films. To illustrate how critical this issue was and how indiafm.com tackled the challenge, let me return to the press kit that Saleem Mobhani handed me.

In addition to the brochure which explained why "indiafm.com is the No. 1 Bollywood portal," the press kit contained thirteen issues of a trade-focused magazine published by indiafm.com called "*70MM*: Movie Marketing at Its Best!" In the first issue, the editor, Venetia Fernandes, outlines the magazine's mandate (December 2003): "Through *70MM*, we endeavour to provide you with a sneak peek into various facets of the world of movie marketing globally, right from the official websites of the latest Bollywood and Hollywood films, to promotions on the mobile platform and inventive marketing case studies." Neatly positioning Bollywood and Hollywood in the same frame, Fernandes continues,

> A movie release today goes beyond mere promos and eye-catching headings. Marketing a movie today is all about an amalgamation of online and offline activities. Hollywood has been a pioneer in the movie marketing arena showcasing a trend in film tie-ups with prominent brands . . . back home, we are also witnessing a greater shift towards in-film branding and use of new media platforms.

Every issue of *70MM* included "case studies" of film marketing and branding in Hollywood that were featured alongside reports of indiafm.com and hungama.com's innovations in promoting and marketing Bollywood films. For instance, the November 2004 issue began with a two-page "spotlight" section that explains how Hollywood animation films such as *The Incredibles* and

Madagascar invited audience participation through innovative online contests and other branding exercises. Following this is a two-page spread that
details indiafm.com's efforts at bringing the same "global" level of innovation
to Bollywood. Framed by case studies of movie websites created by indiafm.
com, the text in the center of this page reads:

> With the Indian Internet Usage projected to go up to 100 million by 2007
> even as the Indian Film Industry is estimated to boom, the Internet just
> cannot be ignored in the movie marketing mix. Internet surveys con-
> ducted abroad are clearly indicative of the trend towards users logging on
> purely to seek entertainment. With a whole slew of Bollywood movies due
> for release, along with some big launches, we at hungama-indiafm have
> been busy doing our bit to *put Indian entertainment on the world (digital)
> map* (my emphasis).

70MM also includes interviews with a diverse array of film industry professionals who comment on the growing importance of marketing and
promotions, the value of working with companies like hungama.com and
indiafm.com, and the importance of the Internet in the long run. Carefully produced, *70MM* is very much a part of indiafm's PR efforts. However, I would argue that it needs to be seen in the first instance as a
trade artifact that addresses a range of professionals in the film, television,
advertising, and marketing sectors in Bombay and only then as publicity
material that seeks to promote indiafm.com to Internet users in India and
abroad. *70MM* invites producers, directors, marketing executives, and stars
in Bollywood to imagine and understand the Web as an index of globality vital to the larger process of reimagining the Hindi film industry as
"Bollywood Inc." Thus, *70MM* serves as an important cultural-industrial
artifact—in John Caldwell's terms, a "semi-embedded deep text"—in at
least two ways.[42] First, it reveals how indiafm.com and other new media
companies went about negotiating and forging relationships with other,
more established media institutions in Bombay. Second, it alerts us to the
changing business practices and identities of film companies that were
grappling with the challenges of reimagining themselves as global, corporatized companies.

The circulation of trade artifacts like *70MM* were not isolated efforts
and must be seen in relation to the normalization of the overseas territory,
particularly the "dollar and pound" markets of the United States and the
U.K. as Bollywood's route to the global. Consider, for instance, a two-day
marketing summit organized by the Confederation of Indian Industry (CII)

A trade-focused magazine that indiafm.com produced, *70MM* was part of a broader revaluation of marketing and promotions in Bollywood.

in November 2003, dubbed "CineMint: A Fresh Look at Film Marketing," focused on the theme of "making and marketing Indian content to overseas markets."[43] Chaired by Shravan Shroff, the thirty-four-year old CEO of Shringar Cinemas Ltd. who is credited with ushering in the "multiplex revolution" in Bombay, the conference brought together producers, directors, and media executives from film and television companies in Bombay in an effort to "brainstorm with international marketing experts, and look at case studies of movies successfully marketed globally to pick up lessons and insights."[44] Dot-com companies used such events to further reinforce the idea that web marketing would play an important role in targeting NRI audiences worldwide. "Some filmmakers get this," remarked Omar Qureshi of movies.indiatimes.com. "If you want to get NRIs interested in your film, how do you do it? You go online and generate buzz. NRIs use the Web a lot, they're used to Hollywood, and they have certain standards," he explained. Echoing the many articles in business and current affairs magazines that provided "tips from marketers in the know about overseas Indians," Mobhani too asserted that web promotions were what NRIs, who had been exposed to "global brands and service standards," expected. As he understood it, "for NRIs, Bollywood is important, but it is also important to recognize that Bollywood is part of a larger entertainment environment. Especially when you think about youngsters, they have grown up with Tom Cruise and Shahrukh Khan. So for this audience, we have to speak a language they get."[45] In fact, by 2003–04, this line of reasoning was being employed by producers, directors, stars, and publicity and marketing executives across Bombay. Explaining the film industry's interest in using the Web as a platform to "tap NRIs," Rajesh Sawhney, CEO of indiatimes.com, reiterated Qureshi and Mobhani's observations and the larger goal of adapting Hollywood's "best practices" in Bollywood:

> Although a new concept in India, online movie trailers have been widely used abroad. For instance, in the U.S.—which has the biggest film industry of the world—68 percent of moviegoers do not generally watch a movie unless they have seen a trailer. And 85 percent of those who prefer to watch trailers to decide which movie to watch, watch movie trailers online.[46]

Such characterizations of the activities of overseas audiences circulated widely in trade and press coverage of the film industry's forays into overseas markets, particularly the United States and the U.K., and also served to demonstrate to the film industry the value of working with dot-com companies. Simply put, it was about "turf marking," of establishing their presence and value in Bombay's media world by convincing the film industry of their unique capabilities. These tactics, however, would have had little effect were it not for a major structural change in another domain of the industry: overseas distribution and exhibition.

A New Map

Until recently, the distribution of Hindi films has been largely fragmented and controlled by a few powerful independent distributors. Within India film distribution is mapped into five major territories. These territories are divided into fourteen subterritories, which are further divided into smaller areas. The "overseas territory," which constitutes the sixth distribution territory, is typically divided into two categories: traditional and nontraditional. The U.S. and U.K. markets, with a large movie-going population of Indian origin, are referred to as traditional markets, while continental Europe, African countries, and the Gulf states are referred to as nontraditional markets.[47] Until the late 1990s, the most common distribution arrangement for the overseas territories was what is known as an "outright sale." An "outright sale" refers to a transaction whereby a distributor buys a film on an outright basis, paying the producer for the rights to distribute the film overseas over a period of time. In this arrangement, the distributor takes on all the costs associated with marketing and exhibiting the film, and is under no obligation to share revenues with the producer.[48] To a dot-com company like indiafm, this method of distribution offered no advantages and in fact posed a major obstacle. Recalling the many meetings he had with producers and directors who saw no good reason to invest in online marketing, Mobhani explained:

> Outside India, the market was completely controlled by players who would buy interests outright. And it was in their interests to be nontransparent. Producers never showed any interest in doing any marketing outside. "Why should I spend any more?" was the logic at work there. Whatever money is to be made, the distributor has taken that.

This situation began to change during the late 1990s and early 2000s as established production companies like Yash Raj Films and newer entrants like UTV recognized the need to control overseas distribution. Yash Raj Films' experience with *Dilwale Dulhania Le Jayenge* (*DDLJ*, Aditya Chopra, 1995), in many ways the film that established the importance of the overseas territory, sparked a trade story around distribution as well. Narrated by marketing and public relations professionals and circulated through newspaper and magazine articles, *DDLJ* marks a key transition in the film industry's approach to overseas distribution.[49] As the story goes, Aditya Chopra's debut film *DDLJ* went on to earn Rs. 200 million abroad and Rs. 500 million in India, but was sold for just Rs. 6–7.5 million per territory.[50] Anxious not to repeat this mistake, by the time their next film was ready for release in 1997 (*Dil To Pagal Hai*/The Heart Is Crazy, dir. Yash Chopra, 1997), Yash Raj Films had established twelve distribution offices across India, and offices in the United States, U.K., and U.A.E. to distribute their film in overseas markets.[51] The growing financial importance of overseas territories gradually led other companies like UTV, Reliance, and Rajshri to follow Yash Raj Films's example. While this narrative speaks more to Yash Raj Films's canny marketing/PR skills and the company's position in the industry, and glosses over the unevenness of the terrain of overseas distribution, it does serve as a useful point of entry. Let me map this ongoing transition by drawing on an interview with Lokesh Dhar, who oversees UTV's North America and U.K. operations.

Dhar, who had tried his hand at scriptwriting in the Hindi film industry before moving into the distribution and exhibition sectors, arrived in the United States to pursue an MBA degree. With an MBA in hand, he joined Eros Entertainment, a company that until recently had a virtual monopoly on the overseas distribution of Indian films. After two years with Eros Entertainment, Dhar joined UTV and launched the company's overseas operations in 2004 in New York City. "And even Eros, what could one company really do?" Dhar remarked, as he went on to recall that the overseas distribution terrain was defined by a "lot of players, most of them mom-and-pop type setups who would last five to six months or at most one year." Dhar entered the business with the understanding that it would involve interactions with players with questionable reputations and whose accounting practices were anything but transparent. "There were all these companies like Spark, Videosound, Rainbow, Net Effects Media . . . you don't hear about them now. They're all gone," Dhar explained. Positioning himself in relation to the corporatization of the production sector in Bombay with the entry of companies like UTV and Studio 18, Dhar offered his take on the changing landscape of overseas distribution:

> Now things are much more professional and we are not like the wheeler-dealers earlier. There is a different level of transparency and accountability in reporting and other operations. There was a time when some international distributor would acquire a film from a producer in India and there was no information flow. People had no idea what was happening here,

money was underreported, there was no transparency at all. And I'm not even sure what the mode of acquisition was . . . basically, there were people here who thought this was a glamorous business, let me give it a shot. But over the last five to six years, these people were gradually phased out as public limited companies came in and prices for acquisition went through the roof. These mom-and-pop types just could not compete.

According to Dhar, Yash Raj Films' move to formalize distribution influenced other companies, including UTV that had, even as recently as 2004–05, relied on Eros Entertainment for overseas distribution and marketing. Beginning in 2004, Dhar has overseen UTV's overseas operations and played a key role in refiguring Bollywood's relations with North American exhibition chains. "It's much easier to approach companies like AMC once you have a base here," he continued, going on to explain the transition further:

In the 1990s, a big film would get released in ten to fifteen halls and then the prints would move from one place to another. It would get released in a handful of ethnic theaters, owned and operated by Desis who were focusing on non-English films in high-density areas like New York, New Jersey, LA, and so on. Now, with a film like *Jodha Akbar*, for example, we are releasing 130 prints across North America. Seven to eight years ago, a Bollywood film would not have opened in a place like Tulsa, Oklahoma but we ensured that a film would open in every market that matters and we now have established relations with all the mainstream theater chains.

Further, influential filmmakers who have stayed out of the distribution business, such as Karan Johar, have tended to enter into agreements with companies like Yash Raj Films to handle distribution. As I explained in the second chapter, one of the most significant developments in Bollywood has been the growing integration of distribution. This ongoing shift in the practice of film distribution allowed Bombay-based companies to target the lucrative overseas market in a more organized fashion and led to a demand for web promotions. More crucially, it created a need for knowledge about NRI audiences that marketing executives and public relations agents working in Bombay were in no position to provide.

"At the end of the day, every producer, director, and star in Bombay wants to get a sense of the buzz," explained Parul Gossain, a prominent public relations professional in Bollywood. We were in the lobby area of the five-star Marriott Hotel in Juhu, waiting for a film publicity event involving Mallika Sherawat (one of Gossain's clients) and Jackie Chan to begin. "In Bombay, when I travel around, I get a sense of whether people are talking about a certain promo, a film's music, the stars, etc. and I convey that to different people in the industry," she elaborated. A few minutes after she had made this point, Bollywood hero Akshay Kumar entered the hotel. Waving to Gossain as he walked toward a throng of photographers and journalists, he raised his hand to his ear, mouthing, "Call me." "See," said Gossain, turning back to me, "I can call him to talk about an upcoming film, to give him my take on how well the publicity is working. And I can do the same for a producer who takes me on for a film's publicity." Professionals like Gossain, however, had no basis to talk about the "buzz" in London, New York, or other lucrative overseas markets. It is this space, defined by intermediaries like Parul Gossain and marketing executives at television corporations and advertising agencies, which dot-com companies sought to occupy in Bollywood. As Lokesh Dhar confirmed:

> The way we gauge the buzz in the market here is through online sources. Posters, banners and so on are designed specifically for the U.S. or U.K. markets now. Plus, you can watch an ad on Zee TV and other satellite channels. In India, you are seeing it in print, on TV, radio, and you are talking to people. But out here, I don't know what your thoughts and feelings are . . . with the Web, I follow user comments and I can feel the buzz . . . so it's extremely important for us in the overseas market. Out here, given the geographic scattering, online is the only way to go.

Companies like indiafm.com seized this opportunity to position themselves as powerful knowledge brokers who could help filmmakers and stars in Bollywood "get a sense of the buzz" among overseas audiences and imagine the vast and vaguely defined overseas territory in more concrete terms. Charles, who monitors web traffic for indiatimes.com, offered this explanation: "Every Bollywood producer or director or star wants their film to do well in the NRI market. And they will all tell reporters why their film will be a hit with NRIs. But each year, only a few films do well abroad. The question I would ask them is, 'Do you know your NRI?'"

It is this problem of "knowing the NRI" that dot-com companies offered to solve by presenting those in the film industry with a range of metrics—page hits, downloads, subscriptions, number of minutes spent on a page, and so on—that indicated how well a film was likely to do among NRI audiences, and following that up by tracking films' overseas earnings. As Omar Qureshi, waving his hand at the computers in the indiatimes.com office, said to me, "See, the beauty of the Web is, we can track interest in every article, every photograph." Showing me around the office, he went on to explain, "So we track interests, we get feedback, and the industry knows this. On an hourly basis, not even a daily basis, we track web trends. We refresh those pages every three minutes. If I'm going home now, it's early morning in New York, then London, and so on." Pausing for a moment in front of a computer screen, Qureshi turned to me with a smile and declared: "There is always an Indian online."

For a particularly telling instance of dot-com companies leveraging their technical ability to measure audience response worldwide, let us turn once again to indiafm.com's trade magazine, *70MM*. The July 2004 issue offered industry insiders an "indiafm.com Research Exclusive" that promised to chart which movies were "likely to be the biggest blockbusters of them all." The two-page spotlight begins by explaining that indiafm.com's analysis was based on an extensive fourteen-day survey that brought in 621,793 responses. The results, tabulated to present an "India rank" and an "overseas rank," "were based on votes from 67 countries—countries which constitute about 98 percent of revenue towards Bollywood releases." This poll, we are told, "threw up several interesting results, generating quite a buzz in the industry." Evidence of this industry buzz is presented in the form of pithy quotes from media executives. For instance, the vice president of Eros Multimedia, Kumar Ahuja, commends the survey, saying, "indiafm research forms one of the key inputs in our strategic planning for promotion of movies in each of the key overseas markets. Indiafm has always been, and continues to remain, an important reference for the Bollywood Trade, especially overseas." This survey, furthermore, was part of a larger shift whereby indiafm.com positioned the overseas territory within a weekly ritual of considerable importance in Bollywood—tallying box-office earnings. As Rajeev Masand, entertainment editor at the television channel CNN-IBN, reflected, "Back in 2002, when I was writing for *Indian Express*, I wrote about the Naaz Building being the Bollywood Barometer. If you wanted numbers, the distributors and others who had offices in the building had the numbers at their fingertips. But now those numbers are online and yeah, when it came to the overseas market, these guys had no way of knowing."[52] Since 2004, the "trade" section of indiafm.com, where reputed film journalist and trade analyst Taran Adarsh compiles films' earnings in the United States, U.K., and other markets on a weekly basis, has emerged as the virtual equivalent of the Naaz Building where knowledge regarding the "NRI audience" is generated and circulated.

Thus, for companies like indiafm.com and indiatimes.com, the ability to generate knowledge about NRI audiences enabled them to locate themselves in relation to Bollywood's efforts to map, target, and monetize the lucrative

Trade analyst Taran Adarsh's weekly box-office report is highly regarded in the industry.

overseas market. However, asserting their value in these aspirational (the Internet as an index of globality) and strategic terms (the need to understand and target NRIs) was only one part of a larger challenge. To become truly indispensable knowledge brokers, these companies would also have to create engaging content that would attract overseas audiences on a daily basis. As we will see in the following section, success in creating compelling content and attracting audiences was determined by these companies' locations in Bombay and their ability to forge connections in a range of social networks in the industry. Specifically, this meant moving beyond marketing/promotions and becoming part of the world of media/entertainment journalism.

Location Matters

"If you want to be successful as a Bollywood site, you need to have a presence in Bombay," declared Sunil Thakur, founder-CEO of U.S.-based wahindia.com. Thakur had started wahindia.com in 2002 while pursuing an MBA at the University of Michigan-Ann Arbor. Like other Bollywood sites based outside India, wahindia.com offered the usual mix of the latest news about films and stars, film music previews, promotional trailers, and slide shows. Websites like wahindia.com, planetbollywood.com, and bollyvista.com used Bollywood content to attract traffic and generate advertising revenue, particularly from companies interested in targeting American NRIs. Further, obtaining Bollywood content was relatively easy and did not cost these small-scale enterprises much. As Thakur explained, "A lot of content is pretty much free because the incremental costs for producers or distributors are very low. All they have to do is send us a CD with images and text, and sometimes a distributor like Eros will send us a DVD with clips. For them, this was good publicity. Had it been expensive, they might have thought twice." For the latest Bollywood news, these websites relied primarily on syndicated news services such as IANS (India Abroad News Service).

To distinguish themselves in the clutter of Bollywood sites online, Thakur and his team at wahindia.com even produced a weekly countdown and a Bollywood news show. Every Saturday, a four-person team comprising Thakur, a cameraperson, a host, and an editor would create a twenty- to thirty-minute segment using the materials they obtained from distributors like Eros Entertainment and often, DVDs borrowed from the local Indian grocery store. "We did attract audiences from around the world, but we also realized that what we were doing was not sustainable in the long run," said Thakur. Despite concerted efforts at creating "stickiness," a term that refers to how well a website is able to retain a loyal user base, and building a "community" by inviting user-generated content, wahindia.com and other similar websites could not compete with sites like indiafm.com, indiatimes.com, or rediff.com. In the fall of 2006, wahindia.com went offline and was reinvented as a social networking website that would serve as a platform for talented young NRIs to develop a portfolio and establish connections with a range of industry professionals in Bollywood. By November 2006, having obtained an undisclosed amount of venture capital funding, Sunil Thakur had set up an office in Malad, an area of Bombay close to western and northern suburbs such as Bandra, Pali Hill, Andheri, Juhu, Versova, Santa Cruz, and Goregaon where most film studios and television corporations are located and where most stars and other industry professionals live. Giving me an update in April 2007, Thakur remarked, "It has made such a difference to meet industry people face-to-face, to have PROs say they would like to work with you. I tell you, location matters."

The notion that location matters even in the context of dot-com companies and "placeless" networks of images and information, what Castells terms a "space of flows," raises important questions about geography that scholars analyzing media convergence have not addressed in systematic fashion. So far, scholars have tended to focus attention on the migration of content across media forms, without paying adequate attention to the spatial logics that shape the flow of content between "new media" companies and film or television corporations. David Marshall, for instance, writes about the "intertextual commodity" that emerges through the cross-production and marketing of film and television shows in the United States, and argues that promotions serve to expand audiences' "pleasure of anticipation" and "deepen the investment of the audience in the cultural commodity."[53] Building on this, Henry Jenkins uses the term "transmedia storytelling" to analyze how storytellers use multiple media platforms to develop different aspects of a story world like *The Matrix*.[54] While such analyses can certainly be used to understand the promotional campaigns for Bollywood films, I wish to shift the focus to explore how geographic proximity shapes the production and flow of content online and more broadly, relations between new media companies and an established film industry.

In *The Rise of Network Society*, Manuel Castells develops the concept of a "milieu of innovation" to explain why the sociocultural and political dynamics of specific geographic locations play a central role in decentralized, post-Fordist network economies.[55] If we are to understand why Silicon Valley in California emerged as the preeminent region of innovation in the late twentieth century, Castells suggests we must pay attention to the value of spatial proximity that roots the "space of flows" in specific places. He writes:

> Although the concept of milieu does not necessarily involve a spatial dimension, I argue that in the case of the information technology industries, at least in this century, spatial proximity is a necessary condition to the existence of such a milieu, because of the nature of interaction in the innovation process. What defines the specificity of a milieu of innovation is its capacity to generate synergy, that is the added value resulting not from the cumulative effect of the elements present in the milieu but from their interaction.[56]

How do spatial proximity and a "milieu of innovation" matter in the case of cultural industries? In his work on the economic geography of Hollywood, Allen Scott demonstrates how clustering in southern California "enhances the availability of agglomeration economies and increasing-returns effect."[57] He argues that by clustering in one region, companies are able to "economize on their spatial interlinkages, to reap the multiple advantages of spatially concentrated labor markets, and to tap into the abundant information flows and innovative potentials that are present wherever many different skills specialized by complementary producers are congregated."[58] Curtin builds on Scott's analysis of the "dense transactional networks" that shape an industry like Hollywood to argue that media capitals like Los Angeles and Hong Kong are also shaped in important ways by "trajectories of creative migration."[59] Using Hollywood as an example, Curtin observes that remaining competitive and maintaining its position as a media capital "requires maintaining access to reservoirs of specialized labor that replenish themselves on a regular basis, which is why media companies tend to cluster in particular cities."[60] These two concepts—clustering/agglomeration and trajectories of creative migration—prove particularly useful for understanding how dot-com companies like indiafm.com, indiatimes.com, and rediff.com leveraged their physical presence in Bombay to broker a sense of proximity between Bollywood and overseas audiences.

In explaining the success of Bombay-based companies such as indiafm.com, indiatimes.com, and rediff.com compared to websites like wahindia.com and bollyvista.com that operate outside India, we have to begin by acknowledging their advantage in terms of economies of scale and reach. Being larger companies with deep financial pockets meant that the Bombay-based dot-com companies were in a position to offer public relations agents, marketing executives, filmmakers, and stars in Bollywood a more comprehensive transmedia package. For instance, in addition to designing a movie website and managing the online promotions for a film, a tie-in with indiafm.com would typically be part of a larger deal that brings in hungama.com's expertise in creating innovative contests and games for the mobile phone platform that is accessible worldwide. Similarly, from a public relations agent's perspective, movies.indiatimes.com offered not only a large diasporic user base, but also the opportunity to publicize the film and its stars across other properties owned by the Times group, including a nationwide network of FM radio stations (Radio Mirchi), an entertainment and lifestyle television channel (Zoom), and a number of print publications, including *Bombay Times*, *Times of India*, and *Bombay Mirror*.[61] Further, large portals like indiatimes.com and rediff.com were also in a position to leverage their advantage as horizontal portals that cover every major news category, including business, sports, and politics worldwide. As Raja Sen, who creates a range of content for rediff.com's "movies" section, explained, "Stars and PROs know that we have a certain credibility. A star thinks, if I'm doing an interview with rediff, the lead story might be about George Bush and my story will be second or third. So even if an NRI is coming to rediff for politics or cricket news, he or she will see the Bollywood story right there. Bollywood is just a click away." The homepages of rediff.com and indiatimes.com carry a small "movies" box, prominently displayed in the center of the page, which includes a picture of a Bollywood star and four catchy headlines that lead to the movies section of the websites.

Second, promotional material in the form of trailers, behind-the-scenes still, and other images of film stars, gossip, and interviews with stars and film directors were available to dot-com companies regardless of their location. Where Bombay-based dot-com companies distinguished themselves was in the domain of film journalism. By recruiting and retaining established film journalists in Bombay, these companies were able to argue that overseas audiences could not access such "exclusive" content elsewhere. While the migration of actors, directors, music directors, playback singers, costume designers, choreographers, and a range of other creative and technical personnel to Bombay has been, without doubt, central to the city's status as a media capital, popular and scholarly accounts have not investigated film journalism as a key site of creative labor that is also locale-specific and involves established professionals passing their "skills along to succeeding generations and to newly arrived migrants."[62] It is this "trajectory of creative migration" that indiafm.com, indiatimes.com, and rediff.com tapped into in an effective manner by hiring "star" journalists. Bombay-based dot-com companies correctly recognized the importance of hiring experienced film journalists with well-established connections in the film industry. Indiatimes.com, for example, hired Omar Qureshi, a film journalist who had made his reputation as editor of a popular fanzine called *Stardust*. "I was not computer savvy, I wasn't even familiar with the Web. I used to write my articles by hand," exclaimed Qureshi, going on to explain that indiatimes.com executives recruited him because they knew he had access to every director and star in Bollywood. More important, Qureshi put together a team of younger journalists and helped them navigate and become part of a network of social relationships in Bollywood in ways that companies like the U.S.-based wahindia.com or Canada-based bollyvista.com could not. In his view, access built on a foundation of established personal relationships was what mattered the most:

> Unlike how journalists use their organization to get access, here I take my team to the stars and personally introduce them and initiate a relationship. In fact, my entire team is like . . . we are all mini-relationship managers. You won't find them hanging out at parties to get a sound bite, like the TV channels. And some stars will walk off without saying anything. But my journalist will move around, and the star will come up and talk to my journalist. And that is because of the personal relationships that we have developed and maintained. This is much more important than a nameless, faceless journalist trying to get an interview.

The value of being in the city and developing personal connections with stars and filmmakers becomes especially clear when we consider the experiences of a film journalist who is not based in Bombay. A software professional who works in an IT company in Gurgaon, a high-tech cluster on the outskirts of New Delhi, Joginder Tuteja entered the world of film journalism by writing music reviews for indiafm.com and was approached by bollyvista.com, a company based in Montreal, Canada. After nearly two years with bollyvista.com, Tuteja quit and began writing for a U.S.-based website called indiaglitz.com. "Without a senior journalist to show me the ropes and give me phone numbers, it was a constant struggle," he explained. Tuteja pointed out that being outside Bombay also meant that he was not "on the radar of PROs" or part of a network of journalists in the city who would often share tips and information. "When it comes to running around, dot-com journalists are right there with the rest of the journos in Bombay. If you go to a press event, along with the print people and TV reporters, you'll see an indiatimes and an indiafm reporter. I am not there, I am not clued in," he continued. It is difficult to ignore the importance of "running around . . . with the rest of the journos." Omar Qureshi's team of film journalists is located in the historic Times of India Building in south Bombay, a space that also houses film journalists writing for *Filmfare*, *Bombay Times*, and *Mumbai Mirror*. Further, while websites based abroad received the standard set of promotional materials that they could repackage, dot-com companies operating out of Bombay were able to take advantage of their connections with PROs to set up interviews or chat sessions with stars and filmmakers and create "exclusive" content that enhanced their credibility among overseas audiences. Emphasizing his point regarding access and personal relationships, Qureshi pointed out:

> Every film today is promoted by a PR machine. And they have their act together and they know the value of the Internet as a new medium through which to reach people, both in India and the U.S. So if a PR agent is giving out slots to *DNA* and *Times of India*, he or she will give one to us and rediff and indiafm as well. So we get that. But if Shahrukh Khan wants to do a chat, he will not go to some website based outside India. He knows us here personally, end of story.

The personal equations with stars and filmmakers that Bombay-based journalists developed over a period of time have been critical in establishing companies like indiafm.com and indiatimes.com as first-hand sources of Bollywood news. Journalists and other content producers working in these dot-com companies understood that their proximity to Bollywood and personal relationships with filmmakers and stars distinguished them from countless Bollywood websites that clutter the Internet. Further, it became clear as I spent more time in the offices of various dot-com companies and accompanied journalists to film publicity events that proximity was interpreted in exceedingly narrow temporal terms, as providing a sense of dailiness in the film industry's imagination of overseas audiences. As Qureshi had articulated it, "There is always an Indian online." Let me elaborate by turning to a conversation with Sanjay Trehan, manager of indiatimes.com's broadband initiative.

Before arriving in Bombay for my first phase of field research, I had spent a few days in indiatimes.com's corporate office located in Gurgaon, near New Delhi. Toward the end of a week during which I had spent time talking with various members of the company's corporate and research groups, I had a chance to meet Trehan. "Lifestyle and entertainment are often the earliest to adopt new media," he began, before moving on to talk about Bollywood: "Bollywood, of late, has realized that new media is critical. Every film has a good website. The content is very rich, as good as any Hollywood film website. But it's early days for now, in India." Acknowledging that indiatimes.com was diaspora-focused, especially when it came to entertainment, he then turned his attention to the mobile phone lying on his desk. "Have you seen this clip from *Ek Khiladi Ek Haseena* (A Player and a Beauty, dir. Suparn Verma, 2005)?" he asked. This video clip from a forthcoming Bollywood film had been the topic of much conversation in the office that day, but I hadn't seen it.[63] "Here, take a look," said Trehan, holding up the phone for me and adjusting the volume. Even as the clip played, Trehan continued: "It's a 1.4 minute MMS, an intimate scene, doing the rounds of the broadband library in India. In fact, we've put it online on the indiatimes website. It's a well-orchestrated PR and advertising stunt that is creating tremendous word-of-mouth buzz." Putting the phone away, Trehan went on to offer his understanding of indiatimes.com's role in mediating relations between the film industry and audiences abroad: "NRIs miss Bollywood . . . so if we can show them something that came from our television channel Zoom—a party, an interview, a clip from a shooting, and so on, then that works. NRIs should be able *to watch what Indians in India are watching*, and that's why, like I said, Bollywood now realizes the importance of the Web" (my emphasis).

As I have already shown, the diasporic bias that shaped the development of the dot-com sector in India had defined the operations of film-related dot-com companies as well. Trehan's account is telling for it makes it clear that dot-com professionals hoped that a sense of simultaneity, coupled with

Excel spreadsheets presenting an array of web metrics, would render the vast overseas territory more readily imaginable as an "NRI audience." For professionals like Mobhani, Qureshi, and Trehan, this meant that the attempt to envision an overseas audience required the continual navigation of temporal gaps between domestic and overseas, home and abroad. In other words, the question of space—of mediating Bollywood's relationship with an overseas audience—was interpreted and resolved in terms of cultural temporality. This spatiotemporal fix was successful, I would further argue, insofar as it allowed dot-com companies to establish a sense of control over categories like "overseas audience" that are, as Shanti Kumar would suggest, best understood as "unimaginable communities."[64] As distinct from the finite, limited, and bounded nature to the imagined communities of print capitalism that Benedict Anderson defined, Kumar argues that the "unimaginable communities of electronic capitalism . . . are infinite, limitless, and unbounded," given the nature of contemporary media circulation across varied spatial scales.[65] Media flows, Kumar further argues, are "unimaginable both in a literal sense of being at the technological limits of imaginative access and in a figurative sense of becoming limitless in imaginary excess."[66] But the fix that the Bombay-based dot-com companies offered came at a considerable cost. Far from offering Bollywood even a glimpse of an infinite audience—a "multiplex with unlimited seats," in Rajat Barjatya's imagination—and grappling with the uneven and heterogeneous terrain of diasporic media circulation and consumption, Bombay-based dot-com companies reduced the overseas territory to a narrowly construed, primarily U.S.-U.K.-centered "NRI audience." To be sure, these companies did succeed in positioning Bollywood as a cultural industry capable of imagining and institutionalizing an overseas audience. However, the notion of a temporal fix allows us to see how these companies' representational practices and strategies ignored, if not suppressed, the unevenness that marks Bollywood's expansion into new territories.

Conclusion

In this chapter, I have traced the emergence of dot-com companies as key intermediaries who could reconfigure a vast and vaguely defined overseas territory into an enumerable "NRI audience" and thereby shape the film industry's imagination of an overseas territory. I began by situating the development of the dot-com sector in relation to what I have called the diasporic bias of the Internet in the Indian context, and how dot-com companies relied on and leveraged the Indian diaspora in first world countries to become both commercially viable and culturally significant. I then detailed how dot-com companies like indiafm.com positioned themselves as vehicles for market-ing and promoting Bollywood films overseas, and capitalized on structural and symbolic dimensions of corporatization to participate in and shape the larger process of Bollywood going global.

However, the story of Bollywood's relationship with overseas audiences—Indian Americans in particular—is not just about Bombay-based industry professionals' imaginations of a multiplex with unlimited seats. Over the past two decades, Bollywood's cultural geography has also been transformed by the efforts of diasporic media entrepreneurs. The next chapter thus shifts focus to map and analyze the role played by diasporic media produc-ers in rearticulating Bollywood's relationship with the world. Outlining the changing dynamics of migration and relations between "home" and "dias-pora" since the mid-1990s, the next chapter traces changes in the diasporic mediascape from grassroots and community-managed media production, particularly the use of public access television, to the entry and dominance of India-based television channels like ZEE, Star, and Sony Entertainment, and finally the launch and failure of MTV-Desi, a niche television channel for South Asian American youth. This analysis of diasporic television in turn sets the stage for tracing the emergence of Saavn.com, one of the most influ-ential Bollywood-focused diasporic media companies.

Further, all the chapters so far have been concerned with industry prac-tices and the institutional dimensions of convergence between the film, television, and dot-com sectors. In the following chapters, I foreground par-ticipatory culture as a key dimension of Bollywood films and film music's transnational circulations and one that complicates any easy assumptions regarding cultural temporality between "home" and "diaspora." Media circu-lation both within and outside the territorial boundaries of India is defined by a vast and networked pirate culture that crisscrosses not only regional, national, and diasporic boundaries but more importantly, moves beyond the Anglo American diaspora to include countries like Singapore, Malaysia, Fiji, and Nigeria as key nodes in Bollywood's emergent cultural geography. The next two chapters thus reflect on what it takes to conjure the diaspora as a viable scale of media production and circulation in a terrain defined not only by changing relations between Bombay and Los Angeles but perhaps more crucially, by informal networks of media circulation that commercial media ventures find nearly impossible to match in scale and scope.

5

"It's Not Your Dad's Bollywood"

Diasporic Entrepreneurs and the Allure of Digital Media

In June 2003 the publicity event for Rajshri Productions' film *Main Prem Ki Diwani Hoon* in New York City was attended primarily by journalists and public relations professionals working for various South Asian newspapers, magazines, and popular diaspora-centric web portals like Sulekha.com. The entire event lasted a hour, and went largely unnoticed by anyone besides this small group of diasporic media professionals. By the fall of 2008, when the South Asians in Media and Marketing Association (SAMMA) organized its second annual convention, the influence that Indian media had come to wield in the South Asian American mediascape and indeed, American public culture at large, had changed dramatically.

Declaring that 2007–08 had been the year of South Asian entertainment, Neal Shenoy, founding member of SAMMA, kicked off the 2008 SAMMA-Summit (October 31–November 1) held at the Time Warner conference center in New York City. In a glitzy room packed with over three hundred professionals from film, television, advertising, and digital media companies, Shenoy set the stage for a day-long series of panel discussions focused on the growing influence of South Asian media and the increasingly prominent role that South Asian media professionals of South Asian origin were playing in shaping media and entertainment on a global scale. As images of Padma Lakshmi (*Top Chef*), Sendhil Ramamurthy (*Heroes*), Mindy Kaling (*The Office*), Kal Penn (*The Namesake*), and other instances of South Asian representation in American film and television flashed behind him on a large screen, Shenoy delivered his opening lines:

We learned that South Asians could play heroes outside of Bollywood films; that we could evolve to far more substantive and accurate depictions of our culture beyond the irate taxi driver and the equally irate terrorist; that good books with universal storylines that feature India as a character could make exceptional cinema. This year, we learned that

Sylvester Stallone, Arnold Schwarzenegger, and "I am Legend's" [sic] Will Smith all declared that I am, in fact, Bollywood. Steven Spielberg recognized that Reliance Entertainment's capital actually comes with a potential consumer base of 1.2 billion new ET fans. And we read in the now prophetic words of *Fortune* magazine that one should short Facebook and buy Bollywood.

Bollywood did, in fact, dominate proceedings for the rest of the day. While one panel (*Bollywood Meets Hollywood*) brought together a Bombay-based producer-director (Rohan Sippy) and executives from Disney, Sahara One, and Gotham Entertainment to discuss relations between Indian and American media corporations, a second panel (*It's Not Your Dad's Bollywood*) focused attention on diasporic entrepreneurs who had established digital media companies with the goal of creating new trajectories and models of circulation for Bollywood films and film music outside India. In addition, convention organizers had roped in Pradeep Guha, former CEO of ZEE TV, to deliver a keynote address that would provide an overview of ongoing changes in the Indian media and entertainment industries.

Further, it was clear from the schedule of panels and list of attendees that South Asian-origin media professionals were no longer working within the confines of "ethnic" media companies. Several panelists and speakers at the SAMMA-Summit held prominent managerial and creative positions within mainstream media companies and, pertinent to the present chapter, a growing number of young South Asians were turning into entrepreneurs and establishing digital media companies that revolved, in one way or another, around Bollywood films and film music. The extent of Bollywood's hold on the imaginations of these diasporic media entrepreneurs became even clearer when I began looking through the package that I had collected at the registration desk for the SAMMA-Summit. Along with a conference badge, notepad, pen, and a brochure with details of panel sessions and keynote presentations for the day was another artifact: a dark blue "Passport to Bollywood." Setting the "passport" on an empty chair beside me, I scribbled on my notepad: "Bollystan."

My note was a reference to a widely circulated article titled "Bollystan: The Global India," in which the author Parag Khanna reflected on how processes of globalization had reframed relations between India and the vast Indian diaspora. Khanna wrote: "Increasingly linked by culture and technology, they form a Global India, which I call Bollystan. 'Bolly' connotes culture (e.g., Bollywood), and 'Stan' (Farsi for "land") represents the transcendence of borders and sovereignty."[1] Khanna's neologism first appeared in

PASSPORT

Bollywood

Produced by Saavn.com, a New York-based digital media company, and distributed to everyone who attended the SAMMA-Summit, such industry artifacts signal how crucial Bollywood has become for diasporic media professionals.

the Fall 2004 issue of *Another Magazine*, a now defunct publication targeted at "young, upwardly mobile South Asians." Featuring Bollywood star Aishwarya Rai on the cover, the magazine declared: "Bollystan is a state without borders, defined by a shared culture and common values." Using the term Bollystan to refer to a vast space of transnational cultural production that included everything from henna tattoos and remix music to literature and films, Khanna and other writers sought to map how rapid flows of people, culture, and capital across national borders have rendered difficult any easy separation between nation and diaspora. In fact, Khanna proceeded to argue that Bollystan is "cosmopolitanism's inversion: instead of one person being at home anywhere, it is re-rooting Desis everywhere in a real and imagined shared cultural space."[2]

In this chapter, I examine the production of this "real and imagined shared cultural space" by focusing on the role played by diasporic media entrepreneurs in shaping Bollywood's transnational circulation. Diasporic media companies have historically operated as small-scale and often, though not always, family-run enterprises. Tracing how this has changed over the past decade, I examine two recent diasporic media initiatives—MTV-Desi, a television channel that sought to target South Asian American youth but only lasted eighteen months, and Saavn.com, a New York-based digital media company that has emerged as the most prominent aggregator and distributor of Bollywood content in North America. The central question that drives this chapter is: what does it take to conjure the diaspora as a viable scale of media production and circulation in an age of global media capitals? The goal is to examine MTV-Desi and Saavn.com as a way to understand both the possibilities and challenges facing diasporic media entrepreneurs as they negotiate a decidedly new phase of links between Bombay and Los Angeles, and at the same time, a vast and networked culture of Desi media that crisscrosses and transcends regional and national boundaries. Thus the stories I narrate here about MTV-Desi and Saavn.com are also stories about Non-Resident Indian and diasporic entrepreneurs working in a space defined on the one hand by a rapidly changing American media system, and on the other hand by increasingly influential Indian film and television companies that are actively courting diasporic audiences and reshaping the terrain of Desi culture.

"Desi," which means "from the homeland," is a term increasingly used to refer to people of South Asian origin in various locations around the world (but most prominently in North America and the United Kingdom). More importantly, the term signals, as Shalini Shankar points out, "the shift from South Asians as immigrants longing to return to a homeland to public consumers and producers of distinctive, widely circulating cultural and linguistic forms."[3] The term Desi thus moves discussions of cultural identities past territorial boundaries and distinctions between those who reside in the Indian subcontinent and those who live outside. There is, of course, a politics to the term Desi, especially given the hegemonic position that India assumes in terms of culture, politics, economics, and geography. Moreover, as Amardeep Singh points out, "Dravidian languages, for instance, do not have the word desi, thus potentially limiting the recognition or usefulness of the term even within South Asia."[4] I will return to this issue in greater detail at a later point in this chapter to explore how such issues involving Desi identity shape media industry practices. But for now, I want to signal the fact that where commercial media ventures are concerned, Bollystan has a very specific Anglo American cultural geography and as a consequence, reroots only certain kinds of Desis. As we will see, the network of cities that are part of diasporic entrepreneurs' imagination of Bollywood's global reach include cities such as London, New York, Los Angeles, and Toronto but not, for instance, Durban in South Africa. And even within these cities in the Global North, it is only a certain narrow, largely middle- and upper-middle class cultural sphere of South Asians that informs the imaginations and practices of media industry professionals.

Between India and the United States: Repositioning
Diasporic Media and Desi Culture

Over the past two decades, media scholars have built on the work of social
theorists including Arjun Appadurai and Stuart Hall to provide us with a
rich vocabulary and set of tools to analyze the relationship between media
and migration.[5] In this scholarship, diaspora and diasporic media production have been privileged sites for understanding the shifting, often disjunc-
tive, relations between cultural production, geography, and identity. Further,
in the South Asian context, it is possible to now trace an arc beginning with
Marie Gillespie's analysis of media use in a predominantly Punjabi community in a London neighborhood, through Sunaina Maira's exploration of
Indian American youth culture in New York City, to Shalini Shankar's ethnography of Desi youth culture during the tech boom in Silicon Valley as a
way to foreground transformations in understandings of South Asian diasporic identity and the South Asian mediascape.[6]

Where Gillespie documented the creative and strategic ways in which
youth in diasporic communities drew on media and popular culture to initiate dialogues between their parents' ideas of culture and their experiences
in British society, Maira illustrated how a range of media (from mainstream
Indian films to subcultural remix music) functioned as triggers for discussions and contests over broader issues of ethnic authenticity and cultural
hybridity, assimilation and race relations, multiculturalism and citizenship. While these issues remain deeply relevant in the lives of Desi teenag-
ers that Shankar documents and analyzes, her ethnography also illustrates
the extent to which being and becoming Desi has changed as South Asians
from diverse class, linguistic, religious, and geographic backgrounds have
established themselves in places like California. Arguing that it is no longer productive to characterize second-generation youth as being "culturally
and intergenerationally conflicted"—of being "American" at school, "Indian"
at home, and "caught in limbo" between these two worlds—Shankar asserts
that Desi youth now "exhibit a far more nuanced consciousness about what
it means to be Desi."[7] As we will see, the heterogeneity of Desi youth culture
that scholars like Shankar foreground poses a formidable challenge to media
industry professionals' efforts to forge a Desi demographic.

Further, where the South Asian diaspora is concerned, popular and scholarly accounts have tended to privilege cinema, Hindi-language films from
Bombay and English-language diasporic films in particular, over print,
television, and other forms of cultural production. While one could argue
that this provides too narrow a template for understanding the relationship

between media and diasporic identity, there are several reasons for the privileged position cinema occupies. The first is simply the enduring popularity of films and film music (mainly Hindi-language cinema from Bombay) among South Asian families who migrated to the United States following changes in U.S. immigration law in 1965.[8] From the late 1960s, when enterprising families began screening films in university halls and other venues, to the recent forays into film exhibition by Bombay-based media companies like Reliance Entertainment, Hindi-language Bollywood films continue to dominate the Desi mediascape. These film screenings were usually held in university halls rented for a few hours during the weekend, with films screened off 16mm, and later, 35mm reels. These weekend screenings, with an intermission that lasted thirty to forty-five minutes, were an occasion, apart from religious festivals, for people to wear traditional clothes, speak in Hindi or other regional languages, and participate in a ritual reminiscent of "home." At a time when there were no cultural institutions in place and little on offer in mainstream media that resonated with their emotions, nostalgic longing, and cultural values, leave alone addressing the difficulties of life in a new cultural space, these screenings were marked as an exclusively *Indian* space, away from mainstream society, where families could meet and participate in a ritual of sharing personal and collective memories of life in India.[9]

A second reason that films and film music figure prominently in discussions of Desi youth culture relates to Desi youth appropriating and remixing film songs and dance sequences in college events, dance clubs, and so on.[10] Third, it is in and through cinema that diasporic writers and directors like Hanif Kureishi, Mira Nair, and Gurinder Chadha began addressing the complexities of claiming and defining South Asian identities in countries such as the U.K. and the U.S. As Jigna Desai observes, Bollywood has shaped South Asian diasporic filmmaking in multiple ways:

> One primary example is the frequency with which Bollywood is referred [to] thematically within the films themselves . . . in addition, Bollywood conventions are reflected in the aesthetic forms and narrative structures in a variety of films . . . also, there is crossover in terms of performers: Shashi Kapoor, Zohra Sehgal, Om Puri, and Shabana Azmi are all actors who have appeared in Indian and diasporic productions. Finally, diasporic filmmakers have employed the networks of distribution that circulate Indian films.[11]

Finally, the limited influence of television production in the South Asian American context (and more broadly, the Asian American one), can be attributed to the relatively small-scale nature—both in terms of finance and geographic reach—of the many initiatives that were launched in the United States during the 1980s and early 1990s. While radio programs featuring Hindi film music, Indian classical music, and other forms, including *ghazals* and *qawwalis*, had been on the air in areas with large concentrations of South Asian immigrants, it was only toward the mid-1980s that television became part of the Desi mediascape.[12] The limited reach of this early phase of South Asian television programming in the United States was largely a function of policies and regulatory frameworks that created the opportunity for such programming in the first place.

On September 9, 1980 the Federal Communications Commission proposed the creation of a "new television broadcast service with low-power mini-stations" that could meet the needs of Americans in rural areas that did not "receive even the basic complement of three or four signals."[13] In addition to viewers in rural areas, this policy shift was also seen as a response to the needs of underserved and underrepresented minority and ethnic groups in large urban areas. These stations, such as KSCI-TV (Channel 18) in Los Angeles, would enter into agreements with private producers—often a husband-and-wife team that sometimes expanded to include their extended family—who used the equipment and other facilities at the stations to produce and broadcast their own programs. In return, these producers would pay a small fee or in some cases, share any revenues generated through advertising. These programs, such as "Bombay Connection" that aired on KSCI-TV, would typically be an hour-long mix of song sequences from Hindi-language Bombay films and coverage of local events relating to South Asian viewers (festival celebrations, dance competitions, interviews with prominent artists from South Asia on tour in the United States, and so on).

Without exception, content from the Bombay film industry was vital to every such local television production. However, given the small scale and limited reach of these television programs, there were no formal links established with industry professionals in Bombay. The only notable exception to this was a weekly television series (*Indigo*) produced by a New York-based company called the Bombay Broadcasting Network (BBN). Established and managed by a husband-and-wife team (Anita Raj and Giri Raj), BBN claimed that it reached "7 million South Asian immigrants from coast to coast, in 9 cities across the country."[14] This program premiered in August 1987 on what was then the newly launched Travel Channel, but ended by February 1989 when the company went bankrupt.

Broadly speaking, then, South Asian diasporic media production has always occupied a space between "national" media capitals, between Bombay and Los Angeles. However, I would argue that for diasporic media producers, preliberalization Bombay had no specificity either as a "switching point" for capital or as a center of media production capable of and/or interested in mediating the experience of migration and diaspora. It is this dynamic that changed in significant ways as India embarked on a program of economic liberalization during the late 1980s and early 1990s. As I have outlined in previous chapters, three interrelated shifts and emergences defined this sociohistorical conjuncture: the growing cultural, political, and economic influence of the Indian diaspora on different spheres of life in India and conversely, the growing influence of Indian media in the diaspora; the transformation of film, television, and advertising industries in cities like Bombay, Chennai, and Hyderabad with the entry and establishment of transnational media corporations; and the state's creative responses and efforts to refigure its relationship with both the Indian diaspora and the media industries. How have these shifts reconfigured the field for diasporic media production and circulation?

To begin with, several scholars have argued that Bollywood films played a major role in mediating the newfound centrality of the diaspora, particularly the late modern, "first world" diaspora, to India's navigation of a global economy. As I detailed earlier in this book, films such as *Dilwale Dulhania Le Jayenge* (*DDLJ*, Aditya Chopra, 1995), *Pardes* (1997, Subhash Ghai), and *Kabhi Khushi Kabhie Gham* (*K3G*, Karan Johar, 2001), which resonated strongly with viewers in India and abroad and count among the most successful films of the 2000–10 decade, began exploring the cultural space of Non-Resident Indians in new ways. By exploring and cautiously legitimizing the cultural space of Indian life in the diaspora, films like *K3G* rendered the diaspora's version of Indianness less transgressive or impure and a more acceptable variant, and in doing so set the stage for the state to reterritorialize Non-Resident Indians and remap the sociocultural boundaries of the "national family." Moreover, as Sujata Moorti has shown, such narrative strategies whereby "India and Indians . . . imaginatively accommodated the diaspora, encompassing it within the folds of a globalized Indian identity," can also be traced in popular magazines and prime-time television programs.[15] Further, when we examine these representational shifts alongside significant institutional and industrial changes, including the emergence of influential television companies like ZEE, Sony, STAR, and Sahara One that have also established themselves in diasporic markets since 2000, it becomes clear that diasporic media producers have to negotiate and grapple with the challenges and opportunities that the growing influence of Bombay-based media corporations present.

I have framed this discussion so far by positioning diasporic media and culture between Bombay and Los Angeles, but it is crucial to also take into account the influence that Chennai and Hyderabad, two other centers of media production, wield. Chennai and Hyderabad are centers of Tamil- and Telugu-language film and television production, and home to power-ful media conglomerates, including the SUN TV network (Chennai) and the Ramoji Group (Hyderabad). In contrast to Bollywood during the 1990s, Tamil and Telugu cinema did not address diasporic communities or wrestle with the issue of reterritorializing diasporic Indians.[16] Further, the distribu-tion of Tamil and Telugu films across the world remains largely unorganized and defined by informal networks involving merchants and grocery stores that cater to South Asian communities, pirate networks that ensure the avail-ability of DVDs within a few days of the film's release in India, and a large number of streaming video and BitTorrent websites. Television, however, is a different story, as Divya McMillin's overview of the SUN TV network makes clear.[17] Managed by Kalanidhi Maran, member of the powerful Karunanidhi family in the south Indian state of Tamil Nadu, SUN TV was launched as a Tamil-language channel in 1993. Beginning with just three hours of pro-gramming, SUN TV developed into a twenty-four-hour channel by 1995, and went on to expand its line up by adding a news channel in 2000 (Sun News), a music channel in 2002 (Sun Music), and a film-based channel (KTV) in 2004. During this time, the network also expanded into Telugu (Gemini TV), Kannada (Udaya TV), and Malayalam-language (Surya TV) programming. By 2002, audiences in the United States had access to SUN TV via the Dish Network, and on other carriers in Australia, New Zealand, the U.K., Singa-pore, Malaysia, China, and Russia. What McMillin's account of the landscape of Indian television companies' global reach makes clear is the segmented nature of the diasporic audience for Indian television and more importantly, the difficulty of imagining a pan-Desi audience demographic. It is in relation to these transformations in the media industries in India, particularly their growing capacity to define media circulation in the diaspora, that I explore the launch and failure of MTV-Desi.

MTV-Desi marks an important moment in the history of South Asian dia-sporic media production and as a productive failure that signals a key shift in the relationship between television and diasporic cultures. As Vicki Mayer points out, examining such initiatives involves listening to stories about fail-ure that media professionals narrate, including how they move on to the next project, and often sheds light on what constitutes success in a given media landscape.[18] But there is another perspective that I want to introduce. MTV-Desi can also be seen as an experiment in situating Bollywood in relation to second-generation diasporic youth culture as distinct from the other television channels that also draw on Bollywood content to address first-generation immigrants from the Indian subcontinent. Instead of regarding Bollywood as a link to "home," as the advertising campaigns of television channels like ETV and ZEE TV proclaim, MTV-Desi could have positioned Bollywood as part of a larger arena of cultural production that reflected the particular life experiences of South Asian American youth. As we will see, MTV-Desi was in some ways emblematic of "ethnic" media companies that operate in the United States today, and in other ways was strikingly different, given that it was firmly established within and in relation to mainstream media corporations in the United States and India.

"I Want My Hyphenated-Identity MTV"

In July 2005 MTV Networks announced the launch of MTV-Desi, a niche channel for South Asian American youth. Launched with great fanfare, MTV-Desi sought to respond to ongoing changes in South Asian American culture and create a space within mainstream media that would speak to the particular experiences of Desi youth. In addition to Bollywood song sequences and Indi-pop music videos, the channel would feature U.S.- and U.K-based artists like DJ Rekha, M.I.A., and Jay Sean alongside popular American stars in order to create a multiethnic, multigenre playlist that would resonate with Desi youth. While music would remain the primary focus of programming, MTV-Desi would also develop new segments covering a range of topics related to life in South Asia and the South Asian diaspora worldwide, including original shows such as "Live From," which would track Desi youth culture in cities across North America and the U.K., "Desi Sweet 16," which was modeled on the Sweet 16 series on MTV USA, and hit shows like *Roadies* from MTV-India. Recognizing the transnational nature of Desi youth culture, writers, producers, and VJs worked hard to define MTV-Desi as a unique site of cultural production that neither mainstream American television nor the India-centric programming on Dish TV and DirecTV could match.

Declaring that MTV-Desi would soon become the "pop culture destination for Desis," Nusrat Durrani, General Manager and Senior Vice President of MTV World, explained: "But more than the music, it is also about articulating the stories from this community—young South Asian Americans who have grown up in the country, but have not seen themselves on TV."[19] At the same time, Durrani aimed to fashion MTV-Desi not simply as a channel for South Asian American youth but as a space that would showcase South

Asian cultural production and invite participation from as diverse an audience as possible. MTV-Desi, furthermore, was part of a larger MTV World initiative that involved channels targeting Korean American (MTV-K) and Chinese American youth (MTV-Chi).[20] As the very first mainstream media initiative that targeted diasporic youth culture, these "hyphenated-identity" MTV channels attracted a great deal of positive attention despite the fact that they were available only through an international programming package on DirecTV's satellite television service. MTV-Desi was part of the "Hindi Direct" package that included five other Indian television channels and cost $29.99 per month.

Eighteen months later, MTV Networks pulled the plug on MTV-Desi, MTV-K, and MTV-Chi, stating that the premium distribution model had failed to attract audiences and hence advertising revenues. In press releases and interviews, MTV executives also pointed out that the decision was shaped by a larger process of corporate restructuring undertaken by the parent company Viacom. On the one hand, the cancellation of the MTV World initiative did not come as a major surprise to either audiences or media journalists. As one prominent journalist remarked on the widely read blog of the South Asian Journalists' Association, "We published next to nothing on the channel, because I couldn't find anyone who watched the satellite channel: no college students, no twenty-somethings with spare change. And it wasn't just me. All the tastemakers I interviewed—DJs, other music types—said they didn't know any MTV Desi subscribers either."[21] On the other hand, given the fact that all other attempts to carve out a space for Asian American programming on television—AZN, American Desi, and ImaginAsian, for instance—had failed or struggled to remain viable, the dismay among Desis and other Asian American groups was understandable.

Relying on advertising and marketing discourse that had, over the 2000–10 decade, constructed the "Asian consumer" and the Asian American community as an increasingly important audience demographic, protest letters and petitions suggested that these failures reflected a lack of commitment on the part of mainstream media corporations to develop and sustain Asian American programming. Although letters to MTV Networks urging the company to keep MTV World alive and to make these channels more widely available did not have any effect, they may have influenced MTV's decision to rethink its content production and distribution model. In December 2008 MTV Networks announced the launch of mtviggy.com, a website for Desi, Chinese, Korean, and Japanese youth across the world. While media attention has moved on, focusing instead on mainstream American television networks' attempts to create South Asian-themed programming, analyzing this moment of "failure" is crucial, for it brings into sharp relief the challenges facing media professionals in imagining diasporic audiences.[22] In this case, it also encourages us to reflect on the limits of television as a site for the articulation of Bollywood with contemporary diasporic youth culture.

The Limits of Niche Television

Nusrat Durrani, who was largely responsible for developing the MTV-World initiative, understood very well that the relationship between "diaspora" and "home" was much more ambivalent for Desi youth compared to their parents' generation, and that MTV-Desi could not succeed by mimicking MTV-India or other Indian television channels. Born and raised in north India, Durrani had worked for a decade in India and Dubai before moving to the United States and joining MTV in the early 1990s. Indeed, his background as a media professional of South Asian origin who had lived and worked in India and Dubai before moving to the United States, and whose taste in music and popular culture had been shaped by transnational circuits of cultural flows that were not limited to the Anglo American cultural sphere that his colleagues at MTV were steeped in, seems to have played a key role in shaping his approach to the MTV-Desi initiative. Recalling his early years as a junior executive at MTV, Durrani reflected on the music channel's narrow programming outlook as something that came as a surprise to him. He went on to narrate one particular incident as he tried to explain to me how his early experience at MTV spurred him to think beyond established industry paradigms when it came to MTV-Desi:

> ND: Disappointed might be a strong word. I think I was surprised. I was surprised that people in New York City, particularly in the entertainment side of things, just didn't know and weren't exposed to what else was happening around the world. They had no concept of Bollywood, for example, they had no concept of any entertainment icon outside of what was kind of, you know, almost endorsed by the U.S. media, and those things really bothered me for some time. I recall an incident, I think it was in '97 . . . in those days by the way, MTV or the entertainment industry, generally speaking, didn't have too many South Asians. . . . So maybe that's part of the reason, maybe I was the only dude, sort of, trying to tell people stuff. Anyhow, do you remember this band called Cornershop?
>
> AP: Yes, I do.

ND: So right, '97, I think that was the year. Cornershop made an album called *When You're Born for the 7th time*. Have you heard it?

AP: Yes, I have. And I could be wrong, but I think Channel [V] or MTV-India did play one of their music videos.

ND: Ok, so you know what I'm talking about. When I heard that, I remember, specifically, I was actually on a VH1 floor. And they used to have these piles of CDs that people didn't like, thrown away because they had two copies or whatever. So I was walking by and I saw two copies of this new album lying outside somebody's door and I picked it up. I had this little Discman and I listened to the entire album on my way home. It's one of the first albums that meaningfully, substantially, integrated South Asian influences and other types of influences like Allen Ginsberg reciting one of his poems, Paula Frazier singing a duet with Tjinder Singh. So the next day I looked up our system, our video library system and I found that they had a video but it wasn't being played on the channel. So I actually walked into the programmer's room and said, why aren't you playing this stuff? I was talking about "A Brimful of Asha," which had a cool video. A few months later we started playing the video, but only after we heard from elsewhere that this is cool. I'm relating this particular incident because it has stayed with me. I yearned to do something, but I didn't have the power to do anything at the time.

Durrani went on to talk at length about other diasporic artists and groups, including Talvin Singh, Fun-Da-Mental, Nitin Sawhney, and others associated with the Asian Underground, a music and cultural formation involving primarily second-generation British-born youth with ties to different countries in the Indian subcontinent. His immersion in this diasporic cultural phenomenon during the mid-to-late 1990s shaped his understanding of diasporic youth culture and its location between and betwixt "national" cultures. However, despite Durrani's efforts to position and brand MTV-Desi as a uniquely diasporic space, MTV Networks entered into a distribution deal with DirecTV and located MTV-Desi firmly within an India-centric programming package. This decision was partly a function of television industry professionals grappling with a changing distribution landscape in the United States, and certainly spoke to their uncertainty about a channel like MTV-Desi reaching audiences via satellite television. As Durrani explained:

When the project was green lit, the distribution landscape was kind of weird. We were still living in the world of linear TV and traditional distribution partners—cable or satellite companies. And you know, there was pressure from our linear TV partners, so we partnered with them and launched the channels as premium TV services, and, you know, everybody loved the idea. They said, let's align ourselves to the model that exists, you know, the premium TV model, where there is enough hunger within these audiences to actually pay a premium to get the channel.

Even though Durrani and others at MTV-Desi recognized that it would be a mistake to imagine Desi youth and their engagement with media and popular culture in the same terms as their parents or, generally speaking, as first-generation migrants from the Indian subcontinent, statements from others at MTV Networks revealed that this was how Desi identity continued to be mobilized. A particularly telling press release from MTV described the entire MTV World initiative as an attempt to "tap into the rich transcultural nature of the target audiences in a manner that uniquely connects local audiences to *their homeland*" (my emphasis).[23] Statements from other industry executives also revealed how this advertising/marketing discourse positioned Desi youth outside the boundaries of American national culture, rehearsing the contradictory nature of American responses to Asian immigration that has tended to position "Asians 'within' the U.S nation-state, its workplaces, and its market, yet linguistically, culturally, and racially marked Asians as 'foreign' and 'outside' the national polity."[24] This understanding of Desi identity also held implications for how industry professionals thought about the interest that South Asian media might attract from audiences at large.

Consider this exchange that took place during the opening keynote session of the SAMMA-Summit in 2008. Peter Liguori, who was the chairman of Fox Broadcasting at the time, delivered a keynote address replete with banal industry catch phrases (such as "content will be king") and did not in any way speak to the interests of a convention on South Asian media and marketing in the United States. But the convention organizers seemed to have anticipated this. SAMMA cofounder and moderator for the session, Rajan Shah, opened the question and answer session by directing Liguori's attention to the lack of South Asia-themed television programming in the United States. Even before the applause to Liguori's keynote speech had ended, the lights in the hall dimmed and Shah drew everyone's attention to a clip from a FOX reality TV program called *So You Think You Can Dance*. During the 2008 season, one of the groups on the program had choreographed a dance to a Bhangra song. Shah posed his question, to loud cheers from the audience:

SHAH: Speaking about the South Asian market, and I'm going to put you on the spot here. Indian, and South Asian, influence is all over the map now. In wellness, retail, even clothing. But we don't see, other than individual characters appearing on shows, South Asian families on television. Can you address why this is so? Do you think there is a chance an Indian family will be on television soon?

LIGUORI: Frankly, I don't think the answer I am going to give you will be popular. I don't think it's going to be too far in the future before we see a South Asian family, an Indian family, portrayed on television. Let's start with why there isn't greater representation. It's just simply a numbers game. Right now, there are 2 million South Asians in this country. And it's very, very difficult when your job is on the line, day in and day out, to say that I'm going to put someone in a show that frankly doesn't have an audience outside the walls of our offices.

Liguori's racialized assumption that only South Asian audiences would be interested in a television program featuring a South Asian family hardly merits attention. But it does signal how niche marketing/programming strategies that have become so well-entrenched in the American media system over the past two decades intersect with the "discovery" and configuration of ethnic identities as viable marketing segments. The phrase—"It's just a numbers game"—and the specific number that Liguori mentioned—2 million South Asians—point to the fact that MTV-Desi and other South Asian media initiatives were working in a context in which advertising and marketing professionals had succeeded in constructing Asian Americans as a consumer demographic that remained untapped and moreover, had unique needs that were unfulfilled by mainstream media and marketing.

While the intersections of South Asian cultural production and American public culture can be traced through the work of artists like DJ Rekha and subcultures in cities like New York, Chicago, and Los Angeles, media companies' interest in this hitherto marginalized community was sparked in part by the results of the 2000 U.S. census, which revealed that Asian Americans were the fastest growing ethnic minority as well as the most affluent of all groups. In much the same way that advertisers and marketers worked to commodify Latinos during the mid-to-late 1990s, companies such as *Ethnik PR* and *Evershine Group* took on the task of constructing a Desi demographic.[25] As one widely circulated arcle entitled "Chasing Desi Dollars" in *Time Magazine* proclaimed:

> There are some 2.5 million Desis in the U.S., and the vast majority is
> Indian. That may not seem terribly significant compared with, say, 40 mil-
> lion Hispanics, but consider how premium a customer a South Asian is:
> Indians alone commanded $76 billion worth of disposable income last
> year . . . median household income is nearly $64,000—50 percent higher
> than the national average. The U.S. has always welcomed the world's poor
> and working classes. India has sent its professionals."[26]

It hardly needs to be pointed out that this particular logic of enumeration
papers over the diversity of South Asian histories and cultural practices in
North America. What is perhaps most problematic is the manner in which
these marketing and media reports use the terms "Desi" and "South Asian"
but reduce them to "Indian" in order to conjure a highly educated, well-
adjusted, and affluent demographic. In fact, the 2000 census reveals that
the median household income for South Asian Americans is $50,723, well
below the $64,000 figure that was widely circulated. As a policy analysis
from a South Asian nonprofit group pointed out, while this is considerably
higher than the national median household income ($41,994), "the per cap-
ita income at $21,765 is only marginally higher than the national per capita
income of $21,587."[27] Minor differences like these assume greater impor-
tance when situated alongside data that reveal, for instance, particularly low
employment rates among Pakistani and Bangladeshi women, higher rates of
children living below the poverty line when compared with the general population, and lower levels of home ownership. As Sunaina Maira and other
scholars have documented, "popular accounts of Indian immigration to the
U.S. have tended to conceal harsh realities, painting the Indian-American
community as well-educated, well-adjusted immigrants likely to be doctors,
scientists, engineers and business professionals."[28] And given the relative
lack of research on immigrant communities with ties to Pakistan, Bangla-
desh, and other South Asian nations, the Indian experience tends to inform
debates concerning the South Asian American diaspora.

These differences were set aside in the dominant marketing discourse,
which focused on the experiences and cultural practices of a very specific
class of Indian families to construct a "Desi audience." This narrow imagination of the Desi audience, one that flattened out linguistic, regional, and other
forms of diversity in the diaspora, had an impact on programming decisions
as well. A majority of the programs on MTV-Desi relied on content that was
either sourced from MTV-India or adapted from MTV-USA's programming
lineup. Not surprisingly, Bollywood-inspired material dominated the content that was imported from MTV-India—programs such as *Bollywood on*

The home page of *EthnikPR*, one of many companies that have constructed the "South Asian consumer" demographic in North America.

Ice and a countdown program called *MTV 123*—and did little to distinguish MTV-Desi from the other India-centric channels available through DirecTV or other satellite and cable systems.

However, MTV-Desi's failure cannot be explained by focusing on the logics of American television alone. The growing influence of Indian film and television companies in defining media circulation in the diaspora that I detailed earlier also played a crucial role in shaping MTV-Desi's programming, distribution, and reception. It would not be an exaggeration to state that television in India has undergone major changes since the mid-1990s. As Shanti Kumar and several other scholars have documented, the establishment of influential transnational networks such as Star TV and translocal networks such as ZEE, Sun, and Eenadu during the 1990s transformed the ways in which television operated as a cultural institution.[29] What began with local cable operators stringing cables across rooftops to connect homes to the new and fascinating world of Star Plus, Star Sports, MTV, and BBC News had, by the mid-1990s, grown into a stable satellite and cable industry with rapidly expanding viewership. Since the late 1990s, these television companies have invested considerable effort in reaching diasporic audiences (particularly in North America and Western Europe). As Rajinder Dudrah points out, taking advantage of the mainstream media's neglect of Asian audiences in Britain and Europe, companies like ZEE TV quickly established

Table 5.1. Prominent Television Initiatives Targeting South Asian American Audiences

Company Name	Launch date	Ownership	Carriage
TV Asia	May 1998	TV Asia	Cable (various local networks), DBS (Dish Network)
Asian Variety Show (AVS)	July 1988	Private	Cable (various local networks); DBS (Dish Network, DirecTV)
ZEE TV	July 1998	ZEE TV USA	Cable (various), DBS (Dish Network)
Bollywood On Demand (BODVOD)	August 2004	212 Media/Schramm Sports & Entertainment	Cable (Comcast, Time Warner Cable, Cox)
ImaginAsian TV	August 2004	Private	Cable (Comcast, Time Warner, Charter, Champion Broadband, Patriot Media), Broadcast Stations (W36AS, Edison, NJ; KTVY, Las Vegas; KBCB, Seattle)
American Desi	January 2005	Private	DBS (Dish Network)
AZN	May 2005	Comcast	Cable, telecom (AT&T U-Verse, Verizon FiOS)
MTV Desi	July 2005	MTV Networks	DBS (DirecTV)

Note: DBS stands for Direct Broadcast Satellite.
Sources: *Cable and Broadcasting, India Abroad,* and *India West.*

themselves as an alternative, offering a "variety of programs that visibly manifest themselves as South Asian for South Asian viewers."[30] This holds true in the United States as well, where a range of Indian television channels targeting different linguistic groups are offered through Dish and DirecTV's satellite television services. But even a cursory look would confirm that India-centric media, nonsubtitled television programming in particular, also ends up marginalizing Desi youth who might have neither the linguistic skills nor the level of immersion in the politics and culture of the Indian subcontinent to engage with its soap operas, sitcoms, and reality shows.

In one sense, then, MTV-Desi is symptomatic of a larger problem confronting diasporic television production—of being caught between the nationalist logics of two powerful media industries. But we could also understand MTV-Desi as an initiative that represented an opportunity for Bollywood to become part of a broader arena of diasporic cultural production instead of remaining ensconced in the ethnic cable and satellite TV packages that target primarily first-generation immigrants. However, given the difficulties of creating programming that cuts across and speaks to the diversity of Desi youth culture while also becoming commercially viable, perhaps it is also worth asking if we can expect television, in its current form and structure, to play a crucial role in expanding Bollywood's reach. Do digital media platforms allow for more flexible and productive links across spatial scales? What might the fortunes of a company like Saavn.com tell us about the work of creating a circuit of media circulation that is able to leverage changing relations between national, global, and diasporic audiences in ways that a television channel like MTV-Desi could not?

"It's Not Your Dad's Bollywood"

The last panel of the SAMMA-Summit of 2008, titled "It's Not Your Dad's Bollywood: The Upstarts behind a New Generation of South Asian-Inspired Content and Distribution Companies," brought together three diasporic entrepreneurs who had launched digital media companies with ties to Bollywood. Given that the title signals a generational break, we might begin by asking: What was Dad's Bollywood for Vin Bhat (Saavn.com), Anjula Acharia-Bath (Desihits.com), and Geetanjali Dhillon (Jaman.com)?

As Bhat and Dhillon recalled, Dad's Bollywood was what they grew up with in their homes and communities in the United States: weekend screenings at a community hall or in a university auditorium, often arranged by an enterprising South Asian family; film music played at home or in cars on road trips with other South Asian families; dances performed at community events; and most crucially, one-hour programs featuring Bollywood songs on the local Public Access Station every Saturday or Sunday morning. Supported by advertising from South Asian grocery stores, restaurants, and companies like Western Union, these television shows were also locally produced or, at best, purchased from the New Jersey-based *Asian Variety Show*. For Acharia-Bath, who grew up in the U.K. and moved to the United States as a working professional, the experience was not that different either. Nodding along as her copanelists recalled their experiences growing up as Indian Americans, Acharia-Bath added that her own experience as a British Asian was much the same, the only difference being that Indian content was far more widely available in the U.K. All the panelists, as well as the moderator for the session, Vipin Goyal, agreed that this was not *their* Bollywood.

What, then, was their Bollywood? The answer, it turned out, rested on a set of shifts in cultural production and perceptions of value—of what was "cool"—that unfolded in seemingly parallel tracks. The first site of change involved these entrepreneurs' rejection of "Dad's Bollywood" early in their lives as they struggled with and against films and film music that resonated deeply with their parents but that they themselves could not draw upon to articulate their hybrid identities. Well into their teenage years, Bollywood films, film music, and indeed all things Indian were embarrassing. However, their tastes as well as modes of valuing Bollywood changed dramatically when they entered college and encountered a larger, if still marginal to the mainstream, Desi cultural space in which Bollywood songs, as remixed dance tracks, for instance, were deemed "cool." In one-on-one interviews that I conducted with each one of these entrepreneurs, they all narrated a similar story of coming to terms with Bollywood. Here is how Acharia-Bath explained it:

> I spent my whole life balancing two cultures. In terms of life at home, my parents were not hugely traditional. But they were very Indian. We're Punjabis, we eat Punjabi food, and when I walked out of my house, I really shed most of that. I wanted to be like an English girl. I even used the name Angela, I was very anglicized. I'd come home and listen to my mum's Bollywood or Zee TV or whatever, but when I went out, that just wasn't part of my life at all. I remember shunning a lot of Indian music and Bollywood music, being embarrassed by it, because that's what my friends made me feel. They didn't make me feel like it was cool or interesting. They were like what's that funny music or what's that funny food. I was embarrassed about it, 'cause it was different. So I kind of let go of most of my Indian heritage during my high school years. But secretly I loved it, I remember loving it. And I remember walking into this club in London—when I was in college—and seeing a sea of Indians, and black kids and white kids, it was just this multicultural mish mash and this melting pot. I walked in and saw this guy—who would become my husband actually!—mixing bhangra and hip-hop. And I remember going ahh, this is amazing, this is really cool, and this is really happening. And I could just see this multicultural sea of kids just enjoying the music, and it wasn't just Indians, I remember seeing some of the friends from my village saying this is really cool. This is the music that my parents listen to, this is the music that my friends thought was funny. But being in a different environment and embracing the music made it okay. I remember this defining moment.

Acharia-Bath's account of growing up in England, initially under pressure to shun Desi markers but gradually coming to terms with her sense of self and belonging in a larger Desi community echoes comments from a range of Indian American youth that Sunaina Maira has documented in her ethnography of Desi culture in New York City. The stories I heard from these three entrepreneurs spoke to the difficulties faced by diasporic youth in navigating two starkly different cultural fields. On the one hand, diasporic youth have to deal with parental pressure to preserve an "authentic" ethnic identity that is, as Maira and others have argued, fraught with the politics of nostalgia and often constructed on the basis of a highly "selective importing of elements and agents of Indian culture."[31] On the other hand, they have to contend with their positions as minorities in the racial and class economies of the United States or the U.K. as they spent the week in schools and colleges. And it is when they enter college that they discover a community of students with more or less similar backgrounds, with comparable stories of growing up "Indian" in the United States or the U.K. Away from home for the first time, many of them begin engaging with issues of cultural identity through coursework concerning multiculturalism, postcolonial literature, South Asian studies, and so on, but also in a more lived way through involvement in events such as the "India Night" shows on multicultural college campuses across the United States. As Kavoori and Joseph suggest, India Night works as a "space-clearing gesture" and as a place for diasporic youth to come to terms with their identities "before they enter the workplace, or parts of regular America, where the place/space for a hybrid, cosmopolitan, and ethnic identity are often absent."[32] It is this very particular experience of coming to terms with Desi culture and identity, especially through remixed Bollywood songs and other hybrid forms of popular culture, that these diasporic entrepreneurs all narrated as they tried to explain what *their* Bollywood meant.

The stories of growing up and coming to terms with Desi identity and culture that I heard from Acharia-Bath, Bhat, and Dhillon, and that I also came across in newspaper and trade press coverage of their companies, do need to be understood in relation to policies of multiculturalism in the United States and U.K., especially as they play out on college campuses. They also need to be situated in relation to the commodified nature of "Indo chic" or "Asian cool" that has become such a prominent part of American and British public culture over the past two decades.[33] In addition, I also want to draw attention to how these stories about their selves, their sense of being and becoming Desi, became intimately tied to media industry logics. In the United States, these entrepreneurs' lived experiences as second-generation diasporic youth was regarded as crucial to their ability to understand the particularities of Desi culture, and thereby positioned them uniquely well to build a commercially viable Desi media business. In other words, these entrepreneurs came to be regarded as representatives of a larger ethnic market and in this capacity, they had to render themselves knowable and intelligible to media industry professionals and venture capitalists in the technology sector. Their personal life histories had become a crucial source of cultural capital at a historical conjuncture in which marketing discourse surrounding the South Asian American consumer and the growing presence of Bollywood in the global media landscape had generated new opportunities.

If their own lives and identities as diasporic subjects constituted one trajectory of change, the other sense of a generational break for these entrepreneurs involved Bollywood itself. Echoing the Indian state and FICCI's narratives of corporatization, these entrepreneurs emphasized that their ventures would not have been possible had it not been for changes in the film industry in Bombay and in particular, the emergence of corporate studios such as UTV Motion Pictures and Reliance Entertainment. In fact, a key panel discussion that took place earlier in the day at the SAMMA-Summit had set the stage for an interpretation of corporatization as a much-needed and smooth transition to more globally recognizable industry practices. Titled "Bollywood Meets Hollywood: How Indian and U.S. Entertainment Partnerships Are Shaking Up the Industry," the panel included Michael Andreen, a senior vice president in Disney's International Production division, Sanjay Chitale, a senior executive in the Indian conglomerate Sahara One, and Rohan Sippy, a Bollywood producer and director who belonged to one of the most storied family businesses in the Bombay film industry. In much the same way that Vishesh Bhatt did a few months later at the FICCI FRAMES convention in 2009, Rohan Sippy struck the lone note of dissent by arguing that corporatization did not necessarily mean the adoption of Hollywood-like practices of speculation, production, and marketing. But the other panelists were quick to point to Hollywood studios' investments in Bollywood, UTV's coproduction deals with Hollywood studios, and the deal between Reliance Entertainment and Steven Spielberg's DreamWorks as signs that established practices would change or simply fade away. In this sense too, it was not their "Dad's Bollywood," one represented by family businesses and kinship-based practices. Rather, their Bollywood was a corporatized media industry with global ambitions that they, as professionals embedded in the American media system, could work with.

Thus, these diasporic entrepreneurs argued that they were uniquely positioned to respond to the transcultural dimensions of diasporic culture and establish new trajectories of circulation for Bollywood films and film music in ways that were not possible either for professionals working primarily in Bombay or American media professionals who at this point simply did not possess the necessary cultural expertise. In the following section, I draw on an in-depth interview with Vin Bhat in addition to his presentation at the SAMMA-Summit to narrate the emergence of Saavn.com as one of the largest and most influential Bollywood-centric digital media companies. While all three companies are interesting cases to consider, I concentrate on Saavn.com because it is focused exclusively on Bollywood, unlike Desihits. com or Jaman.com. Saavn.com's industrial identity is defined by its focus on Bollywood, as evident not only in the slogan that accompanies all Saavn.com advertisements—"Bringing Bollywood to the World"—but also in its claim to offer a "Passport to Bollywood."

Saavn.com: "Bringing Bollywood to the World"

The story begins in the early 2000s when Vin Bhat decided, after a few years in the world of investment banking in New York City, to try his hand at being an entrepreneur. With three other colleagues, Bhat launched a software company that focused on servicing media clients and designing contextual advertising. As with several such ventures in the postboom dot-com economy, Bhat and his colleagues sold their company to a venture capital firm and, in a move that would bring them in close contact with the media world in Bombay, decided to spend a few months in India. "This was 2003–04 and we didn't really have a plan. It was about taking some time off while also getting to know the media industry in a place that was attracting attention across the world," Bhat recalled. Through contacts at major banks in India, Bhat and his colleagues were able to meet a range of media industry professionals across the film, television, and music sectors in Bombay. According to Bhat, this experience was formative. In particular, what sparked their interest was the recognition that Bombay-based professionals were struggling to establish a presence in overseas territories. "When we heard from so many people that it was difficult to get a sense of the [overseas] market when there isn't proper reporting and the distribution chain is opaque, it got us thinking," Bhat recounted. "We wanted to go back to the drawing board, to figure out how to solve this problem in the industry."

Back in the United States, Bhat and his colleagues began by approaching cable operators. With the help of former advisors, one of whom had been an executive vice president at Fox Broadcasting and another a vice president at Bravo, they were able to initiate conversations with major companies such as Time Warner Cable early in the fall of 2003. As it happened, their visit took place in the context of cable companies across North America exploring the possibilities of Video-on-Demand (VOD) services as a way to tap into the sought-after "Asian American audience." To be sure, cable television in the United States has been a vital space for a range of transnational, ethnic, and exilic media. This has, however, been limited to public and leased access television. As Naficy and others have shown, exilic and diasporic media producers have had to work "at the intersection and in the interstices of culture industries; transnational, national, federal, state, local, private, ethnic, commercial and non-commercial funding agencies."[34] In 2003, Vin Bhat and his colleagues entered into conversations with companies that now aimed to create a space for diasporic audiences within mainstream cable television. "It was a surprise, yes," Bhat continued: "Time Warner Cable was telling us that customers were emailing call centers and calling customer service asking for Bollywood channels. But of course, in 2004, Time Warner could not carry those channels. Unlike Dish and DirecTV, their issue was one of space, of capacity. So they wanted to get individual Bollywood movies that they could put on VOD, which was a new service they had launched. And this is where we came in."

Vin Bhat and his team struck a deal that involved securing licensing agreements from film producers in Bombay, designing a marketing campaign for Time Warner, and developing a revenue-sharing agreement. In October 2003, Bhat and his colleagues launched BODVOD Networks in partnership with two New York-based companies, [212]Media and Schramm Sports & Entertainment, and began supplying Bollywood films and other South Asian media content to cable operators and creating marketing plans for cable operators to attract South Asian audiences. Over the next few years, BODVOD expanded to other cable carriers (Comcast and Rogers, for example) and was able to claim a distribution base of 19 million homes across North America. Further, having negotiated rights for global distribution, Bhat also explained that their objective was to expand to other overseas markets as well.

Securing distribution arrangements with film producers in Bombay was not, however, a straightforward affair. When Vin Bhat and others at BODVOD approached various production companies and studios with a revenue-sharing proposal, they found themselves unable to persuade anyone that focusing on the cable television market and subsequently, online and mobile phone platforms would be just as crucial as intervening in theatrical distribution and exhibition practices. The fact that BODVOD was primarily a New York-based company managed by people who did not have deep ties in the film industry did not help matters either. According to Bhat, one production company finally agreed to a revenue-sharing agreement and this in turn made it possible for BODVOD to raise investor capital. These funds were used to pay minimum guarantees to the production company, an arrangement that soon attracted several other producers with interests in the overseas market. "Once we had minimum guarantees in place and got prominent companies like UTV and Adlabs to sign up, things got easier," recalled Bhat, going on to explain that BODVOD positioned itself in relation to the rhetoric of "corporatization" that had come to define the transformation of the Bombay film industry into Bollywood. Industry professionals in Bombay, for their part, were interested in the increasingly lucrative overseas territories and were more than pleased with the level of transparency in reporting when it came to video-on-demand services. With pirate networks remaining robust and the theatrical distribution chain just as opaque and unreliable, BODVOD seemed to offer a way forward.

Having forged relations with the media industries in India and the United States, BODVOD moved beyond Bollywood films and the cable business to enter the Internet and mobile phone sectors as well. Adopting the name "Saavn.com," Vin Bhat and his colleagues entered into a joint venture with Hungama Mobile, a Bombay-based media company that is one of the largest aggregators of content for the mobile phone platform across Asia (Hungama also owns indiafm.com). By 2007, Saavn.com had established a distribution network that included films and film music, and more importantly an audience network that spanned the globe. In contrast to South Asia-centric television channels, Saavn.com's distribution network held the potential to move Bollywood beyond a niche audience. As one of the largest aggregators of Bollywood content, Saavn.com could track consumer purchases across a wide range of media platforms, including Apple's iTunes, Amazon.com, and a number of mobile phone services. In turn, this meant that Saavn.com could aggregate audience demographics for marketing and advertising companies on a scale that no "ethnic" media company could match. As Bhat explained, "A lot of South Asian media isn't measurable, Nielsen doesn't come in and rate any South Asian television network which prevents advertisers from entering, and there is only one newspaper, *India Abroad*, that is audited."

Thus, while Durrani and his team at MTV-Desi found themselves unable to forge links between the national scale-making projects that Indian and American television corporations were invested in, Bhat and his colleagues at Saavn.com succeeded by positioning themselves as brokers between Indian and American media companies to forge a lucrative audience interested in Bollywood films and film music. The distribution network that Saavn. com had built in collaboration with the Bombay-based company Hungama Mobile enabled the circulation of Bollywood content beyond the realm of "ethnic television" and into other media networks that included prominent players in the television, Internet, and mobile phone industries. By 2008, Vin Bhat could declare at the SAMMA-Summit that Saavn.com had worked toward, and in large measure succeeded in accomplishing, its declared goal of "Bringing Bollywood to the World."

On the ground realities notwithstanding, Saavn.com defines itself as a company that targets audiences worldwide and not just a diasporic audience.

Conclusion

Narrating the fortunes of two recent diasporic media initiatives, this chapter has examined how the restructuring of the media industries in Bombay, and changing relations between Bombay and Los Angeles, have reconfigured the space of South Asian diasporic media production and circulation. MTV-Desi and Saavn.com are without a doubt mainstream media ventures and are strikingly different in comparison with diasporic film and television production up to the mid-1990s. Far from being exilic or interstitial, the scale at which these media initiatives operate cannot be grasped without accounting for the ways in which relations between global media capitals—in this case, Bombay, New York City, and Los Angeles—have begun to define media circulation in the diaspora and structure the conditions for diasporic media production.

Projects such as establishing and operating a digital media company do not just reveal the interpenetration of scales (national, global, regional, diasporic, urban)—that is surely recognizable from the operations of a company like Saavn.com. To return to Anna Tsing's terms, one could say that such projects "cannot limit themselves to conjuring at different scales—they must conjure the scales themselves."[35] Focusing on the rhetorics and practices of scale-making allows us to understand MTV-Desi and Saavn.com as projects that sought to reimagine the diaspora as a commercially viable scale of media production and circulation. And surely this is what Vin Bhat, Nusrat Durrani, and their colleagues were doing—imagining and mobilizing different visions of the South Asian diaspora, from New York City, as Desis, in collaboration with professionals in Bombay, Los Angeles, and other cities in the world, building on shifting notions of Desi identity and ongoing changes in Indian and American media industries. The two ventures I have described conjured the Desi diaspora in different ways and encountered different sets of challenges and opportunities. Where MTV-Desi was limited by the niche marketing logics of the American television industry, Saavn. com managed to not only construct an enumerable and commercially viable "Desi audience" but also define itself as a company interested in bringing Bollywood to the world. After all, it was Saavn.com that gave every convention attendee a "Passport to Bollywood." It is worth asking, then, what kind of a world is being imagined? Who gets to hold and use this passport and who doesn't?

The information provided in this "passport" makes it clear that it is an artifact designed, in the first instance, for media industry professionals. Flipping open the passport reveals a center page that clarifies Saavn.com's role as a key intermediary for anyone interested in leveraging the worldwide interest in Bollywood: "Saavn hereby grants the holder of this passport the right to use the best Bollywood entertainment to engage affluent consumers globally." But this claim on consumers anywhere in the world is quickly scaled back as the accompanying page specifies and narrows down Saavn.com's sphere of operations. To begin with, the list of cities that form the global circuit that Saavn.com is invested in includes New York, London, Bombay, Los Angeles, and Toronto. These are all cities in which Saavn.com has a presence—it has employees in all these locations, its main business partner (Hungama Mobile) is based in Bombay, and its center of operations in the United States is New York City. But as we have seen, this particular network of cities also speaks to an emerging hierarchy in which media industries and diasporic communities in the Global North shape Bollywood's cultural geography, setting aside other key diasporic locations and in the process flattening out varied histories and patterns of Bollywood films' circulation and reception. Moreover, this passport indicates that even within this specific network of cities in the world, the cultural sphere in question is defined by a marketing discourse about the affluent Desi consumer demographic, one that is comprised of the "South Asian Consumer" who is a citizen of the United States

NEW YORK · LONDON · MUMBAI · LOS ANGELES · TORONTO

Saavn hereby grants the holder of this passport the right to use the best Bollywood entertainment to engage affluent consumers globally.

PASSPORT
PASSEPORT
PASAPORTE

Priyanka Chopra
Film: Fashion
UTV Motion Pictures

BOLLYWOOD

Market
SOUTH ASIAN CONSUMER

Nationality
UNITED STATES OF AMERICA

Affluent
$76K AVERAGE HOUSEHOLD INCOME

Educated
61% HOLD COLLEGE DEGREES

Booming
4 MILLION CONSUMERS WITH 8% ANNUAL GROWTH RATE

Tech-Savvy
86% HAVE HIGH SPEED INTERNET

Big Spenders
OVER INDEX ON TRAVEL, FINANCE, FASHION, AUTO AND CONSUMER ELECTRONICS

Purchasing Power
$90 BILLION

<<<SAAVN<<<<WWW<SAAVN<COM<<<<SAAVN<<<<WWW<SAAVN<COM<<<<<<<<

Saavn.com's "Passport to Bollywood" reveals how marketing and industry discourse imagines Bollywood's cultural geography in narrow cultural and spatial terms.

of America, is part of a family that earns on average $76,000 a year, is highly educated, and is tech-savvy.

Thus in one sense, this passport can be interpreted simply as a digital media company's claim that it is uniquely positioned to mediate American media companies' relations with a lucrative "ethnic market" and at the same time create opportunities for Bollywood to extend its reach in the American media market. But I would argue that this "Passport to Bollywood" can also be read as a marker of media industry professionals' anxieties that stem from the recognition that Bollywood's cultural geography does in fact extend well beyond the world that companies like Saavn.com are able to conjure. The very notion of a "passport" suggests that there are borders to be defined, maintained, and policed. It also speaks to the desire among industry professionals to control practices of sharing and circulating Bollywood content in ways that transcend the traditional boundaries of the nation-state, linguistic barriers, and market segments.

From the media industry's perspective, copying and sharing media content constitutes piracy and little else. The issue of piracy has been a major concern for the Bombay film industry for well over three decades now, and especially since the late 1980s when recording technologies and the rapid expansion of the cable TV market generated a new moment of crisis. But it is only since the late 1990s that piracy has emerged as *the* challenge facing Bollywood. Taking their cue from Hollywood, consultancy reports as well as institutions like FICCI have dedicated considerable attention to the issue of piracy, framing it as a problem that Bollywood and the Indian state together need to address. In fact, virtually every FRAMES convention since 2006 or so has included a panel discussion on this topic, with several industry professionals citing fantastic figures of lost revenues and jobs as they frame piracy as the singlemost important obstacle in Bollywood's otherwise smooth path to becoming a global media industry. Not surprisingly, discussions at venues like FRAMES, and state and industry discourse generally, approach the issue of piracy in terms of a highly reductive legality/illegality binary. These discussions have also led to some high-profile initiatives such as the "antipiracy coalition" launched in 2010 by the Motion Picture Association of America (MPAA) in collaboration with leading Bollywood professionals and companies, including Yash Chopra (Yash Raj Films), Siddharth Roy Kapur (UTV), Ram Mirchandani (Eros International), and Sandeep Bhargava (Studio 18).[36] In addition to these initiatives, the decade 2000–10 has also been marked by highly publicized and periodic raids of piracy hubs within India and in other countries. Saavn.com's "Passport to Bollywood" can therefore also be understood in relation to this larger anxiety surrounding Bollywood and the Indian state's inability to tackle piracy.

But there is another dimension to copying, remixing, and circulating that this "passport" ignores. I am referring, of course, to the vast range of fan practices that shape the circulation of Bollywood content around the world. For example, srkpagali.net is an immensely popular website that archives videos of Bollywood star Shahrukh Khan—clips from his films, television advertisements, awards shows, and interviews. The small group of fans who manage this website have also, through a networked effort that drew in other popular fan-maintained websites and blogs, subtitled many of these videos for the benefit of those who do not understand Hindi. Needless to say, srkpagali.net is part of a world-encircling pirate infrastructure defined by easy and cheap access to technologies of media reproduction. However, to approach an initiative like srkpagali.net simply in terms of the market logics of companies like Saavn.com or in relation to the question of piracy that defines industry and state discourse, is to misunderstand the nature of participatory culture that surrounds Bollywood. It is this dimension of Bollywood's presence in the world that I address in the final chapter.

CONCLUSION

Fandom and Other Transnational Futures

I began this book with an account of a spectacular media convention designed to celebrate Bollywood's growing prominence in the world. Held in Bombay and attended by industry professionals, policymakers, and bureaucrats from across the world, the 2009 FICCI-FRAMES convention seemed to mark Bollywood's arrival on the world stage. Yet as we saw, discussions at this gathering revealed the messy, uneven, and contradictory nature of industrial change. As with other domains of cultural, political, and economic life in India, the consequences of globalization where the Bombay film industry is concerned have been far from predictable or, for that matter, easily managed. Gatherings like FRAMES in Bombay and the SAMMA-Summit in New York thus served as rich ethnographic sites from which to begin mapping and analyzing the reconfiguration of the Hindi-language film industry in Bombay as Bollywood. Beginning with these sites and moments of celebration, introspection, and predictions regarding Bollywood's global futures, I have moved across a range of other media spaces in an attempt to craft a narrative of industrial and cultural transformation. In examining the reconstruction and performance of industrial identity, the impact of the rapid growth of the television and advertising sectors on the film industry, dot-com companies and their conjuring of an overseas territory on a daily basis, and the social and professional worlds of diasporic entrepreneurs, the overarching question that has guided this book has been: How is Bollywood in the world today? In this concluding chapter, I want to address this question by first highlighting a few broad themes and issues that this question brings into play and that various chapters in this book have tackled. Following this, I want to direct our attention to fan participation as a domain of media culture that is intimately connected with industry practices and offers an alternative perspective and vantage point from which to explore Bollywood's emergent cultural geography.

* * *

First, *Bollywood is a transnational cultural and industrial formation.* I begin with this broad statement to reiterate that the emergence of Bollywood has to be situated within the sociohistorical conjuncture of the period since the early 1990s. This was a period that witnessed a number of sociocultural and political transitions engendered by the Indian state's adoption and gradual legitimization of neoliberal economic policies, including the privatization of different sectors of the economy and, broadly speaking, attempts to leave behind a developmentalist imaginary and integrate the nation into a global economy. As I outlined in the first chapter, this was a pivotal moment marked not only by dramatic changes in various sectors of the Indian economy and the emergence of a globally competitive IT and software services sector, but also by a reworking of the symbolic boundaries of the nation to include the diaspora. In particular, this entailed a sharp turn in the Indian state's relationship with the diaspora and the reimagination of the figure of the Non-Resident Indian as central to India's fortunes in a global economy. Among other arenas of cultural production, Hindi-language films and television shows played a crucial role in mediating these concerns regarding national identity. The state's decision to grant "industry" status to cinema in the late 1990s and the ongoing transformation of the Bombay film industry into a multimedia cultural industry intent on reimagining its position in the world has to be understood in relation to these broader political, economic, and cultural shifts.

In invoking the term transnational, I also want to signal that asking how Bollywood is in the world today entails dealing with a larger problematic: the role played by nation-states and the prominence of the national in processes of economic and cultural globalization. Since the late 1980s, media and cultural studies scholars have played a crucial role in moving the debate on globalization past totalizing conceptions of modernization, cultural imperialism, and homogenization. The idea that the production, circulation, and consumption of media are processes that involve interactions among a range of actors and institutions and across multiple scales seems now to be a basic starting point. The challenge that an emergent terrain of cultural production like Bollywood poses, then, is how we might acknowledge the continued relevance of the national without privileging it as *the* dominant scale at which the processes and politics of media globalization are worked out. Adopting a transnational perspective does not mean ignoring the fact that the national, as Nitin Govil has argued, "has given the media industries a way to think both globally and locally."[1] Rather, it is to carefully account for the ways in which the national has come to be articulated with other scales and in the process been reconfigured. As scholars like Saskia Sassen and Michael Curtin have argued, what we are contending with are new geographies in which relations between cities or regions, for instance, may determine the movement as well as the reterritorialization of capital, creative labor, and of course a range of cultural commodities.[2] Throughout this book, one of my main aims has been to reveal the contingent nature of claims about urban, national, diasporic, and global scales that inform the imaginations and practices of everyone from bureaucrats and state officials to media professionals and, as we will see later in this chapter, pirates and fans.

Second, *Bollywood is part of ongoing transformations in relations between capital, space, and cultural production.* As early as 1995, when the multinodal media world that we are familiar with today was beginning to take shape, David Morley and Kevin Robins argued that a "social theory that is informed by the geographical imagination" was crucial to understanding changes in media and communication.[3] Surveying the political and economic transformations that had transformed national economies across the world since the late 1970s, they focused in particular on the increasingly complex spatial relations that the mobility of capital had engendered as the "essential context for understanding the nature and significance of developments in the media industries."[4] Informed by this spatial approach, I have attempted to show here that Bollywood is shaped by the uneven and highly differentiated nature of capitalist transformation in India and specifically the city of Bombay since the early 1990s. For instance, examining the impact that the discourse of corporatization has had on the film industry by analyzing the construction of industrial identities suggests that the narrative of transition from one established mode of production to a new one, say Fordism to post-Fordism, does not adequately explain the industrial logics and practices that characterize Bollywood.

In fact, Madhava Prasad's observation that the Hindi film industry adopted a "heterogeneous form of manufacture in which the whole is assembled from parts produced separately by specialists, rather than being centralized around the processing of a given material," troubles stagist narratives of media industries in the non-Western world catching up with those in the West. After all, the dominant mode of production in the Bombay film industry could be described using terms like flexible accumulation and decentralization that theorists like David Harvey use to describe the logics of late capitalism in the West.[5] In other words, the particular histories of capital in Bombay cannot be easily set aside. Understanding how contemporary speculative capital is reconfiguring Bombay's media world requires us to pay careful attention to entrenched practices associated with mercantile capital that are in turn underpinned by long-standing kinship ties and interpersonal relationships.

The dialectic of homogenization and localization does shape developments in various domains of the media industries in a city like Bombay. At the same time, it would be too reductive to say that the model of capitalist media production that characterizes Bollywood is simply another manifestation of what is an essentially "Indian" history of capital. The panel discussions at FRAMES 2009 that I discussed spoke precisely to this issue. Of course, it is understandable that media professionals routinely invoke notions of "Indian culture" as a way to negotiate a position of difference in the global media landscape, particularly in relation to the universal claims that Hollywood makes. But the larger problem remains. As Ritu Birla, among other historians, has argued, "[T]he affirmation of an authentic *Indian* capitalism repeats the structural logic of the economy/culture distinction, validating culture on the grounds of its consistency with capitalist economic rationality."[6] A Bollywood producer-director like Karan Johar comes to represent, by this logic, an *Indian* capitalist. A closer look at the operations of family firms, including the one that Karan Johar manages, suggests, however, that production relations defined by mercantile capital and kinship networks are neither static nor contained within national boundaries. And when we move beyond family businesses to consider a wider range of companies and professionals, it becomes clear that every domain of Bollywood, including production, distribution, marketing and promotions, and exhibition involves negotiations among actors and institutions enmeshed in multiple, asymmetric, and seemingly incongruent cultures of capitalism.

Third, *Bollywood is a site of technological and industrial convergence.* Film and media scholars have identified a number of key factors that explain how Bombay emerged and maintained its position as the preeminent media capital in India: the city's position as a center of trade and commerce, and the influx, through the decades, of mercantile capital into filmmaking; its status as a vibrant cultural center with established theater movements initially providing the film industry with a range of creative personnel; the use of Hindi, which accorded the Bombay-based film industry (located in a multilingual city and in a state where the official language is Marathi) "national" status whereas film industries in cities like Madras and Hyderabad were ascribed "regional" status; and the impact of India's partition on other centers of film production, most notably Calcutta and Lahore, and the migration of a number of producers, directors, actors, and technicians to Bombay during this period.

In this book, I have argued that there is another important factor that accounts for why Bombay has managed to maintain its position as a national media capital and claim global status in ways that no other center of media production in India has been able to: the role played by new media—radio, television, the Internet, and the mobile phone—in enabling the Bombay film industry to consistently imagine and mobilize a national and now, transnational audience. Moving past a film-centric approach, the case studies of television and dot-com companies' relations with the film industry that I have presented here invite us to consider to how various "new media" have historically reconfigured the cultural geography of Bombay cinema and Bombay's status as a media capital. Considering the case of Radio Ceylon, which broadcast a range of film-based programs that reached audiences across the Indian subcontinent, South Africa, and even some cities in east Africa, encourages us to ponder how other technological and institutional developments influenced the circulation of films and film music, transforming the Bombay film industry's spatial coordinates and engendering new sites and forms of consumption. This does not necessarily mean that we think only about continuities from the 1950s to the present. Rather, my goal here has been to open up a space for more grounded explorations of the interwoven histories of different media technologies and institutions and in the process, expand our understanding of the histories and patterns of media convergence.

In developing these and other arguments, I have so far taken a primarily industry-centric approach. As I explained at the outset, media scholarship in the Indian context and indeed global media studies at large, has tended to focus on questions of form, representation, and to an extent, audience reception. Thus in the broadest sense this book aims to make a timely contribution to an emerging body of scholarship on the media industries and how the imaginations and practices of media industry professionals give shape to the media worlds we inhabit and engage with. There is, however, another closely related perspective from which one could map and analyze Bollywood's cultural geography: fandom and participatory culture. In the final section of this book I want to position this vibrant yet largely neglected realm of transnational media culture as a vital site for understanding not just how Bollywood is in the world today, but perhaps more importantly, how the world is in Bollywood.

From Piracy to Media Consultancy and Everything in Between

Part of the difficulty involved in charting the terrain of participatory culture surrounding Bollywood, especially in an era of networked audiences and publics, stems from the sheer range of sites and modes of participation one encounters. So the two stories I start with here are not intended to be representative of fan activity but rather to serve to highlight some of the questions regarding cinema, new media, and state and industry discourses of legality, citizenship, and audience practices that arise.

The first one is from Hari Kunzru's novel, *Transmission*, which revolves around Arjun Mehta, a software engineer in New Delhi. We learn that Mehta is also a Bollywood fan and a regular at a basement cybercafé that supplies him with bootleg films, film songs, and pornography.[7] Body-shopped to West Coast U.S.A., he navigates the racial and cultural fields of the high-tech sector with great tenacity and verve, only to lose his job in unceremonious fashion. Enraged and desperate to come up with a ploy to hold on to his job and live in America, he exacts revenge by unleashing one of the most deadly computer viruses ever conceived. As the code paralyzes and wreaks havoc on computer systems worldwide, the only thing visible on screen is a simulation—Leela Zahir, a Bollywood heroine, dancing suggestively.

The second story concerns an online fan community that has cohered around the renowned music director A. R. Rahman (arrahmansfans.com), and specifically the labor of a group of fans that wanted to ensure the success of a Rahman concert in Bangalore. Working closely with the concert sponsors, these fans managed everything from promotions and ticket sales to stage construction and crowd control on the day of the concert (October 8, 2005). As part of their effort to gain recognition as the "official" Rahman fan group, they also decided to present Rahman with a gift—a montage, composed of thumbnail images of all his album covers, which formed the contours of his face. Faced with the prospect of buying expensive software, a smaller group (some of whom run a design company called 3xus.com) went on to develop their own software. After many sleepless nights of painstaking coding, they finally got to meet Rahman and present the gift.

Acknowledging these fans' perseverance, technical and marketing savvy, and transnational network established through online activities, Rahman and his team decided to collaborate with them to promote and organize concerts in different cities worldwide, evolve new modes of music distribution, and work together to tackle piracy. As the moderator of arrahmanfans.com pointed out to me when we met a few days after the concert, this story of fan activity went largely unreported in mainstream media. Media attention was focused instead on violent clashes between fans of Tamil film star Vijaykanth and activists of a political party who took offense at Vijaykanth's remarks directed at their leader. Referring to these stories, the moderator remarked, "We're online, not on the streets. We would never venture into street battles, and that does not attract media attention."[8]

The media world that the character Arjun Mehta inhabits in New Delhi resonates with descriptions of spaces such as Palika Bazaar, an underground market in the central district of Connaught Place. One of several sites in New Delhi that Ravi Sundaram describes in his analysis of media urbanism,

Palika Bazaar is a major node in the circulation of pirated media. As the media landscape began changing with the introduction of cable television in the early 1990s, Palika Bazaar emerged as "the nerve center of a complex web of operations linking local cable networks, neighborhood video rentals, and an elaborate courier system between shops and pirate factories in neighboring states, Pakistan, and South East Asia."[9] Such networks of media circulation provide an alternative perspective on media globalization.

This perspective on piracy as a constitutive dimension of media circulation in the contemporary world becomes even more apparent when we consider the dramatic reconfiguration of the mediascape in countries like Nigeria. As Brian Larkin observes, "instead of being marginalized by official distribution networks, Nigerian consumers can now participate in the immediacy of an international consumer culture—but only through the mediating capacity of piracy."[10] But there is, as my account of the Rahman fan community suggests, another dimension to the culture of the copy and the networked media terrain in question. If VCDs/DVDs in stores a few steps from multiplexes across urban India, BitTorrent sites, and other modes of copying and circulation constitute one end of the spectrum of participation, the other end involves industry and fan interests coming together. These are, of course, two extremes. But taken together, they do signal that the space in between is likely defined by a range of practices that we have yet to consider seriously.

In the Indian context, our understanding of participatory culture remains tied to a very specific history of fan associations and their links to electoral politics in south India. This narrative of fan/cine-politics has been so dominant that other modes and sites of participatory culture have not been considered, leave alone studied in systematic fashion, for no apparent reason other than their seemingly "nonpolitical" character. In fact, the topic of fan activity has not even been raised in relation to Bollywood. In what follows, I argue against framing participatory culture surrounding Bollywood and more generally, film and television across India, in terms of devotional excess or in relation to political mobilization. How might we reframe fan activity and in doing so, position participatory culture as an important site for mapping and analyzing Bollywood's emergent cultural geography?

Rethinking Participatory Culture

Let me begin by returning to the case of arrahmanfans.com and provide a brief account of the group's formation and activities. In 1998, less than three years after the state-owned telecommunications provider VSNL (Videsh Sanchar Nigam Limited) offered dial-up connections to the Indian public in large metropolitan areas, Channel [V], a popular music television channel, announced that votes for "best music director of the year" could be submitted via the Internet.[11] Gopal Srinivasan, a Rahman fan based in Bangalore, spent the next few months surfing websites and discussion forums, gathering email addresses, and coordinating an online campaign that would ensure that Rahman won the music award. Srinivasan came into contact with a large number of Rahman fans around the world, mostly students and young expatriate Indians in countries such as the United States, U.K., and Singapore who were participating in popular newsgroups, including rec.arts.movies.local.indian and rec.music.indian.misc, and in some cases had developed websites of their own. Having developed a database of close to a hundred fans, he decided to launch a group focused on Rahman and his music. Many of the fans Srinivasan contacted in 1998–99 continue to participate in the group, and several have gone on to develop contacts with Rahman and his team in Chennai. Arrahmanfans.com now involves nearly 12,000 members from twenty-six different countries, and is a space that brings together, for instance, Tamil Malaysians, second-generation Indian Americans, Indians settled in Gulf countries like Dubai, youth in urban India, and a growing number of non-Indian fans.[12]

Arrahmanfans.com, like most online fan groups that cohere around films and film music, consists of a filmography, a member directory, a folder for creative works where fans post various clips of music they create, a music library where mp3 clips are stored, and a list of FAQs for new members. The group also maintains a large collection of photographs of Rahman from various occasions, and has recently developed a collection of Rahman-related videos hosted using YouTube. The "links" section contains URLs to a range of Rahman-related resources such as fan sites and blogs, newspaper and magazine articles, interviews, and websites about others in the film industry who work with Rahman. Within the group, there is an emphasis on the need for all members to participate, and an acknowledgment of different competencies—knowledge of Tamil and Hindi, for instance, in order to translate complex lyrics, or knowledge of the technicalities of music that might be helpful in discussions. Rahman fans also monitor print publications, radio and television shows, and different websites for news and trivia about their star and, like other fan communities, perceive themselves as guardians of Rahman's image and attempt to control the circulation of negative coverage of Rahman's music or personal life. The community also includes people who work with Rahman on a professional basis, and these members have played a key role in getting this group recognized as Rahman's official fan group. Over the last few years, fans based in different cities around the world have also begun meeting offline to extend discussions conducted online, help organize concerts, and in some cases to form bands and perform film songs. Enabled by the Internet, constituted by individuals from different parts of the world, and driven by an interest in film music that reaches across the world, there is no doubt that the Rahman fan community is strikingly different when compared with fan associations such as those that form around Tamil film stars like Vijaykanth.

We could begin by noting that the Rahman fan community is an elite space and one that is defined explicitly in opposition to "rowdy" fan associations. We could point out that compared to fan associations that meet at street corners, tea shops, and in and around cinema halls in India, online fan communities are not dominated by men. It is also evident that the Rahman fan community is not invested in mobilizing around caste or linguistic identity. Given that it is first and foremost a community realized online, and that fans bring diverse stakes and affiliations to bear on their participation, mobilization along axes of caste or language is, at a basic level, rendered structurally impossible. For example, fans based in Malaysia, for whom participation in the Rahman fan community is part of a larger process of claiming a Tamil ethnic identity, share little in common with second-generation Indian Americans for whom dancing to a remixed Rahman song at a club speaks to a very different set of concerns. Embedded as citizens in disparate ways, each fan brings his or her own linguistic and regional background, experiences of varying racial and ethnic politics, religious affiliations, and different registers of knowledge and affiliation with India and "Indian" culture, to bear on his or her engagement with Rahman's music. Therefore, while useful to start with, such comparisons only take us so far. It is not enough to merely point out that the fan in question here is a middle-class subject or a diasporic subject. We are still left with the problem of approaching and defining such new modes of participatory culture, a defining aspect of Bollywood, in opposition to a specific and idealized mode of participation that is explicitly political. The pressing challenge, then, is to reconceptualize the relationship between cinema and public culture and broaden the very notion of participatory culture.

S. V. Srinivas' path-breaking work on fan associations is the obvious starting point for any discussion of participatory culture in the Indian context. Focusing on the Telugu film star Chiranjeevi, Srinivas situates the formation of fan associations in Andhra Pradesh in relation to a broader history of subaltern struggles and considers fan practices as a domain of political activity that does not fit within classical liberal accounts of citizenship and political representation, but one that has clear links to linguistic and regional identity.[13] For Srinivas, the performative dimensions of fan practices, especially as they cohere in and around the cinema hall, lead to a conception of a cinematic public sphere where "the consumption of film becomes an occasion for a range of performances that are broadly *political* in nature," one manifestation being the links to party politics and election campaigns (emphasis in original).[14] Further, while he argues that we also need to understand the political nature of fan associations beyond their "linkages with the politics of linguistic/identity nationalism," he maintains that fan activity is political mainly because it "develops around the notion of spectatorial rights."[15] He writes:

> The cinema exists because of my presence and for me. Further, the "I" at the cinema is always a member of a collective: *we make the film happen.* Anyone who has watched a Chiranjeevi or Rajnikanth film knows exactly what I am talking about. Not only do these stars address spectators in rather direct ways (including by looking at the camera) but seem to perform according to "our" demands.[16]

This articulation of cinema's relationship to public culture and democracy, with the figure of the "fan" occupying center stage, lies at the heart of our understanding of participatory culture surrounding film and television in India. Even as Srinivas exhorts us to examine the various "webs of public transactions" involving cinema, and to rethink what constitutes the "political" beyond the narrow sense of the term, his analysis remains bound by one particular, highly visible, mode of participatory culture and the film industry's perception and management of such activity. He goes on to say: "[M]uch work needs to be done across the spectrum of activities and organizations that fade into the cinema hall at one end and the political party at the other."[17]

In light of Indian cinema's flows worldwide, the question of who comprises the "we" in the cinema hall and what "our" demands might be complicates the notion of "spectatorial rights."[18] For it would be difficult to maintain that Tamil Malaysian fans of Rajnikanth are positioned as spectators in precisely the same way as fans in Tamilnadu or, for that matter, Japanese fans who watch subtitled prints of Tamil-language films. I am not arguing that the figure of the fan is not constructed by the filmic text.[19] However, we need to recognize that the notion of "spectatorial rights" certainly does not help us explain the kind of activity that Rahman fans are involved in.[20] While opening up an important line of inquiry, Srinivas's analysis needs to be extended in at least two directions.

The first question we need to address is: Are the two poles of the spectrum—the cinema hall and the political party—adequate sites or analytic categories to begin with? If one were to consider film music, a component of films that circulates in the public realm much before and long after the film itself does, it forces us to consider the radio, television, the Internet, and mobile phones as sites constitutive of the publicness of cinema as much as the cinema hall itself, if not more so. Radio, television, the Internet, and cell phone networks are spaces of public culture with intimate ties to the film, but with distinct institutional, cultural, and political histories that have shaped our experience of films. I would argue, then, that a focus on fan practices that emerge at the intersection of film and various new media and shape their interaction opens up the possibility of developing accounts of participatory culture that does not necessarily originate in the cinema hall and culminate in the sphere of political parties and electoral campaigns.

The second question we have to grapple with concerns the image of the fan that we derive from a focus on the cinema hall and its surroundings, and fan associations of stars like Vijaykanth: obsessive, male, working class, and rowdy. The "excessive" behavior that marks viewers in front rows of cinema halls, what Lawrence Liang calls the "protocols of collective behavior"—whistling and commenting loudly, throwing flowers, coins, or ribbons when the star first appears on the screen, singing along and dancing in the aisles, and so on—is routinely cited as what distinguishes fans from the rest of the audience.[21] Further, the public nature of fan associations' activities—celebrating a star's birthday or hundred days of a film, organizing special prerelease functions, adorning street corners with giant cutouts of the star, decorating theaters where the film has had a successful run, and the like—and press coverage of such activities have further served to both marginalize and circumscribe fan activity as undesirable, vulgar, and at times dangerous. As Srinivas, drawing on Vivek Dhareshwar and R. Srivatsan's analysis of rowdy-sheeters (individuals with a criminal record), writes:

> The fan is a rowdy not only because he breaks the law in the course of his assertion or his association with criminalized politics—the fan becomes a rowdy by overstepping the line which demarcates the legitimate, "constructive," permissible excess, and the illegitimate [. . .] as far as the "citizen" is concerned, the fan is a blind hero-worshipper (devoid of reason) and a villain. The rowdy/fan is an agent of politics which is de-legitimized.[22]

Fans, in this view, are imperfect citizens, or even noncitizens, in aesthetic, sociocultural, and political terms. Middle-class constructions of norms of excess are, without doubt, designed in part to maintain hierarchies of cultural production and taste. In other words, it is clear that the fan-as-rowdy is constructed in semantic and social opposition to the idea of the fan-as-rasika—rowdy fans of the actor Vijaykanth as opposed to rasikas of Carnatic musician M. S. Subbulakshmi, for instance.[23] Where, then, do we position film music fans like members of radio listener clubs (*Srota sanghs*) across India who wrote hundreds of letters to Ameen Sayani, the anchor of *Binaca Geet Mala*, the popular program on Radio Ceylon, and played a critical role in the consolidation of playback singers and music directors' aural stardom? How do we account for a show like *Lift Kara De*, hosted by Karan Johar on Sony Entertainment Television, which relies so centrally on fan participation and labor? Finally, how do we understand the online life-worlds of fans in diverse locations worldwide who come together as online and offline communities on the basis of shared attachments to film culture? Moving past the rowdy/rasika binary is crucial if we are to broaden the arena of inquiry to include spaces such as the Rahman fan community.

Academic interest in "rowdy" fan associations has resulted in a romanticization of fan associations as belonging to the realm of "political society," a term that Partha Chatterjee has proposed to conceptualize relationships between individuals or groups that are outside the rule-bound and legal framework of bourgeois civil society and the state in postcolonial societies such as India. Chatterjee writes:

> Most of the inhabitants of India are only tenuously, and even then ambiguously and contextually, rights-bearing citizens in the sense imagined by the constitution. They are not, therefore, proper members of civil society and are not regarded as such by the institutions of the state. But it is not as though they are outside the reach of the state or even excluded from the domain of politics. As populations within the territorial jurisdiction of the state, they have to be both looked after and controlled by various governmental agencies. These activities bring these populations into a certain *political* relationship with the state.[24]

Chatterjee argues that the "sites and activities characteristic of . . . political society" have become particularly visible since the 1980s owing to changes in the techniques of governance and a "widening of the arena of political mobilization, prompted by electoral considerations and often only for electoral ends."[25] This is shaped, he points out, not only by organized political parties but also by "loose and often transient mobilizations, building on communication structures that would not be ordinarily recognized as political."[26]

Thus, for Chatterjee political society is the domain of the population, not citizens. Using the example of illegal settlements in the city of Calcutta, Chatterjee further argues that such individuals and groups are not completely outside the purview of the state. As individuals who reside within the territorial and juridical boundaries of the state, they have to be cared for and controlled by government agencies. Even if it is clear that such individuals and groups "transgress the strict lines of legality in struggling to live and work," the state cannot ignore them and is forced to enter into different kinds of negotiations.[27]

Chatterjee's formulation can certainly be employed to understand relationships between fan associations and the democratic process, especially given that such extralegal domains have typically been neglected in political theory. Using the term "political society" accords this domain of participation a certain visibility previously denied it. Film star Vijaykanth mobilizing his fan base in the state of Tamilnadu does speak to the ways in which cinema serves as a staging ground for contests over regional and linguistic identity. Vijaykanth's decision to articulate a vision of a "Dravida Nadu" (Dravidian Nation), one in which there would be "no blind opposition to Hindi," was seen as a significant departure, given the history of conflict over the imposition of Hindi as a national language and the resistance that this faced in states like Tamilnadu where film stars-turned-politicians campaigned on a pro-Tamil platform.[28] The entanglement of language- and caste-based politics is also evident in Andhra Pradesh where, as Srinivas has shown, Chiranjeevi, as the first non-kamma star, became the basis for the formation of non-kamma publics.[29]

However, to bracket fans as a nonelite public and theorize "rowdy" fan practices as an expression of subaltern politics can also be misleading if it leads us to ignore the overlaps and intersections between different sites and modes of fan expression. Consider the issue of illegal networks of film and music piracy in a city like Bangalore and the Rahman fan community, a space of participation constituted by a large number of elite youth in urban India with access to new media technologies. While the Internet remains the main site of interaction, it is crucial to recognize that in cities like Bangalore, Rahman fans also navigate and participate in the extralegal world of pirated VCDs, DVDs, and mp3 collections. The extralegal world is not an exclusive and closed-off subaltern space but rather one that intersects with online fan communities. In fact it informs the practices of Rahman fans online. It is also critical to recognize the ambivalence that marks Rahman fans' attitudes and practices when it comes to the issue of being part of the "illegal city."[30] While some Rahman fans create ftp sites and upload collections of Rahman's songs and pieces of background music ripped from DVDs, others police music stores (makeshift stores set up on pavements in busy shopping areas, in shopping complexes, and so on), threatening to call the police if pirated CDs of Rahman's music are not taken off the shelf.

Part of the work that lies ahead of us, then, involves examining a greater range of sites and modes of participation surrounding the media industries in Bombay and other emerging media capitals. Doing so will allow us to rethink the figure of the fan: part rowdy, part rasika, part pirate, part copyright enforcer, the fan is as much a figure operating within pirate networks as she or he is caught up in media industry logics. In an era in which media industries across the world are making concerted efforts to tap into fan participation and labor, we can enrich our accounts of transnational media and expand the boundaries of media industry studies if we stop treating participatory culture as mere epiphenomena. Paying sustained and systematic attention to patterns of audience reception and modes of participation in varied social and geographic contexts will likely generate new insights into the three major problematics that I have focused on throughout this book—Bollywood as a transnational cultural and industrial formation, as a site of technological and industrial convergence, and as a site of cultural production that is part of broader realignments of relations between space, capital, and culture. But even more broadly, to look closely at fan participation is to imagine transnational media worlds that are intimately tied to, but not always constrained by, statist or industrial imperatives. The world that fans of A. R. Rahman have created, or the one that a group of Shahrukh Khan fans have built (srkpagali.net), disclose to us not only the multiple and fragmentary ways in which Bollywood is already in the world today, but also suggest the possibility of different transnational futures for Bollywood.

Profiles of Key Bollywood Companies

I provide profiles of the following companies because taken together, they represent the range of models and practices prevalent in Bollywood—small-scale family-owned production companies (Dharma Productions), small-scale star-owned companies (Aamir Khan Productions, Shahrukh Khan's Red Chillies Entertainment), vertically integrated family-owned studios (Yash Raj Films, Rajshri Productions), vertically and horizontally integrated media corporations (UTV, Reliance Entertainment, Studio 18, Eros Entertainment), and newer corporate entrants (Shree Ashtavinayak Cine Vision, Percept Pictures). Needless to say, there are several other production, distribution, and exhibition companies that could have been featured here.

1. *Aamir Khan Productions Private Limited*

Aamir Khan Productions Pvt. Ltd. is a privately held "star studio" established in 1999 by actor Aamir Khan. A member of a prominent film family (his cousin is director Mansoor Khan, and his uncle is Nasir Hussain, a prominent producer, director, and screenwriter), Khan established himself as a star as the lead in Mansoor Khan's *Qayamat Se Qayamat Tak* (1988). Beginning as a child actor and later a teen heartthrob, Khan has recently chosen projects that have cultivated his reputation as a serious, "thinking actor," including *Lagaan* (2001), *Mangal Pandey: The Rising* (2005), and *Rang de Basanti* (2006).

Khan's production credits reflect his carefully constructed persona as an actor. Aamir Khan Productions' first film was *Lagaan* (2001), a film whose script was reportedly passed over by a number of producers and production houses. Directed by Ashutosh Gowariker, and starring Aamir Khan in a leading role, the film tells the story of a group of villagers suffering under British rule who accept a challenge to play a cricket match against the local British administration. Critically acclaimed, the film also received an Academy Award nomination for Best Foreign Language Film in 2002. Since *Lagaan*, Khan has produced only a handful of films, including *Taare Zameen Par* (2007), *Jaane Tu Ya Jaane Na* (2008), *Peepli Live* (2010), *Dhobighat* (2010), and *Delhi Belly* (2011)—all of which have achieved a measure of critical and commercial success. For example, *Taare Zameen Par*, Khan's directorial debut, deals with a child coping with dyslexia, and *Peepli Live* is a low-budget satire focused on the issue of farmer suicides in India.

Aamir Khan Productions crafts an image of a small, independent, artisanal production house that handpicks projects reflecting Khan's social conscience, intelligence, creativity, and unique authorial vision. The production staff consists of the small core creative team of Aamir Khan, executive producer B. Shrinivas Rao, and Associate Producer (and Khan's wife) Kiran Rao. While the company often handles domestic theatrical distribution of its films, it has entered into agreements with a range of large corporations, including UTV, Walt Disney Home Entertainment, and PVR Pictures for overseas distribution.

2. *Studio 18*

Studio 18 is part of Viacom 18, a joint venture between the transnational media conglomerate Viacom and the India-based Network 18. Viacom 18 is a publicly traded, multinational media conglomerate with interests in magazines, the Internet, films, e-commerce, television, mobile content, and related businesses. The company's Indian operations began with a focus on television, with Raghav Bahl and Sanjay Ray Chaudhuri establishing TV18 in 1993. Bahl entered the media and entertainment industries after a career in management and consulting, and Chaudhuri came with extensive experience in television production. By forging strategic partnerships with companies specializing in different media platforms, the company has grown into what is now known as the Network18 Group. In 2006 it was converted into a public limited company, and listed on the Bombay Stock Exchange as well as the National Stock Exchange in 2007. Bahl presently retains controlling ownership in the company. Network 18's partnerships include CNBC, CNN, Yatra, Australia Network, Viacom, the Lokmat Group (Indian newspaper publishing house), and Forbes. Viacom 18, a 50/50 joint venture of Viacom and Network 18, operates four key television channels in India: Colors, MTV-India, Nickelodeon India, and VH1-India. The conglomerate also has a music label and a home video division.

Studio 18 (the new name of the newly acquired Indian Film Company) handles the acquisition, production, syndication, marketing, and worldwide distribution of full-length feature films. Its catalogue includes films such as *Namastey London* (2007), *Bhoothnath* (2008), *Singh Is Kinng* (2008), *Golmaal Returns* (2008), *London Dreams* (2009), and *Rann* (2010). For the most part, Studio 18 has focused on the production, distribution, and management across platforms of domestic films, but the company has also dabbled in the Indian distribution of foreign films. To date, Studio 18 has been more active in distribution, syndication, and movie marketing than in production, although this aspect of the company is currently being actively cultivated.

3. Rajshri Productions Pvt. Ltd./Rajshri Group

Established initially as a film distribution company in 1947 by Tarachand Barjatya, the Rajshri Group is one of India's oldest and most successful family-owned media businesses with a carefully cultivated reputation for "family entertainment." Since 1962 the company's production house has produced over fifty Hindi films, including *Dosti* (1964), *Uphaar* (1971), *Ankhiyon Ke Jharokhon Se* (1978), Sooraj Barjatya's directorial debut *Maine Pyar Kiya* (1989), *Hum Aapke Hain Koun..!* (1994), *Hum Saath-Saath Hain* (1999), and *Vivah* (2006).

The company remains a major distributor and has a strong presence in the distribution of regional films with offices in Kolkata, New Delhi, Bangalore, and other major cities throughout the country. Rajshri has handled distribution for both celebrated producers (Gemini, Prasad Productions, Sippy Films) and entered into distribution arrangements with large corporate film producers as well (Percept, PVR, Reliance, and UTV). However, unlike film distribution ventures launched by corporates like Studio 18, which are focused on the urban multiplex audience, Rajshri does not distribute Hollywood films in India and is not actively courting the international theatrical distribution market.

Tarachand Barjatya's three sons—Kamal Kumar, Raj Kumar, and Ajit Kumar—are the current directors of the Rajshri Group, Tarachand having passed away in 1992. Under the direction of Kamal Kumar's daughter Kavita Barjatya, Rajshri produces family-oriented television serials and dramas, including *Woh Rehne Waali Mehlon Ki* (now in its sixth season on Sahara One), and *Yahaaan Main Ghar-Ghar Kheli* (airing on Zee TV). This recent growth in television production is in keeping with the company's legacy as one of the earliest Indian producers of television programming with its 1985 series *Paying Guest* for Doordarshan. In 1997 the company also formed Rajshri Music, a niche label that specializes in non-film music recordings (overseen by Rajjat Barjatya, son of Ajit Kumar).

Rajshri Media is the company's latest effort to blend "modern technology with traditional Indian values." In 2006, under the leadership of Rajat Barjatya, a third-generation member of the Barjatya film family (he is the son of producer Ajit Kumar Barjatya), the company made its foray into web and mobile distribution in order to reach out to audiences outside India. Today, the company's website (Rajshri.com) provides downloadable as well as ad-supported streaming movies, trailers, television shows, and music in a number of Indian languages including Hindi, Tamil, Telugu, Marathi, Bengali, Punjabi, and Gujarati. The site provides not only a new mode of distribution beyond India, but also a means for producers to continue to profit from their back catalogs. Rajshri also has a mobile site offering ring tones and other mobile content.

Reimagining distribution for a digital age, Rajshri released its film *Vivah* (2006) on Rajshri.com on the same day as its theatrical release, a first for Indian cinema. The company also produced the first serial exclusively for web and mobile platforms, *Akbar Birbal Remixed*. Rajshri boasts one of the earliest, and today the most watched Indian channel on YouTube, logging over 100 million viewers. The company also maintains a strong presence on social networking sites.

4. Percept Pictures

Percept Pictures was founded in 2002 as the film, television, and advertising production arm of Percept Limited, an advertising company founded in 1984 by Harindra Singh. He is now the company's Vice Chairman and Managing Director while his brother, Shailendra Singh, is the Joint Managing Director. Self-consciously seeking to build a company firmly set in and oriented toward the Indian market but with global connections, Percept Limited sought strategic international alliances—such as its work with international marketing organizations including the Aegis Group plc and Hakhodo Inc.—and carefully filled its board with MBAs, chartered accountants, and marketing professionals rather than family members. The company currently has network offices in nineteen countries; the most important offices are in India, the United States, the United Kingdom, Japan, and the Middle East.

Percept's entry into film production is very much about extending its reach and presence in the advertising market by providing vertical solutions for its clients. Percept's film production studios are also a logical result of the company's long-standing emphasis on cross-promotion and synergy. According to the company's website, Percept adheres to an "efficient film making process, by integrating content production, distribution, tie-ups for exhibition, broadcasting and music rights." Some of Percept's recent film productions include the animated film *Hanuman* (2005), *Maalamaal Weekly* (2006), *Return of Hanuman* (2007), *Firaaq* (2008), *Kanchivaram* (2008), *Raat Gayi, Baat Gayi?* (2009), *Bumm Bumm Bole* (2010), and *Aashayein*

(2010). Percept has also handled Indian distribution for a number of Hollywood films, including *Rush Hour 3* (2007), *Spiderman 3* (2007), *Hancock* (2008), and *The Mummy: Tomb of the Dragon Emperor* (2008). In addition to a wide range of advertising films, Percept also produces several television serials, including *A.D.A.* (a teen program about a dancing and acting academy), *Powerr Trip* (a celebrity lifestyle program), *Dial One Aur Jeeto* (a call in, interactive game show), and *Sati* (a serial about a law firm that defends women against oppression).

In 1993 Percept Limited launched Tyger Productions. While the umbrella organization focused on marketing and public relations, Tyger Productions could create media content, specifically television commercials for Percept's clients. In 1999 Tyger Productions produced *Pyar Mein Kabhi Kabhi*. In 2002, the company produced its second film, *Makdee*, under the banner of the newly formed Percept Picture Company (later to be renamed Percept Pictures), which took over the film-related responsibilities of Tyger Productions. Percept Pictures increased its film output each year, reaching its peak of six films released in 2008, and continues to produce new films each year. The parent corporation also brings its considerable marketing resources to bear to promote these in-house productions. While producing a few "masala" or light romance flicks that are more typical Bollywood fare, Percept Pictures has made its mark through limited release and critically acclaimed multiplex films (*Page 3*, 2005) and other kinds of specialized or niche films: animated and live action devotionals (*Hanuman*, 2005) and horror (*Sacred Evil*, 2006). The company has also expanded into distributing Indian-language films (primarily Hindi), including their own in-house productions.

5. *Yash Raj Films Pvt. Ltd.*

Yash Raj Films is a celebrated, privately held, family-run company founded by Yash Chopra in 1970. Consciously identifying with Hollywood's golden age, Yash Chopra's web bio describes him as combining "the producing acumen of a Louis B. Mayer or a David O. Selznick ... with the sublime directorial skills of a Frank Capra or a Michael Curtiz." Chopra began his film career as an assistant to his brother B. R. Chopra, directing such films as *Dhool Ka Phool* (1959, Blossom of Dust) and *Dharmputra* (1961) under the production banner of B. R. Films. He went on to found Yash Raj Films, producing and directing his own films, including classics like *Daag* (The Stain, 1973), *Kabhie Kabhie* (Sometimes, 1976), *Kaala Patthar* (Black Stone, 1979), *Silsila* (Chain, 1981), *Chandni* (Moonlight, 1989), *Darr* (Fear, 1993), and *Dil To Pagal Hai* (The Heart Is Crazy, 1997).

Until 2000 Yash Raj Films had produced nineteen films, one every few years, with Yash Chopra directing more than half of these. Yash Raj Films's reputation was not made, however, until the remarkable box-office success of *Dilwale Dulhania Le Jayenge* (1995), the directorial debut for Yash Chopra's son, Aditya Chopra. The blockbuster reinforced Yash Raj Films's commitment to lavish romantic musicals with middle- and upper-class heroes and heralded significant structural changes in the company. From 2000 to 2009, Yash Raj Films released twenty-seven films, with Yash Chopra credited as the director of only one film. Starting in the mid-1990s, Yash Chopra stepped back from his directing duties and, along with Aditya Chopra, took on a more managerial role in a growing media conglomerate. Yash Chopra's other son, Uday Chopra, is an actor and director and is taking the lead in shaping the company's strategy in the domain of digital and new media. Further, anticipating movements toward corporatization, in 2000 Yash Chopra made Sanjeev Kohli, "probably the first management graduate in the entertainment business," CEO of the company in order to pair his management and business expertise with the Chopras' creative talent.

Yash Raj Films boasts a catalog of over forty films. Since 2000 Yash Raj has consistently produced top-grossing films, including *Veer Zaara* (2004), *Dhoom* (Blast, 2004), *Salaam Namaste* (2005), *Dhoom 2* (2006), *Fanaa* (Destroyed in Love, 2006), *Chak De India* (2007), *Rab Ne Bana Di Jodi* (A Match Made by God, 2008), and *New York* (2009). As the liberalization of the Indian economy and the corporatization of the film industry introduced new pressures and players, Yash Raj Films adapted by extending its reach into domestic and overseas distribution, music production, home entertainment, television, documentaries, advertising, and music video production. According to its website, the company's goal is to become "the most complete entertainment conglomerate" in India. In 2006 Yash Raj produced *Kabul Express*, its first film specifically aimed at an international audience. In 2008, Yash Raj partnered with Walt Disney Studios to produce a series of feature-length Hindi-language animated films. Likewise, in 2010 Yash Raj began production of five new television programs in partnership with Sony Entertainment Television.

In terms of film distribution, Yash Raj Films had laid a formidable foundation even before the rhetoric of corporatization gained prominence, distributing its own films and those of other companies across India and internationally for theatrical and home video audiences. As the 2000s progressed, the company began exclusively managing its home video and international theatrical releases, and elaborately orchestrating its domestic releases. The company currently has offices for this purpose in eleven major Indian cities as well as an office each in the United Kingdom, the United States, and the United Arab Emirates. Its business plans in U.A.E. also include a joint venture with Dubai Infinity Holdings to build a Yash Raj Films-themed amusement park that is slated to open in 2014. While Yash Raj Films remains a private family-run company, it has taken steps to diversify and build partnerships in order to look more like the new conglomerates that have increasingly made inroads into the Indian film market. The most notable feature of Yash Raj Films's activities in an era of Bollywoodization surround Yash and Aditya Chopra's efforts to style the company as "India's leading Entertainment Conglomerate" by promoting it as "veritably a 'Studio' in every sense." Toward this end, the company launched a subsidiary studio, Y-Films, in 2011 to cater to the youth market and built studio grounds, which include three sound stages, elaborate technical capacities, and amenities intended to match international tastes.

6. *Dharma Productions Private Ltd.*

Dharma Productions Private Ltd. was established in 1976 by the late Yash Johar and it began releasing films four years later. Yash Johar had a long history in the movie business, having worked on production units on both Indian and foreign films since 1952. In 1976 he formed his own production company, Dharma Productions Private Ltd., and in subsequent years produced a host of films, including *Dostana* (*Friendship*, 1980), *Duniya* (*The World*, 1984), *Muqaddar Ka Faisla* (*Decision of Fate*, 1987), *Agneepath* (*Path of Fire*, 1990), and *Gumraah* (*Lost*, 1993). The company's current trajectory, however, was launched with the release of *Kuch Kuch Hota Hai* (*KKHH*, 1998), the directorial and screenwriting debut of Yash Johar's son, Karan Johar. Prior to this, from 1976 to 1998 Dharma Productions released six films, none directed by the Johars, with the majority of them being action thrillers. Beginning with *Kuch Kuch Hota Hai*, as the company entered the Bollywood era, production increased (the company released four films in 2011, for instance), and was accompanied by a shift toward romantic, family-oriented melodramas. Maintaining less control than other companies over film distribution, Dharma Productions depends heavily on companies, including Yash Raj Films and UTV for much of its theatrical and home video distribution, and Sony BMG for its film music releases.

Dharma Productions's catalog includes Karan Johar's directorial debut and the first Indian film to make the U.K. Top Ten, *Kuch Kuch Hota Hai* (1998), *Kabhi Khushi Kabhie Gham* (2001), *Kal Ho Na Ho* (2004), and *My*

Name Is Khan (2010). As a testament to the company's mission to provide family-friendly stories, *Kuch Kuch Hota Hai* (1998) won the "Indian National Award for Best Popular Film Providing Wholesome Entertainment." According to the company's website, *Kabhi Khushi Kabhie Gham* remains the highest grossing Indian film in the overseas market, debuting at No. 3 on the U.K. Top Ten Chart and breaking records in the U.K. and the United States. With the internationally successful release of his second film, *Kabhi Khushi Kabhie Gham* (2001), Karan Johar cemented the glorification of the Indian family and the depiction of family drama as a central theme for the company (e.g., *We Are Family*, 2010). Many of these movies are filmed and set in foreign countries, heightening the import for the characters of retaining a connection with one's cultural heritage and family, and helping the movies achieve significant international sales at the box office.

With Yash Johar's passing in 2004, Dharma Productions came under the leadership of Karan Johar who has taken the company in a new direction by funding the work of independent directors. While some of these films are youth-oriented fare, such as *Wake Up Sid* (2009) and *I Hate Luv Storys* (2010), others tackle more challenging social and ethical problems, particularly the disconnect between traditional values and the cosmopolitanism of a new generation of young, upwardly mobile Indians. For example, *Dostana* (2008) tackled the issue of homosexual relationships, while *My Name Is Khan* (2010) dealt with racialized intolerance and suspicion in the United States after 9/11. Karan Johar's fame, and thus Dharma Productions's prominence in Bollywood, rests not only on his directorial skills but also on his transmedia presence. He has hosted two celebrity-oriented television shows (*Koffee with Karan* and *Lift Kara De/Helping Hand*), and is also a celebrated brand ambassador with numerous product endorsement deals.

7. Red Chillies Entertainment Private Ltd.

In 2000 Shahrukh Khan, Juhi Chawla, and Aziz Mirza founded *Dreamz Unlimited* as a film distribution and production company, but their first few films did not garner significant box office success. In 2002 Shahrukh Khan, with his wife Gauri Khan, sought to rebrand and reboot the company as Red Chillies Entertainment Pvt. Ltd. (RCE), which released its first film, *Main Hoon Na*, in 2004. Red Chillies Entertainment is now a prominent "star studio" in Bollywood, and releases three or fewer films each year, most featuring Shahrukh in a starring role. These include box office blockbusters such as *Om Shanti Om* (2007), and critical successes like *Billu* (2009), as well as less successful ventures.

Branding itself a "film production house," Red Chillies Entertainment's business portfolio reflects its greater interest in product across media platforms, although the company has considerable control over the domestic home video distribution of its films and some theatrical distribution oversight. TVC, the television commercial subunit of the company, has been producing commercials for domestic Indian consumption since 2001. Most of these feature celebrity endorsements, often given by Shahrukh himself. RCE VFX is its postproduction studio, which has focused on special effects work in commercials, television, and film since its inception in 2006. The company's "Idiot Box" division has been producing television shows since 2008 for Channel [V], Disney Channel India, NDTV channels, STAR Plus, and other general entertainment channels as well as telefilms. Having acquired, rather than rented, the equipment necessary for its various filming project, Red Chillies Entertainment also loans out its cameras and filming gear to other production companies. Red Chillies Entertainment also has a majority share in the Kolkata Knight Riders, a cricket team associated with the Indian Premier League that was formed in 2008. A major reason for the Knight Riders' financial success has been attributed to Shahrukh Khan's elaborate promotion campaigns in which Red Chillies Entertainment's commercials and other promotional materials have figured prominently.

8. *Reliance Entertainment*

Reliance Entertainment is the entertainment division of Reliance Anil Dhirubhai Ambani Group (ADAG), which also includes Reliance Communications, India's largest telecommunications provider serving over 50 million subscribers, Reliance Capital, Reliance Infrastructure, Reliance Power, and Reliance Health. The conglomerate has over 11 million shareholders and over 100,000 employees. Reliance ADAG was created when the founder of Reliance Industries (established in 1966 as a polyester firm), Dhirubhai Ambani passed away in 2002 and his sons divided his business empire. Founded by Anil Ambani, Reliance Entertainment's operations today include film production, local and international distribution, exhibition, television production and distribution, postproduction services, Internet and mobile portals, online and mobile gaming, radio, and live events coordination and marketing.

Reliance Entertainment's entry into Bollywood was defined by its acquisition of a controlling stake in Adlabs Films in 2005. Adlabs Films Limited was established in 1978 in Bombay as a film processing laboratory primarily catering to the advertising industry. The company moved into film exhibition in 2000, opening its first multiplex in Bombay in 2001. In 2002, through its wholly owned subsidiary Entertainment One, Adlabs also began producing films. In 2005, the Reliance Anil Dhirubhai Ambani Group (ADAG) acquired Adlabs Films Ltd. and in 2009 the company was renamed Reliance MediaWorks Ltd. Association with Reliance ADAG has allowed what was once Adlabs Films to exploit and support ventures in other media platforms, including telecommunications, television, music, and radio. At present, Reliance MediaWorks' assets include a worldwide cinema chain with over 550 screens (spanning India, the United States, Malaysia, Nepal, and the Netherlands), postproduction offices in New York and London (specializing in film processing, special effects, and 2D to 3D conversions), and a television production company. Reliance Synergy, the television production arm, produces primarily quiz and contest formats, including *Quiz Time, India Quiz, Big Money, Kaun Banega Crorepati?* (Who Wants to Be a Millionaire?), and *India's Got Talent.* Having gained a significant stake in the domestic film production industry, in 2008 Reliance ADAG signed a $1.5 billion deal with the U.S.-based DreamWorks, providing DreamWorks with $325 million in equity so that it could become a stand-alone company and end its partnership with Paramount Pictures. In return, the Steven Spielberg-championed Hollywood studio is 50 percent owned by Reliance ADAG's Chairman, Anil Ambani.

9. UTV Software Communications Pvt. Ltd./UTV Motion Pictures PLC

United Software Communications Pvt. Ltd., founded in 1990, became UTV Software Communications Ltd. when it went public in 1998. Ronnie Screwvala, its founder, chairman, and CEO, had made his fortune and reputation as an entrepreneur who built and managed one of the first and most profitable cable television subscription networks in Bombay and later, a producer of several hit television programs for the state-run network (Doordarshan). This led in 1992 to lucrative television production work for ZEE TV and forays into related media business ventures through expansion and acquisition: in-flight entertainment (1992), producing daily soap operas (1994), television distribution (1995), dubbing Disney's film library into Hindi (1996), producing animated films and shows (1998), and Internet content creation and aggregation (2000). In 1995 the company acquired its own Tamil-language channel (formely known as Vijay TV), which it sold to STAR TV by 2004. In 2004 UTV launched a children's television channel Hungama TV, which it subsequently sold to the Walt Disney Company in 2006. Presently UTV has a library of over 5,000 hours of television programming, covering all genres, and has provided programming for 26 channels in 19 countries.

In 1996 UTV also entered the film production and distribution business, with Screwvala producing his first film in 1997 (*Dil Ke Jharoke Main/In the Heart's Window*). Although UTV Motion Pictures PLC would not be incorporated until 2007, beginning in 1996 Screwvala and UTV became increasingly involved in film production, theatrical distribution, and television/satellite syndication until it developed into a major pillar of the corporation. Unlike the heads of other film companies in India run by charismatic leaders, Screwvala is neither a megastar nor an auteur. Instead of carefully crafting a library of its own work, UTV works most often in partnership with a wide array of foreign and domestic companies to diversify its investments, producing and distributing films in Tamil, Telugu, Hindi, English, and other languages, and making the most use of its film content to promote its other media platforms (television, games, broadcasting, the Internet). UTV currently distributes films in more than 45 countries and is one of the top 20 distributors in the United States. Since 2000 UTV has produced a number of successful and high-profile films, including *Rang de Basanti* (Color of Sacrifice, 2006), *Jodha Akbar* (2008), *Fashion* (2008), *Kaminey: The Scoundrels* (2009), and *Raajneeti* (Politics, 2010). UTV has also collaborated on a number of recent Hollywood productions, including Mira Nair's *The Namesake* (2006), Chris Rock's *I Think I Love My Wife* (2007), and M. Night Shyamalan's *The Happening* (2008).

Today the company is a major media conglomerate with interests in film production, distribution, broadcasting, television programming, digital media, and gaming. In addition to the new possibilities for cross-promotion and brand development afforded by new media, Screwvala's strategy includes a focus on developing "young India" as an audience and a market. This focus has led to a new emphasis on gaming and young adult programming, as well as an ongoing partnership with the Walt Disney Company, which acquired a 50.4 percent stake in UTV in 2006. UTV went public in 2005 and listed on the Bombay Stock Exchange and the National Stock Exchange. Shortly after its incorporation in 2007, UTV Motion Pictures was admitted to trading on the Alternate Investment Market of the London Stock Exchange. In January 2012 the Walt Disney Company acquired UTV and announced plans to delist UTV from the Indian stock exchange and create Walt Disney Company India.

10. *Eros International Media Ltd./Eros Entertainment*

Eros International Media Ltd. was founded in 1977 by its honorary life president, Arjun Lulla. His son, Kishore Lulla, took over as executive director in 1988. In no small part because of the 1980s video boom in India, Kishore Lulla cofounded the United Kingdom Eros International branch. Much of the company's considerable wealth, then, is premised on its dominance in the international home entertainment distribution market, originally catering to the large NRI population in countries like the United States and the United Kingdom. Not limiting themselves to film recordings for home entertainment use, Eros International also distributes music videos worldwide, and syndicates its music video and film content to domestic and international satellite television channels. Throughout they have also been involved in Indian film production, with an eye toward vertical integration. Nevertheless, most of the selections available from their massive film (over 2,000 titles) and music video home entertainment catalog were not produced by Eros International. In 2006 they also moved into the film music production business, starting their own Eros Music label.

In 2003, Eros International began distributing VCDs and DVDs of original and dubbed non-domestic films for the Indian audience (e.g., both volumes of *Kill Bill,* 2003 and 2004, and *The Aviator,* 2004). In 2005 Eros International began dubbing its international Bollywood releases into foreign languages in the hope of courting the burgeoning non-South Asian audience for Bollywood in various markets worldwide. In 2006 Eros International became the first Indian company to be admitted to trading on the Alternate Investment Market of the London Stock Exchange. Having established their presence in distributing films in Punjabi and Marathi, Eros International went on to acquire a controlling stake in Ayngaran, a major Tamil-language film content and distribution company, in 2007. Beyond the Indian media market, Eros International has arrangements and joint ventures with EMI, Comcast, and Universal. In 2007 the company launched a visual effects studio that now works on Hindi-, regional language-, and (international) English-language films.

11. *Shree Ashtavinayak Cine Vision Ltd*

A film production and distribution company, Shree Ashtavinayak Cine Vision Ltd. was founded in 2001 by a small group of business professionals— three with MBAs, the fourth a computer engineer. Dhillin Mehta, a first-generation entrepreneur, currently serves as the CEO of the company. With a number of hit films to its credit, Shree Ashtavinayak Cine Vision positions itself as a company that offers a "corporatized" and secure model for Indian film finance and production. In fact, the most striking aspect of this company's website and branding strategy is the emphasis it places on how well its mission is aligned with the "corporatization" of the Bombay film industry. Shree Ashtavinayak Cine Vision's industrial identity fits neatly in relation to an apparently seamless transition from Bombay cinema to Bollywood, defined in particular by the adoption of rational systems of management and the formalization of business practices in production, financing, and distribution. On its website, the company declares itself to be "the pioneering corporate structure in the tinsel town."

Beginning with the low-budget film *Fun 2shh* in 2003, which Shree Ashtavinayak Cine Vision produced and distributed, the company slowly built itself up, leveraging past successes into larger budget films. In subsequent years the company produced and released films with notable action and comedy stars (Akshay Kumar, Ajay Devgan), and went on to produce the hit *Jab We Met* (When We Met) in 2007. Beginning in 2004, Shree Ashtavinayak Cine Vision also began distributing films produced by other companies. Focusing originally in Bombay, they have spread their network into other Indian regions and some international markets. In 2005 SACV also entered into the exhibition business in the Bombay territory, but has since pulled back from this venture. SACV does not have a home entertainment division and typically sells home video rights to companies such as Eros International.

Top Box-Office Successes, 2000–2009

Year	Film	Producer	Production Company	Domestic Distributor	Overseas Distributor
2000	Kaho Naa Pyaar Hai	Rakesh Roshan	Film Kraft	Film Kraft, Yash Raj Films	
	Mohabbatein	Yash Chopra	Yash Raj Films	Yash Raj Films	Yash Raj Films
	Mission Kashmir	Vidhu Vinod Chopra	Vinod Chopra Productions	Vinod Chopra Productions, Destination Films	
	Josh	Ganesh Jain, Ratan Jain, Balwant Singh	Venus Movies	United Seven Creations	
	Refugee	J. P. Dutta	J P Films	H. R. Enterprises	Yash Raj Films
2001	Gadar: Ek Prem Katha	Nitin Keni	**Zee Telefilms**	**Zee Telefilms**	Video Sound
	Kabhi Kushi Kabhie Gham	Yash Johar	Dharma Productions	Yash Raj Films	Yash Raj Films
	Lagaan	Aamir Khan	Aamir Khan Productions	Aamir Khan Productions	**Sony Entertainment**
	Indian	Dharmendra	Vijayta Films	Vijayta Films	N/A
	Jodi No. 1	Dhirajlal Shah, Hashmukh Shah, Pravin Shah	Time Magnetics Pvt. Ltd.	Time Magnetics Pvt. Ltd.	N/A
2002	Devdas	Bharat Shah	Mega Bollywood	Mega Bollywood	**Eros International**
	Raaz	Mukesh Bhatt	Vishesh Films	Vishesh Films, Tips Films Pvt. Ltd.	N/A
	Kaante	Pritish Nandy Communications, Sanjay Gupta	**Pritish Nandy Communications**, White Feather Films	White Feather Films	Raju Patel

Year	Film	Producer	Production Company	Domestic Distributor	Overseas Distributor
	Aankhen	Gaurang Doshi	V. R. Pictures	V R Films	Video Sound
	Humraaz	Ganesh Jain, Ratan Jain	Venus Movies	Venus Movies	
2003	Koi Mil Gaya	Rakesh Roshan	Film Kraft	Film Kraft Productions	Yash Raj Films
	Kal Ho Na Ho	Yash Johar	Dharma Productions	Yash Raj Films	Yash Raj Films
	The Hero	Dhirajlal Shah, Hasmukh Shah, Pravin Shah	Time Magnetics Pvt. Ltd.	Time Magnetics Pvt. Ltd.	Video Sound
	Baghban	B. R. Chopra	B. R. Films	B. R. Films	**Eros International**
	Munna Bhai MBBS	Vidhu Vinod Chopra	Vinod Chopra Films	Vinod Chopra Films	**Entertainment One**
2004	Veer Zaara	Aditya Chopra, Yash Chopra	Yash Raj Films	Yash Raj Films	Yash Raj Films, MG Distribution
	Main Hoon Na	Shahrukh Khan	Red Chillies	Red Chillies Entertainment, **Shree Ashtavinayak Cine Vision**	**Eros International**
	Mujhse Shaadi Karogi	Sajid Nadiadwala	Nadiadwala Grandson Entertainment	Nadiadwala Grandson Entertainment, **Shree Ashtavinayak Cine Vision**	**Zee Telefilms**
	Dhoom	Aditya Chopra	Yash Raj Films	Yash Raj Films	Yash Raj Films
	Khakee	Keshu Ramsay	DMS Films	DMS Films Pvt. Ltd.	N/A
2005	No Entry	Boney Kapoor	S. K. Enterprises, **Sahara One Motion Pictures**	S. K. Films Enterprises, **Sahara One, K Sera Sera**	N/A

Year	Film	Producer	Production Company	Domestic Distributor	Overseas Distributor
	Bunty Aur Babli	Aditya Chopra, Yash Chopra	Yash Raj Films	Yash Raj Films	Yash Raj Films
	Mangal Pandey	Bobby Bedi	Kaleidoscope Entertainment	Kaleidoscope Entertainment, Tfk Films, **INOX Leisure Ltd.**	Yash Raj Films
	Garam Masala	Ganesh Jain	Venus Movies	Ashco Media Arts Pvt. Ltd., Venus Movies	Venus Movies
	Maine Pyaar Kyun Kiya?	Seema Kar	**Shree Ashtavinayak Cine Vision**	**Shree Ashtavinayak Cine Vision Ltd.**	N/A
2006	Dhoom 2	Aditya Chopra	Yash Raj Films	Yash Raj Films	Yash Raj Films
	Krrish	Rakesh Roshan	Film Kraft	Film Kraft, Yash Raj Films	**Eros International**
	Lage Raho Munna Bhai	Vidhu Vinod Chopra	Vinod Chopra Productions	Vinod Chopra Productions	**Eros International**
	Fanaa	Aditya Chopra	Yash Raj Films	Yash Raj Films	Yash Raj Films
	Don	Farhan Akhtar, Ritesh Sidhwani	Excel Films	Excel Films	**Eros International**
2007	Om Shanti Om	Gauri Khan	Red Chillies Entertainment	Red Chillies Entertainment, **Shree Ashtavinayak Cine Vision Ltd.**	**Eros International**
	Welcome	Firoz A. Nadiadwala	Base Industries Group	Base Industries Group, Shree Ashtavinayak Cine Vision Ltd.	N/A
	Chak De India	Aditya Chopra	Yash Raj Films	Yash Raj Films	Yash Raj Films
	Partner	Sohail Khan	**K Sera Sera**	**K Sera Sera,** Shree Ashtavinayak Cine Vision Ltd.	**Eros International**

Year	Film	Producer	Production Company	Domestic Distributor	Overseas Distributor
	Tare Zameen Par	Aamir Khan	Aamir Khan Productions	Aamir Khan Productions	**PVR Pictures**
2008	Ghajini	Tagore Madhu, Madhu Mantena	Geetha Arts	Geetha Arts	**Reliance Entertainment**
	Rab Ne Bana Di Jodi	Aditya Chopra	Yash Raj Films	Yash Raj Films	Yash Raj Films
	Singh Is Kinng	Vipul Amrutlal Shah	Blockbuster Movie Entertainers, Big Screen Entertainment	**Viacom 18**	**Adlabs Films Ltd.**, Slide Screen Entertainment
	Race	Ramesh S. Taurani, Kumar S. Taurani	Tip Films	Tips Music Films, **UTV Motion Pictures**	**UTV Motion Pictures**
	Jodhaa Akbar	Ronnie Screwvala,	**UTV Motion Pictures**	**UTV Motion Pictures**	**UTV Motion Pictures**
2009	3 Idiots	Vidhu Vinod Chopra	Vinod Chopra Productions	**Reliance Entertainment**	**Reliance Entertainment**
	Love Aaj Kal	Saif Ali Khan	Illuminati Films	**Eros Entertainment**, Illuminati Films	**Eros International**
	Ajab Prem Ki Prem Ghazab Kahani	Ramesh S. Taurani, Rajkumar S. Taurani	Tips Films	**Shemaroo**	**Shemaroo**
	Wanted	Boney Kapoor	**Sahara One Motion Picture**	**Sahara One Motion Pictures**, S K Films Enterprises	**Eros International**
	De Dana Dan	Ganesh Jain	Venus Movies	**Eros Entertainment**	**Eros International**

Note: **Boldface** *indicates corporate entities.*

NOTES

INTRODUCTION

1. My use of the term "media capital" is informed by Michael Curtin's work which foregrounds the spatial dimensions of transnational media flows (2003; 2007). I will elaborate how the term informs this book at a later point in this introduction. For now, I am using it to simply indicate the position that cities like Bombay and Los Angeles occupy as major centers of media production.

2. Anna Tsing, *Friction: An Ethnography of Global Connection* (Princeton: Princeton University Press, 2005), 58.

3. Ibid.

4. Shanti Kumar, "Mapping Tollywood: The Cultural Geography of 'Ramoji Film City' in Hyderabad," *Quarterly Review of Film and Video* 23, no. 2 (2006): 129–38; S. V. Srinivas, *Megastar: Chiranjeevi and Telugu Cinema after NTR* (New Delhi: Oxford University Press, 2009).

5. For a more detailed consideration of the changing cultural geography of Hyderabad, see Kumar, "Mapping Tollywood."

6. Brian Larkin, *Signal and Noise: Media, Infrastructure, and Urban Culture in Nigeria* (Durham: Duke University Press, 2009); Sudha Rajagopalan, *Indian Films in Soviet Cinemas: The Culture of Movie-Going after Stalin* (Bloomington: Indiana University Press, 2008).

7. Ravi Vasudevan, "The Meanings of 'Bollywood,'" *Journal of the Moving Image* 7 (2008).

8. Ashis Nandy, introduction to *The Secret Politics of Our Desires: Innocence, Culpability, and Indian Popular Cinema*, ed. Ashis Nandy (New York: St. Martin's Press, 1998), 2.

9. Ibid.

10. Bhrigupati Singh, "The Problem," *Seminar*, May 2003.

11. Ibid.

12. The notable exception here is Manjunath Pendakur. See, for example, his article, "New Cultural Technologies and the Fading Glitter of Indian Cinema," *Quarterly Review of Film and Video* 11 (1989): 69–78.

13. Bhrigupati Singh, "The Problem" Also, Amit Rai makes a similar argument in approaching Bollywood as a "new media assemblage." Rai argues that "neither formalist analyses of film culture nor representational theories of subjectivation" are adequate for understanding a media ecology that is defined by complex interconnections among media forms, industries, and modes of consumption. However, Rai does not focus on actual industry dynamics and practices. Amit Rai, *Untimely Bollywood: Globalization and India's New Media Assemblage* (Durham: Duke University Press, 2009), 20.

14. While some scholars have written about "regional" language films and the film industries based in the four southern states of Tamilnadu, Kerala, Andhra Pradesh, and Karnataka, and the eastern state of West Bengal, scholarship on cinema in India has predominantly focused on Hindi-language films produced in Bombay.

15. Sumita S. Chakravarty, *National Identity in Indian Popular Cinema, 1947–1987* (Austin: University of Texas Press, 1993); Madhava M. Prasad, *Ideology of the Hindi Film: A Historical Construction* (New Delhi: Oxford University Press, 1998); Ravi S. Vasudevan's anthology,

Making Meaning in Indian Cinema (New Delhi: Oxford University Press, 2000); Jyotika Virdi, *The Cinematic ImagiNation: Indian Popular Films as Social History* (New Brunswick: Rutgers University Press, 2003); Neepa Majumdar, *Wanted Cultured Ladies Only! Female Stardom and Cinema in India, 1930s–1950s* (Urbana: University of Illinois Press, 2009); Monika Mehta, "Selections: Cutting, Classifying, and Certifying in Bombay Cinema" (Ph.D. dissertation, University of Minnesota, 2001); Rachel Dwyer and Divya Patel, *Cinema India: The Visual Culture of Hindi Film* (New Delhi: Oxford University Press, 2002); Gayatri Gopinath, *Impossible Desires: Queer Diasporas and South Asian Public Cultures* (Durham: Duke University Press, 2005).

16. Ranjani Mazumdar, *Bombay Cinema: An Archive of the City* (Minneapolis: University of Minnesota Press, 2007).

17. Henry Jenkins, *Convergence Culture: Where Old and New Media Collide* (New York: NYU Press, 2006), 2.

18. Ravi Sundaram, *Pirate Modernity: Delhi's Media Urbanism* (New Delhi: Routledge, 2010), 3.

19. The key text in this regard is Michele Hilmes's pathbreaking *Hollywood and Broadcasting: From Radio to Cable* (Urbana: University of Illinois, 1990). More recently, Jennifer Holt has shown that understanding the history of media regulation calls for an approach that takes into account the fact that different media industries (film, cable, and broadcast) have been intertwined for several decades now and as such cannot be studied in isolated fashion. Jennifer Holt, *Empires of Entertainment: Media Industries and the Politics of Deregulation, 1980–1996* (New Brunswick: Rutgers University Press, 2011).

20. This account of Radio Ceylon is based on newspaper records as well as an in-depth interview I conducted with Ameen Sayani, the legendary broadcaster affiliated with Radio Ceylon and later, All India Radio.

21. G. C. Awasthy, *Broadcasting in India* (New York: Allied Publishers, 1965); David Lelyveld, "Upon the Subdominant: Administering Music on All-India Radio," *Social Text* 39 (1995): 111–27.

22. Awasthy, *Broadcasting in India*, 51; "Compulsory Study of Music," *The Hindu*, September 29, 1957.

23. Lelyveld, "Upon the Subdominant," 121.

24. "Vividh Bharati: New Programme over All India Radio," *The Hindu*, September 29, 1957.

25. Lelyveld, "Upon the Subdominant," 57.

26. In fact, given that Radio Ceylon's programs reached audiences in Pakistan and as far afield as South Africa and parts of East Africa with significant concentrations of immigrants from the Indian subcontinent, one might even argue that Radio Ceylon created a transnational audience community in a historical conjuncture in which national identity was being defined in territorial terms by newly independent nation-states in South Asia.

27. Prasad, *Ideology of the Hindi Film*.

28. Ashish Rajadhyaksha, "The Curious Case of Bombay's Hindi Cinema: The Career of Indigenous 'Exhibition' Capital," *Journal of the Moving Image* 5 (2006).

29. Tejaswini Ganti, "Casting Culture: The Social Life of Hindi Film Production in Contemporary India" (Ph.D. dissertation, New York University, 2000), 14.

30. Michael Curtin, "Thinking Globally: From Media Imperialism to Media Capital," in *Media Industries: History, Theory, and Method*, ed. Jennifer Holt and Alisa Perren (Malden, Mass.: Wiley-Blackwell, 2009), 109. There are, of course, a few exceptions, the most notable one in the Indian context being William Mazzarella's ethnography of the advertising

industry in Bombay—*Shoveling Smoke: Advertising and Globalization in Contemporary India* (Durham: Duke University Press, 2003).

31. Serra Tinic, *On Location: Canada's Television Industry in a Global Market* (Toronto: University of Toronto Press, 2006); Michael Curtin, *Playing to the World's Biggest Audience: The Globalization of Chinese Film and TV* (Berkeley: University of California Press, 2007).

32. Michael Curtin, "Media Capital: Towards the Study of Spatial Flows," *International Journal of Cultural Studies* 6, no. 2 (2003): 204.

33. Ritu Birla, *Stages of Capital: Law, Culture, and Market Governance in Late Colonial India* (Durham: Duke University Press, 2009); Kajri Jain, *Gods in the Bazaar: The Economies of Indian Calendar Art* (Durham: Duke University Press, 2007).

34. Arjun Appadurai, "Spectral Housing and Urban Cleansing: Notes on Millennial Mumbai," *Public Culture* 12, no. 3 (2000): 627.

35. Jain, *Gods in the Bazaar*, 37.

36. Curtin, "Media Capital," 205.

37. Alexandra Alter, "A Passage to Hollywood," *Wall Street Journal*, February 6, 2009. For more details on the Reliance Entertainment-DreamWorks deal, see Lauren Schuker, "Spielberg, India's Reliance to Form Studio," *Wall Street Journal*, September 20, 2008.

38. See, for example, Mrinalini Sinha, *Colonial Masculinity: The "Manly Englishman" and the "Effeminate Bengali" in the Late Nineteenth Century* (Manchester: Manchester University Press, 1995).

39. David Morley and Kevin Robins, *Spaces of Identity: Global Media, Electronic Landscapes and Cultural Boundaries* (New York: Routledge, 1995).

40. Nandini Lakshman and Ronald Grover, "Why India's Reliance Is Going Hollywood," *Business Week*, June 18, 2008, http://www.businessweek.com/print/globalbiz/content/jun2008/gb20080618_504190.htm

41. Ibid.

42. Ashish Rajadhyaksha, *In the Time of Celluloid: From Bollywood to the Emergency* (Bloomington: Indiana University Press, 2009); also see Neepa Majumdar's discussion of the translocation of Hollywood stardom in the Indian film industry in the interwar period (*Wanted Cultured Ladies Only!*) and Nitin Govil, "Something to Declare: Trading Culture, Trafficking Hollywood and Textual Travel" (Ph.D. dissertation, New York University, 2005).

43. Holt and Perren, ed., *Media Industries*; Vicki Mayer, Miranda Banks, and John Caldwell, ed., *Production Studies: Cultural Studies of Media Industries* (New York: Routledge, 2009).

44. John Caldwell, *Production Culture: Industrial Reflexivity and Critical Practice in Film and Television* (Durham: Duke University Press, 2008).

45. Caldwell, *Production Culture*, 4.

46. George Marcus and Michael Fischer, *Anthropology as Cultural Critique: An Experimental Moment in the Human Sciences* (Chicago: University of Chicago Press, 1986). Also see "Ethnography in/of the World System: The Emergence of Multi-Sited Ethnography" and other chapters in George Marcus, *Ethnography through Thick and Thin* (Princeton: Princeton University Press, 1998), 79–104.

47. Interviews with industry professionals were open-ended and followed an emergent approach. While I did have a set of questions for each industry professional regarding his or her business practices, the interviews would often spiral outward into a conversation about broader changes in the media industries in Bombay. Further, interviews were conducted not only with high-level executives but also with on-the-ground professionals,

including marketing executives, public relations agents, film journalists, web analysts, and those involved in various aspects of production and distribution in film, television. and dot-com companies. Unless otherwise noted, all quotes from industry professionals are from personal interviews.

48. Caldwell, *Production Culture*, 4.
49. See, for instance, Sherry B. Ortner, "Studying Sideways: Ethnographic Access in Hollywood," in *Production Studies*, ed. Holt and Perren, 179.
50. Ibid., 176.
51. Vicki Mayer, Miranda Banks, and John Caldwell, introduction to *Production Studies*, 4.
52. George Yudice, *The Expediency of Culture: Uses of Culture in the Global Era* (Durham: Duke University Press, 2005), 26.

CHAPTER 1

1. Yudice, *The Expediency of Culture*, 28.
2. Leela Fernandes, "The Politics of Forgetting: Class Politics, State Power, and the Restructuring of Urban Space in India," *Urban Studies* 41, no. 12 (2004): 2415–30.
3. Ibid., 2416.
4. Amitav Ghosh, "The Diaspora in Indian Culture," *Public Culture* 2, no. 1 (1989): 73–78.
5. However, as Tejaswini Niranjana points out, it is difficult to categorize the "older diaspora as being 'immigrant' in the sense in which Indians in the metropolitan countries can be described today, since the term suggests a certain recentness in the achievement of that status." See Tejaswini Niranjana, *Mobilizing India: Women, Music, and Migration between India and Trinidad* (Durham: Duke University Press, 2006), 21.
6. Kathinka Sinha-Kerkhoff and Ellen Bal, " 'Eternal Call of the Ganga': Reconnecting with People of Indian Origin in Surinam," *Economic and Political Weekly* 38, no. 38 (2003): 4010.
7. M. C. Lall, *India's Missed Opportunity: India's Relationship with the Non-Resident Indians* (Ashgate: Aldershot, 2001), 169; quoted in Sinha-Kerkhoff and Bal, "'Eternal Call of the Ganga,'" 4010.
8. Srikant Dutt, "India and the Overseas Indians," *India Quarterly* 36 (1980): 307–35.
9. Ibid.
10. Aditya Nigam, "Imagining the Global Nation: Time and Hegemony," *Economic and Political Weekly* 39, no. 1 (2004): 72.
11. Ibid.
12. Ibid.
13. Sinha-Kerkhoff and Bal, "Reconnecting with People of Indian Origin." For further details, see N. E. Vadodera, *BJP Foreign Policy Agenda for the Future* (New Delhi: Bharatiya Janata Party Publication, 1994).
14. L. M. Singhvi, *Report of the High Level Committee on the Indian Diaspora* (New Delhi: Ministry of External Affairs, 2000), accessed August 2, 2010, http://www.indiandiaspora. nic.in/contents.htm. Also see Nasima Khan, "Dual Deal," India Today, January 21, 2002, 28–32.
15. Lall, *India's Missed Opportunity*, 98.
16. "NRIs All Set for Diasporic Meet," *Rediff*, January 8, 2003, http://www.rediff.com/money/2003/jan/08pbd.htm.
17. See http://www.cgidubai.com/press47.htm.

18. Bakirathi Mani and Latha Varadarajan, "'The Largest Gathering of the Global Indian Family': Neoliberalism, Nationalism, and Diaspora at Pravasi Bharatiya Divas," *Diaspora: A Journal of Transnational Studies* 14, no. 1 (2005): 45–73.

19. Ashish Rajadhyaksha, "The 'Bollywoodization' of the Indian Cinema: Cultural Nationalism in a Global Arena," *Inter-Asia Cultural Studies* 4, no.1 (2003): 28–34.

20. All these films were directed by Sooraj Barjatya, son of Tarachand Barjatya who established Rajshri Pictures in 1947 as a film distribution company. Rajshri Productions, the film production division, was set up in 1962. Sooraj Barjatya's films are generally known for their conservatism and focus on the ideals of a large, joint Hindu family.

21. As Selvaraj Velayutham writes, "[W]hile Bollywood represents to its local and global audience a kind of pan-Indian cultural identity—whereby the territorial, cultural and ethno-linguistic identity of India's diverse population becomes narrowed and compressed into an Indian identity which exalts the notion of a Hindi speaking, Hindu, middle class Indian—Tamil cinema persistently aims at anchoring Tamil identity." "The Diaspora and the Global Circulation of Tamil Cinema," in *Tamil Cinema: The Cultural Politics of India's Other Film Industry*, ed. Selvaraj Velayutham (New York: Routledge, 2008), 179.

22. Vijay Mishra, *Bollywood Cinema: Temples of Desire* (New York: Routledge, 2002), 236–37.

23. Purnima Mankekar, "Brides Who Travel: Gender, Transnationalism, and Nationalism in Hindi Film," *Positions* 7, no. 3 (1999): 731–62; Patricia Uberoi, "The Diaspora Comes Home: Disciplining Desire in DDLJ," *Contributions to Indian Sociology* 32, no. 2 (1998): 305–36.

24. Such a positioning of women as the primary custodians of "Indian" culture in the diaspora is neither new nor surprising. The repositioning of women in relation to changing configurations of public/private domains can in fact be traced to representational shifts in Bombay cinema during the 1980s. Examining changes in Bombay cinema's representations of romance and the romantic couple, Sircar argues that the shift in Bombay cinema's love-story genre during the 1980s, coinciding with the project of "liberalization," marked a key change in the configuration of the "Indian woman." She observes that "paralleling the 'celebrations' of the identity of the New Woman there also appeared in the media a whole spate of features asserting the continuity of traditional institutions in the new time." Ajanta Sircar, "Love in the Time of Liberalization: *Qayamat Se Qayamat Tak*," *Journal of Arts and Ideas*, no. 32–33 (1999): 35–60. Also see Virdi, *The Cinematic ImagiNation*, 185, 152.

25. Sircar, "Love in the Time of Liberalization," 38.

26. Virdi, *The Cinematic ImagiNation*, 185.

27. Focusing on television, Purnima Mankekar also demonstrates how women-oriented television narratives such as Rajani and Udaan, and the state's projects and policies pertaining to nation-building during the 1980s, worked to position the "New Indian Woman" as "middle-class and modern but not Western." See Purnima Mankekar, *Screening Culture, Viewing Politics: An Ethnography of Television, Womanhood, and Nation in Postcolonial India* (Durham: Duke University Press), 152.

28. See, for instance, Anjali Ram, "Framing the Feminine: Diasporic Readings of Gender in Popular Indian Cinema," *Women's Studies in Communication* 25, no. 1 (2002): 33.

29. Mishra, *Bollywood Cinema*, 267.

30. Virdi, *The Cinematic ImagiNation*, 202.

31. Madhava Prasad, "This Thing Called Bollywood," *Seminar*, no. 525 (2003), http://www.india-seminar.com.

32. Rajadhyaksha, "The Curious Case of Bombay's Hindi Cinema," 32.

33. Prasad, "This Thing Called Bollywood."

34. Nigam, "Imagining the Global Nation," 72.

35. Ibid.

36. Ibid., 72–73.

37. Mazzarella, *Shoveling Smoke*, 101.

38. Ibid.

39. Quoted in Naunidhi Kaur, "The Dreams of a Diaspora," *Frontline* 20, no. 2, January, 13–21, 2003, http://www.frontlineonnet.com/fl2002/stories/20030131008112700.htm.

40. Sushma Swaraj, "Keynote Address on Entertainment, Ethnic Media, and Diasporic Identity" (speech, Pravasi Bharatiya Divas, New Delhi, January 9, 2003). Accessed April 6, 2007, http://www.indiaday.org/pbd1/pbd-sushmaswaraj.asp.

41. "Film Accorded Industry Status," *Business Line*, October 19, 2000, accessed April 2, 2007, http://www.indiaserver.com/businessline/2000/10/19/stories/141918re.htm; "Sops Set Film Industry on a Roll," *Business Line*, March 2, 2000, accessed April 2, 2007, http://www.indiaserver.com/businessline/2000/03/02/stories/03024482.htm; "Finally an Industry," *Indian Express*, May 12, 1998, http://www.expressindia.com/ie/daily/19980512/13250064.html

42. "Focus, Please (Indian Movies)," *The Hindu*, September 23, 1998, http://www.webpage.com/hindu/daily/980923/05/05232512.htm; quoted in Monika Mehta, "Globalizing Bombay Cinema: Reproducing the Indian State and Family," *Cultural Dynamics* 17, no. 2 (2005): 135–54.

43. Dalal, 2001. Cited in Ashish Rajadhyaksha, "The Curious Case of Bombay's Hindi Cinema: The Career of 'Indigenous' Exhibition Capital," *Journal of the Moving Image*, 5 (2006), available online at http://jmionline.org/film_journal/jmi_05/article_01.php#article_text_9.

44. For more details, see Brian Shoesmith and Noorel Mecklai, "Religion as Commodity Images: Securing a Hindu Rashtra," in *Hindu Nationalism and Governance*, ed. John McGuire and Ian Copland. New Delhi: Oxford University Press, 2007.

45. "Film Industry Becomes Eligible for Bank Finance," *India Abroad Daily*, October 18, 2000, accessed April 3, 2007, http://www.indiaabroaddaily.com/2000/10/18/18filmfin.html.

46. A report in the *Financial Express* (2001) explained the norms for IDBI financing:

> The scheme says no two films should be the same and the investment would vary depending on the "treatment" of the story or concept and scale of production. Materials and technicians' cost should constitute about 55% of the capital outlay. Said IDBI executive director RS Agarwal, "The film should be comprehensively insured and a guarantee for the timely completion within the estimated cost of film should be provided by the applicant. The borrower should be a corporate entity, backed by established directors/producers having a satisfactory record. The quantum of assistance will be normally not less than Rs. 5 crore and not exceeding 50 percent of the film's cost. The promoter's contribution should be normally not less than 30 percent of the cost of the film. The period of loan should not be more than two years. The security towards the loan will be a lab letter, assignment of Intellectual Property Right of the proposed films as also existing rights on old films, hypothecation of movable assets, personal guarantee and receivables IPRs to be routed through TRA."

"IDBI Outlines Norms for Film-Financing," *Financial Express*, March 31, 2001, http://www.financialexpress.com/fe/daily/20010331/fc031005.html.

47. As a *Business Today* article explained:

> There is also talk of private equity money heading for Bollywood. However, Mahesh Chhabria, Co-head (Investment Banking), Enam Financial, believes that this will only happen when the industry boasts several companies that can deliver, not just one or two. "The issue of scalability is important. Apart from Yash Raj, K Sera Sera and Vishesh, there are not too many who are in a position to make four-to-six films each year," he explains. And while several companies have gone in for ipos since 2000 (Mukta and Adlabs are two), issues related to the way the companies are run abound. Chhabria admits that there is still some scepticism in finance and banking circles about companies in Bollywood that are listed.

Ahona Ghosh, E. Kumar Sharma, and Nitya Varadarajan, "The New New Bollywood," *Business Today*, October 23, 2005.

48. V. S. Aiyar, "Badshah in the Red," *India Today*, April 26, 1999. N. Kazmi, "Holier Than Thou," *Times of India*, November 10, 1996.

49. S. Raval and A. Chopra, "The Plot Thickens," *India Today*, January 22, 2001.

50. See Appadurai, "Spectral Housing"; Thomas Blom Hansen, *Wages of Violence: Naming and Identity in Postcolonial Bombay* (Princeton: Princeton University Press, 2001). Also see Ranjani Mazumdar's *Bombay Cinema* for a discussion of how these transitions inform representations of the city in Bombay cinema, and gangster films in particular.

51. There have been several critiques of the impact that such visions had on urban space. See, for example, J. S. Anjaria, "Street Hawkers and Public Space in Mumbai," *Economic and Political Weekly* 41, no. 21 (2006): 2140–2146. For an overview of urban planning as it played out in Bombay in postindependence India, see Gyan Prakash, *Mumbai Fables* (Princeton: Princeton University Press, 2010).

52. Fernandes, "The Politics of Forgetting"; Partha Chatterjee, "Are Indian Cities Becoming Bourgeois at Last?" in *The Politics of the Governed: Reflections on Popular Politics in Most of the World* (New York: Columbia University Press, 2004), 131–148; Darryl D'Monte, *Ripping the Fabric: The Decline of Mumbai and Its Mills* (New Delhi: Oxford University Press, 2002).

53. Mazumdar, *Bombay Cinema*, 114. Also, for a detailed consideration of how this notion of *safai* shaped filmmakers' subjectivities, see Ganti's discussion of gentrification. Ganti, *Producing Bollywood*, 77–118.

54. Ibid., 147.

55. See http://www.ficci.com/entertainment.htm.

56. Cheryl Bentsen, "Don't Call it Bollywood," *CIO Magazine*, December 1, 2000.

57. Sanjay Krishnan, "Narayana Murthy's 5-Pt Plan for Film Sector," *Rediff*, April 8, 2005, http://www.rediff.com/money/2005/apr/08murthy.htm.

58. Lili Tan, "Bollywood Gets Booed," *Asia Media*, April 11, 2003, http://www.asiamedia.ucla.edu/article.asp?parentid=9195; "Film Industry Told to Set Its House in Order," *Business Line*, March 15, 2003.

59. For an account of how previous moments of state intervention shaped the workings of the Bombay film industry, see Prasad, *Ideology of the Hindi Film*, and chapter 5 ("The Moment of Disaggregation") in particular.

60. Rajadhyaksha, "The 'Bollywoodization' of the Indian Cinema," 28.

61. Ibid.

62. Prasad, *Ideology of the Hindi Film*, 32.

63. Ibid., 33. The report was titled "Report of the Indian Film Industry's Mission to Europe and America."

64. See Paula Chakravartty for a discussion of telecommunications policy in postindependence India. "The Democratic Politics of Telecommunications Reform in India, 1947–1997" (Ph.D. dissertation, University of Wisconsin-Madison, 1999).

65. As Ganti notes, cinema has always played a critical part in "state discourses about development, nationhood, and modernity in post-independence India." In addition to the S. K. Patil Film Enquiry Committee, there have been a number of other commissions and inquiries, including the Sangeet Natak Akademi Film Seminar (1955), the Khosla Committee on Film Censorship (1968), the Symposium on Cinema in Developing Countries (1979), the Working Group on National Film Policy (1980), and most recently, the National Conference on Challenges before Indian Cinema (1998). Ganti, "Casting Culture," 48–49.

66. Ashish Rajadhyaksha and Paul Willemen, *The Encyclopedia of Indian Cinema* (New Delhi: Oxford University Press, 1994), 23–24.

67. Prasad, *Ideology of the Hindi Film*, 34.

68. "A Victim of Ad Hocism," *Filmfare* 27, no. 9, May 16–31, 1978.

69. "A Victim of Ad Hocism," 3.

70. Vandana Agarwal and Bonita Baruah, "FMs Have Always Made Budget Speeches Dil Se," *Times of India*, February 27, 2005.

71. Kaveree Bamzai and Sandeep Unnithan, "Corporatization of Bollywood: Show Business," *India Today*, February 24, 2003; Abhay Singh and Nabeel Mohideen, "*Krrish*, Bollywood Blockbuster, Pummels *Superman* in India," *Bloomberg News*, August 22, 2006. For a detailed account of the rise of the multiplex, see Adrian Athique and Douglas Hill, *The Multiplex in India: A Cultural Economy of Urban Leisure* (New York: Routledge, 2009).

72. "Corporatisation Will Kill the Soul of Filmmaking," *Business Line*, March 16, 2003, http://www.thehindubusinessline.in/2003/03/16/stories/2003031601660300.htm.

73. "Indian Entertainment Industry Focus 2010: From Dreams to Reality," report commissioned by the Confederation of Indian Industry (CII) and developed by KPMG Consulting, 45–46.

74. For news coverage of this moment of optimism, see: Ghosh, Sharma, and Varadarajan, "The New New Bollywood." In 2005 ten films grossed over Rs. 350 crore. Also see Kaveree Bamzai, "Hot, Hip, Huge: Bollywood's Firecracker Year," *India Today*, November 14, 2005.

75. See http://en.wikipedia.org/wiki/India_Brand_Equity_Foundation and http://www.ibef. org.

76. Aroon Purie, "Hype and Hardsell," *India Today*, February 13, 2006, 7.

77. Yudice, *The Expediency of Culture*, 38.

78. Shanti Kumar, *Gandhi Meets Primetime: Globalization and Nationalism in Indian Television* (Urbana: University of Illinois Press, 2006).

CHAPTER 2

1. *Luck by Chance*, DVD insert, 2009.

2. Lalitha Gopalan, *Cinema of Interruptions: Action Genres in Contemporary Indian Cinema* (London: British Film Institute, 2008), 71.

3. Caldwell, *Production Culture*.

4. Ibid., 235.

5. Rajadhyaksha, *Indian Cinema in the Time of Celluloid*, 19.

6. For overviews of family businesses in India, see Dwijendra Tripathi, *The Oxford History of Indian Business* (New Delhi: Oxford University Press, 2004); Harish Damodaran, *India's New Capitalists: Caste, Business, and Industry in a Modern Nation* (New York: Palgrave Macmillan, 2008). There is also a rich body of scholarship on kinship, vernacular capitalist practices, and market cultures in colonial and postcolonial India. Among others, see: Rajat Kanta Ray, *Industrialization in India: Growth and Conflict in the Private Corporate Sector, 1914–1947* (New Delhi: Oxford University Press, 1979); Chris Bayly, *Rulers, Townsmen, and Bazaars: North Indian Society in the Age of British Expansion, 1770–1870* (Cambridge: Cambridge University Press, 1983); Anand Yang, *Bazaar India: Peasants, Traders, Markets and the Colonial State in Gangetic Bihar* (Berkeley: University of California Press, 1998); Jain, *Gods in the Bazaar*.

7. Birla, *Stages of Capital*, 233.

8. Ibid., 6. Michael Curtin's analysis of the development of the Shaw Brothers studio in Hong Kong offers a particularly relevant comparative case. See Curtin, *Playing to the World's Biggest Audience*.

9. Caldwell, *Production Culture*, 96.

10. Ibid.

11. Amit Mitra, "Framing Indian Media's Progress," *Picklemag: Indian Entertainment Biz Guide*, March 2009, 4.

12. Ibid.

13. The prominent Bollywood companies listed on the stock exchange—Bombay Stock Exchange and the National Stock Exchange—include: Reliance Entertainment, UTV, Shree Ashtavinayak Cine Vision, Sahara One, PVR, INOX, Cinemax India, Studio 18, Mukta Arts, K Sera Sera, Pyramid Sahara, Pritish Nandy Communications, and Moser Baer. In addition, three companies are listed on the London Stock Exchange's Alternate Investment Market (AIM): Eros International, UTV, and Studio 18. Sources: *Pickle Magazine* (FICCI FRAMES 2009), company websites.

14. Jean Comaroff and John L. Comaroff, "Millennial Capitalism: First Thoughts on a Second Coming," in *Millennial Capitalism and the Culture of Neoliberalism* (Durham: Duke University Press, 2001), 20.

15. Prasad, *Ideology of the Hindi Film*, 49.

16. Archna Shukla and Sagar Malviya, "Business Majors Script New Plot for Bollywood," *Mint*, November 15, 2007.

17. Jason Overdorf, "Bigger than Bollywood," *Newsweek*, September 9, 2007, http://www.thedailybeast.com/newsweek/2007/09/09/bigger-than-bollywood.html.

18. Manjeet Kripalani and Ron Grover, "Bollywood," *Business Week*, December 2, 2002.

19. See http://www.ashtavinayakindia.com/aboutus/introduction.htm

20. Madhava Prasad, *Ideology of the Hindi Film*, 5.

21. Anupama Chopra, "Stumbling toward Bollywood," *New York Times*, March 22, 2009, http://www.nytimes.com/2009/03/22/movies/22chop.html.

22. Mazzarella, *Shoveling Smoke*, 222.

23. Amit Mitra, "Framing Indian Media's Progress," *Picklemag*, 6.

24. As Ravi Vasudevan observed, drawing our attention to firms like Sahara India Limited, the "porousness between corporate firms, apparently defined by transparent financial protocols and audit, and a world of illicit deals suggest the complications concealed by

contemporary discourse of financial probity and industrial regularity." Ravi Vasudevan, *The Melodramatic Public: Film Form and Spectatorship in Indian Cinema* (New York: Palgrave Mcmillan, 2011), 395.

25. Ganti, "Casting Culture."

26. S. K. Patil, ed., *Report of the Film Enquiry Committee* (New Delhi: Government of India Press, 1951), 64.

27. *Indian Motion Picture Almanac and Who's Who*, 1953, 238; cited in Erik Barnouw and S. Krishnaswamy, *Indian Film* (New Delhi: Oxford University Press, 1980), p. 121.

28. Brian Shoesmith, "Changing the Guard: The Transition from Studio-Based Film Production to Independent Production in Post-Colonial India," *Media History* 15, no. 4 (2009): 439–52.

29. Barnouw and Krishnaswamy, *Indian Film*, 117. For accounts of the development of studios in the film industries in South India, see: Swarnavel Eswaran Pillai, "Tamil Cinema and the Major Madras Studios (1940–57)," Ph.D. dissertation, University of Iowa, 2010; and S. V. Srinivas, "Making of a Peasant Industry: Telugu Cinema in the 1930s–1950s," *BioScope: South Asian Screen Studies* 1, no. 2 (2010): 169–88.

30. Mark Lorenzen and Florian Arun Taube, "Breakout from Bollywood? The Roles of Social Networks and Regulation in the Evolution of Indian Film Industry," *Journal of International Management* 14 (2008): 294; Surajeet Das Gupta, "How Bollywood Makes Money," *Rediff*, May 27, 2006, http://www.rediff.com/money/2006/may/27spec1.htm.

31. It is important to note here that box-office earnings do not necessarily serve as a good measure of a producer or production company's earnings. As I document in the next chapter, one of the major consequences of rapid expansion of the television and advertising sectors in Bombay has been the displacement of the box office as the primary and most critical site for profit. Product placement and merchandising deals, music rights, and cable and satellite television rights have emerged as key revenue streams for producers to recover their costs before the film is even released in theaters. Still, there is no denying that box-office performance does serve to establish a producer/production company's reputation, which in turn influences future negotiations for marketing, merchandising, and a range of media rights.

32. Their business plans in U.A.E. also include a joint venture with Dubai Infinity Holdings to build an YRF-themed amusement park that is slated to open in 2012. See http://www.yashrajfilms.com for more on this.

33. It is clear that large media corporations have been successful in reconfiguring distribution. I will address this in detail in chapter 4, where I take up the question of Bollywood's imagination and construction of an overseas territory.

34. Lorenzen and Taube, "Breakout from Bollywood?" 290.

35. Athique and Hill, *The Multiplex in India*.

36. Ibid., 50.

37. For complete details on K Sera Sera, particularly regarding its organizational and financial structure, see K Sera Sera Productions Limited, *Draft Red Herring Prospectus*, September 29, 2005, accessed January 2, 2011, http://*www.sebi.gov.in/dp/kseradraft.pdf*. Also see "From Hong Kong to Bollywood via K Sera Sera and Ram Gopal Varma," *Financial Express*, September 9, 2003, http://www.financialexpress.com/news/from-hong-kong-to-bollywood-via-k-sera-sera-&-ram-gopal-varma/88054.

38. Vasudevan, *The Melodramatic Public*, 395.

CHAPTER 3

1. "The New Marketing Mantra," *Business Today*, April 16, 2005, 134.
2. Ibid.
3. Ganti, "Casting Culture," 176.
4. MMS stands for Multimedia Messaging Service, and refers to the production and circulation of video clips using mobile phones.
5. "*Kaante* Revives Bollywood," *BBC News: World Edition*, January 6, 2003, http://news.bbc.co.uk/2/hi/entertainment/2632445.stm.
6. *Kaante* was released on December 20, 2002 and earned a total of $5,753,991, with $4,712,763 from overseas markets and $1,041,228 within India. Source: http://www.boxofficemojo.com.
7. See http://kaante.indiatimes.com/indexframe.html.
8. Ganti, *Producing Bollywood: Inside the Contemporary Hindi Film Industry* (Durham: Duke University Press, 2012), 132.
9. Ibid., 135.
10. Madhava Prasad, *Ideology of the Hindi Film*, 40.
11. Curtin, *Playing to the World's Biggest Audience*.
12. Caldwell, *Production Culture*, 346–47.
13. "Film Information," April 28, 2001, http://kaante.indiatimes.com/call29.html
14. "Complete Cinema," April 28, 2001, http://kaante.indiatimes.com/call28.html.
15. See http://kaante.indiatimes.com/callarticles.html for a collection of trade and press reports of the *mahurat*.
16. "Mumbai Newsline," April 20, 2001, http://kaante.indiatimes.com/call10.html.
17. In fact, the centrality of personal relationships is evident even in the case of a film like *Kaante*. One of the actors in the film, Kumar Gaurav, is related to Sanjay Dutt, who is considered an A-list star. Further, Kumar Gaurav is also related to Raju Patel, one of the producers of *Kaante*. *Kaante* was as much a "family" affair as a marker of "corporatized" Bollywood.
18. Sibabrata Das, "Bollywood Banks on Corporate Route to the Big League," *Indian Television*, March 21, 2006, http://www.indiantelevision.com/special/y2k6/film-finance.htm.
19. Kaajal Wallia, "Bollywood Spawns Film Marketing," *Times of India*, March 5, 2002, 3.
20. "Changing Face of Cinema," *Screen*, July 29, 2005, http://www.screenindia.com/fullstory.php?content_id=10858.
21. Nitin Govil, "Size Matters," *BioScope: South Asian Screen Studies* 1, no. 2 (2010): 107.
22. "Bollywood Producers Need Specialised Marcom Consultants," *Indian Television*, January 14, 2003, http://www.indiantelevision.com/special/y2k3/valuecreation3.htm.
23. Smita Sadanandan, "Back to films," *The Hindu*, June 14, 2004, http://www.hindu.com/mp/2004/06/14/stories/2004061402110100.htm.
24. Tsing, *Friction*, 57. And as we will see in the next chapter, Sanjay Gupta also staged a performance online as a way of conjuring a "global audience" for *Kaante*. For an interpretation of the *mahurat* as cine-magic, see Ganti, *Producing Bollywood*, 241–51.
25. "Need a Hit? It's All about Marketing and Communications," *Indian Television*, January 14, 2002, http://www.indiantelevision.com/special/y2k3/valuecreation.htm.
26. Archana Shukla, "Bollywood Gears Up with Filmi Marketing Formulas," *Economic Times*, September 27, 2003, http://articles.economictimes.indiatimes.com/2003-09-27/news/27550157_1_film-maker-film-marketing-ram-gopal-varma.

27. Working Group on Software for Doordarshan, Ministry of Information and Broadcasting, "An Indian Personality for Television," 1985, p. 160.

28. Shailaja Bajpai, "How Doordarshan Spends Rs. 133 Crores," *TV and Video World*, February 1985.

29. "Doordarshan's Winner: Manju Singh Makes Waves with 'Show Theme,'" *TV and Video World*, September 1984.

30. Vinod Nagdev, Atul Dev, and Iqbal Malik, "Doordarshan's Great Leap Forward," *TV and Video World*, September 1984; "Film Industry Demands More Revenue," *Business Standard*, April 25, 1985. Doordarshan began responding to film producers' demands, and would periodically increase payments for both song sequences and entire films. See, for example, "Sharp Hike in TV Film Rates," *Economic Times*, November 29, 1982.

31. Iqbal Malik, "TV Film Contracts: Cause for Concern," *Indian Express*, September 28, 1981; "Plan for Socially Relevant TV Films," *Free Press Journal*, May 28, 1982.

32. Ganti, "Casting Culture," 20.

33. Ali, "Thank You, DD," *Screen*, September 5, 1986, 6; "Serial Bazaar," *TV and Video World*, April 30, 1988.

34. V. Verma, "1986 Brings Hope for the Future," *Screen*, January 3, 1986, 1; also see Curtin, *Playing to the World's Biggest Audience*, for an elaboration of how "trajectories of creative migration" shape media industry dynamics.

35. Kumar, *Gandhi Meets Primetime*, 4.

36. Manjunath Pendakur and Jyotsna Kapur, "Think Globally, Program Locally: Privatization of Indian National Television," in *Democratizing Communication?Comparative Perspectives on Information and Power*, ed. Mashoed Bailie and Dwayne Winseck (Creskill, N.J.: Hampton Press, 1997), 195–218.

37. Jocelyn Cullity, "The Global Desi: Cultural Nationalism on MTV India," *Journal of Communication Inquiry* 26, no. 4 (2002): 414. Also see Vamsee Juluri, *Becoming a Global Audience: Longing and Belonging in Indian Music Television* (New York: Peter Lang, 2003).

38. The emergence of the video business and the issue of piracy were catalogued extensively in the trade press. See, for instance: Murli Santanam, "Video Biz: Now Is the Time," *TV and Video World*, September 1988, 62–65; Siraj Syed, "Video Pirates: Copyright Thieves," *TV and Video World*, June 1987, 74–79. The impact that the cable TV business had on the Bombay film industry also received a lot of news media attention. See, for instance: Satish Nandgaonkar, "Producers Fret as *In Mumbai* Gets Set to Beam Blockbusters," *Times of India*, February 2, 1996, A1.

39. See, for instance, Malcolm Gladwell, "The Coolhunt," *New Yorker*, March 17, 1997.

40. In addition to Jiggy George, the other music channel executives I spoke with include Paromita Vohra, Vikram Sathaye, Shashanka Ghosh, and Rajesh Devrai.

41. Ulka Bhadkamkar, "Networks at War Over Ratings of Hindi Film Songs," *Pioneer*, March 23, 1994.

42. As Tarun Tripathi, marketing manager at Yash Raj Films, recalled, "I wasn't here at the time, but yes, *Dilwale Dulhania Le Jayenge* was what started it. We released promotional trailers with different songs from the film, but we also did a 'making of DDLJ' show that got very high ratings. Even today, when I look at those ratings numbers, I am blown away."

43. Rajadhyaksha, *Indian Cinema in the Time of Celluloid*, 67.

44. Ibid.

45. Caldwell, *Production Culture*, 38.

46. Ibid., 47.
47. Mazzarella, *Shoveling Smoke*, 73.
48. Jain, *Gods in the Bazaar*, 34.
49. Ibid., 35.
50. See http://www.madisonindia.com/mate_case.htm#main for a list of case studies including compilations of film clips relating to the product placement.
51. Kajri Jain, "More than Meets the Eye: The Circulation of Images and the Embodiment of Value," *Contributions to Indian Sociology* 36, no. 1–2 (2002): 67.

CHAPTER 4

1. Nikhil Pahwa, "Rajshri.com Is a Multiplex with Unlimited Seats," *Paid Content*, November 10, 2006, http://paidcontent.org/tech/ rajshricom-is-a-multiplex-with-unlimited-seats-rajjat-a-barjatya-md-rajshri.
2. Rai, *Untimely Bollywood*.
3. Curtin, *Playing to the World's Biggest Audience*, 11.
4. Ravi Sundaram, "Beyond the Nationalist Panopticon: The Experience of Cyberpublics in India," in *Electronic Media and Technoculture*, ed. John Caldwell (New Brunswick: Rutgers University Press, 2000), 270–94.
5. Ibid., 275.
6. Ibid., 276.
7. Report on the History of NIC, prepared by the NIC for the National Archives of India. A member of the "corporate group" of Indiatimes.com gave me a copy of this report. According to this report, the NIC was set up in 1975–76 with the following mandate: "provide informatics services to various user agencies in Government; play a promotional role in creating appropriate decision-support information systems in Government; act as a focal point for developing, managing and operating information system in Government; act as a focal point for development of methodologies for designing and implementing national information systems and data management techniques; act as a focal point for maintaining inventories of primary data and computer-based systems for data collection and dissemination; train users in information systems, data management and computing techniques" (2)..
8. Sundaram, "Beyond the Nationalist Panopticon," 277. Also, as described in the report cited above, "the organizational set up of NIC encompasses its Headquarters at New Delhi, State Units in all the 28 State capitals and 7 Union Territory Headquarters and District Centres in almost all the Districts of India. In North-Eastern states and in Jammu & Kashmir, I.T. infrastructure has been strengthened by way of setting up of Community Information Centres (CICs) at sub-district/block levels."
9. Gyanesh Kudaisya, "India's New Mantra: The Internet," *Current History*, April 2001, 162.
10. Ibid.
11. "Internet Users Take Pot Shots at VSNL," *Indian Express*, December 8, 1996. Also see Indranil Ghosh, "Spreading the Net," *Business India*, September 7–20, 1998.
12. "Licenses for Private Internet Providers before Nov 7," *Deccan Herald*, November 2, 1998.
13. Manoj Gairola, "Panel Clears Norms for Private Gateways," *Economic Times*, April 13, 1999. For a detailed discussion of policy changes concerning telecommunications and the Internet, see Stephen McDowell and Karthik Pashupati, "India's Internet Policies: Ownership, Control, and Purposes," in *Internet in Asia*, ed. Sankaran Ramanathan and Jorg Becker (Singapore: Asian Media Information and Communication Center, 1999), 53–70.

14. Sundaram, "Beyond the Nationalist Panopticon," 282.
15. "India: Internet Usage Stats and Telecommunications Market Report," Miniwatts Marketing Group, last modified April 9, 2011, http://www.internetworldstats.com/asia/in.htm.
16. Avtar Singh, "Is Anyone Not Setting Up a Dotcom?" *Man's World*, May 2000, 92.
17. Chakravartty, "The Democratic Politics of Telecommunications Reform in India," 77.
18. Sam Pitroda, "An Experiment at Nation-Building," *Silicon India*, September 2000.
19. Ibid.
20. Sam Pitroda, "Taking Silicon Valley Culture to India," *Silicon India*, April 2000.
21. "Licenses for Private Internet Providers," *Deccan Herald,* November 2, 1998.
22. Pallab Datta, "@India.com: The Frontiers of the New Economy," *India West* 25, no. 17, February 25, 2000.
23. There was a profusion of articles in print media both in India and the diaspora (in publications such as *India Abroad, Little India, India West,* and *Silicon India*) that focused on the new Information Economy as a golden opportunity for India to establish itself as a regional and global power. Titles like "Riding the Net Train in India: Internet Development Evokes Global Aspirations in India" (Madanmohan Rao, *Little India,* February 1, 1998) were typical during the late 1990s and early years of this century.
24. Vidya Viswanathan, "Masters of the Web," *Business World,* May 24, 1999.
25. Vidya Viswanathan, "India Internet World," *Business World,* September 27, 1999.
26. Ibid.
27. Rajiq Dossani and Martin Kenney, "Creating an Environment for Venture Capital in India," *World Development* 30, no. 2 (2002): 227–53.
28. Carol Upadhya, "A New Transnational Capitalist Class? Capital Flows, Business Networks and Entrepreneurs in the Indian Software Industry," *Economic and Political Weekly* 39, no. 48 (2004): 5142.
29. Arvind Padmanabhan, "Of Incubators, Angel Investors, and Venture Capitalists," *India Abroad,* April 14, 2000. Also see "Start-Up Fever in India," *Silicon India,* February 2000.
30. "Homeward Bound," *Silicon India,* June 2000. For a more detailed analysis of how ethnic networks in Silicon Valley and "cross-border" alliances between Silicon Valley and cities like Bangalore shaped the development of a transnational "Indian" IT sector, see Anna Lee Saxenian's article, "Silicon Valley's New Immigrant Entrepreneurs," *California Public Policy Institute,* 1999.
31. E. Kumar Sharma, "The Truth behind Sify's Mega-Deal," *Business Today,* February 7, 2000, 124–27.
32. Ibid.
33. Arvind Padmanabhan, "Surfing for Success," *India Abroad,* April 14, 2000.
34. Radhika Dhawan, "Dotcom Survivors," *Business World,* May 14, 2001.
35. Madhavi Mallapragada, "Home, Homeland, Homepage: The Web, Transnationalism, and Indian-American Identities." Ph.D. dissertation, University of Wisconsin-Madison, 2003.
36. Arun Shankar, "Dot.coms: Will They Make It?" *Business India,* November 11–24, 2002.
37. Ibid.
38. Anshuman Daga, "Dotcom Firm Plays Patriotic Card," *New India Times,* August 24, 2001.
39. "*Filmfare* Is Now in Cyberspace," *Times of India,* October 6, 1996.
40. Consider the case of Pacific Century Cyberworks (PCCW), an ambitious pan-Asian broadband initiative launched by Hong Kong-based media baron Richard Li.

Documenting Li's move from Star TV into the dot-com economy via a detour in the real estate business, Curtin observes that the "most fatal flaw in PCCW's strategy" was Li's failure to recognize the importance of developing and delivering compelling content. Curtin, *Playing to the World's Biggest Audience*, 239.

41. Nithya Subramanian and Ratna Bhushan, "Bollywood Logs On to the Net," *Business Line*, August 5, 2003.

42. Caldwell, *Production Culture*, 346.

43. Rina Chandran, "CII to Host Film Marketing Summit," *Business Line,* January 10, 2003.

44. Sudipto Dey, "Bollywood Goes to the Classroom," *Economic Times*, November 10, 2003. The "international experts" at this conference included director Shekhar Kapur, Paula Silver (marketing strategist for *My Big Fat Greek Wedding*), William Pfeiffer (CEO, Celestial Pictures), Ira Dutchman (CEO, Emerging Pictures), Nicolas Chartier (Arclight Films, head of U.S. office), Tony Stafford (20th Century Fox), Christina Marouda (Director, Indian Film Festival of Los Angeles), and Nadia Dresti (Director, Locarno International Film Festival).

45. Vanita Kohli, "Look, Here's a Booming Market," *Business World*, February 7–21, 1999.

46. Prajjal Saha, "Online Movie Trailers Gain Prominence," *Agency Faqs*, May 25, 2004.

47. Tejaswini Ganti, *Bollywood: A Guidebook to Popular Hindi Cinema* (New York: Routledge, 2004).

48. The other common distribution arrangements include the Minimum Guarantee and the Commission models. In a minimum guarantee arrangement, the distributor acquires rights by paying a minimum guarantee to the producer. The excess of distributor revenues over the minimum guarantee, print and publicity costs, as well as the distributor's commission (referred to as "overflow" in the industry), is shared with the producer in a predetermined ratio. This ratio is determined, of course, by a number of factors, including the stars in the film, genre, the distributor's assumptions regarding the film's appeal among different audience segments, and crucially, the history of interpersonal relations between the producer and distributor. In the Commission model, the distributor retains a commission on the total amount collected from the exhibitor and remits the rest to the producer. In this case, the distributor does not bear any risk arising from box-office collections.

49. The other film that is often included in this narrative is Rajshri Pictures's *Hum Aapke Hain Kaun* (1994).

50. Kohli, "Look, Here's a Booming Market."

51. Ibid. Also see the "about us" section of http://www.yashrajfilms.com.

52. Rajeev Masand, "Bollywood Inc?" *Indian Express*, April 28, 2002.

53. P. David Marshall, "The New Intertextual Commodity," in *The New Media Book*, ed. Dan Harries (London: BFI, 2002), 80.

54. Jenkins, *Convergence Culture*.

55. Manuel Castells, "The Space of Flows," in *The Rise of Network Society* (Berkeley: University of California Press, 1996), 376–428.

56. Ibid., 390. Also see Anna Lee Saxenian, *Regional Advantage: Culture and Competition in Silicon Valley and Route 128* (Cambridge: Harvard University Press, 1996).

57. A. J. Scott, *On Hollywood: The Place, the Industry* (Princeton: Princeton University Press, 2005), 6–7.

58. Ibid., 7.

59. Curtin, 2007, 14.

60. Ibid.

61. Content-sharing across media platforms is, in fact, a core strategy of the BCCL group. Although the various "channels" on indiatimes.com have their own content and editorial staff, often, news content on the website is derived from BCCL's print media properties. Other Internet portals with no print affiliations pay $3,000–5,000 every month for content. See Rajeev Dubey, "Family Support," *Business World*, June 3, 2002.

62. Curtin, 2007, 14.

63. For more details about the made-for-mobile trailer, see Sunaya Nadkarni's article, "Fardeen Koena Caught on MMS," *IBNLive*, November 8, 2005, http://ibnlive.in.com/news/fardeen-koena-caught-on-mms/809-8.html. MMS—Multimedia Messaging Service.

64. Kumar, *Gandhi Meets Primetime*, 14–15.

65. Ibid., 15.

66. Ibid.

CHAPTER 5

1. Parag Khanna, "Bollystan—The Global India," *Globalist*, December 3, 2004, http://www.theglobalist.com/printStoryId.aspx?StoryId=4279.

2. Ibid.

3. Shalini Shankar, *Desi Land: Teen Culture, Class, and Success in Silicon Valley* (Durham: Duke University Press, 2008), 4.

4. Amardeep Singh, " 'Names Can Wait': The Misnaming of the South Asian Diaspora in Theory and Practice," *South Asian Review* 28, no. 1 (2007): 15.

5. See Stuart Hall, "Cultural Identity and Diaspora," in *Identity: Community, Culture, Difference*, ed. Jonathan Rutherford (London: Lawrence & Wishart, 1990), 223–237; Arjun Appadurai, "Disjuncture and Difference in the Global Cultural Economy," *Public Culture* 2, no. 2 (Spring1990): 1–24.

6. Marie Gillespie, *Television, Ethnicity, and Cultural Change* (London: Routledge, 1995); Sunaina Maira, *Desis in the House: Indian American Youth Culture in New York City* (Philadelphia: Temple University Press, 2002); Shankar, *Desi Land*.

7. Shankar, *Desi Land*, 6.

8. As Lisa Lowe carefully recounts in *Immigrant Acts: On Asian American Cultural Politics* (Durham: Duke University Press, 1996), migration from India to the United States can be traced to the early 1900s, but the most significant wave of migration can be dated to 1965 following the Immigration Act of 1965, often referred to as the Hart-Cellar Act. Until 1965, the Barred Zone Act of 1917 and the Asian Exclusion Act of 1924 did not allow Asians to migrate to the United States. Before 1965, the U.S. immigration system limited foreign entry by mandating extremely small quotas according to national origin. In 1965, these laws were changed to permit "occupational migration," and designed primarily to address the shortage of highly educated and skilled labor in the American economy. Thus, the first wave of migration from India and other South Asian countries was comprised of highly educated professionals and their families. For a more detailed account of migration from South Asia to the United States, see, among others, Vijay Prashad, *The Karma of Brown Folk* (Minneapolis: University of Minnesota Press, 2001).

9. The draw that these weekend screenings had also stemmed from difficulties involved in maintaining connections with India. Not only was air travel limited and expensive, but the only means of contact for most families was a monthly phone call and letter writing. I address questions pertaining to viewing practices and reception of films in the diaspora in another essay. See Aswin Punathambekar, "Bollywood in the Indian-American Diaspora:

Mediating a Transitive Logic of Cultural Citizenship," *International Journal of Cultural Studies* 8, no. 2 (2005): 151–75.

10. Maira, *Desis in the House*; also see Shilpa Dave, LeiLani Nishime, and Tasha G. Oren, ed., *East Main Street: Asian American Popular Culture* (New York: NYU Press, 2005).

11. Jigna Desai, *Beyond Bollywood: The Cultural Politics of South Asian Diasporic Film* (New York: Routledge, 2004), 42.

12. For example, "Rang Hi Rang, Zaidi Ke Sang" was a highly popular radio program that covered most of the West Coast of the United States. Launched in 1977 and hosted by Shamim Zaidi, the program aired on KMAX for eighteen years before migrating to KYMS in 1995 (both KMAX and KYMS being Bay Area radio stations).

13. Penny Pagano, "FCC OK's Plan to Let Host of TV Stations on Air," *Los Angeles Times*, September 10, 1980, A7.

14. "The Indian Experience on US TV," *TV and Video World*, December 1987, 23.

15. Sujata Moorti, "Uses of the Diaspora: Indian Popular Culture and the NRI Dilemma," *South Asian Popular Culture* 3, no. 1 (2005): 49.

16. For a detailed consideration of why Tamil cinema has not focused attention on diasporic life and culture, see Velayutham, "The Diaspora and the Global Circulation of Tamil Cinema." Further, Chennai and Hyderabad's influence needs to be understood beyond the issue of capitalizing on diasporic audiences. For an analysis of Hyderabad's Ramoji Film City and its global reach, see Kumar, *Mapping Tollywood*. As major hubs of information and technology industries, these cities are also key nodes for a range of postproduction processes.

17. Divya C. McMillin, "The Global Face of Indian Television," in *Reorienting Global Communication: Indian and Chinese Media Beyond Borders*, ed. Michael Curtin and Hemant Shah (Urbana: University of Illinois Press, 2010), 118–38.

18. Mayer, Banks, and Caldwell, ed., *Production Studies*.

19. Suman Guha Mozumder, "Desi Television Comes Alive," *India Abroad*, January 7, 2005.

20. Deborah Sontag, "I Want My Hyphenated-Identity MTV," *New York Times*, June 19, 2005.

21. Arun Venugopal, "Obit, MTV-Desi," *SAJAforum* (blog), February 18, 2007, http://www.sajaforum.org/2007/02/obit_mtv_desi.html.

22. Nellie Andreeva, "Indian-Themed Comedies a New TV Trend," *Holly-wood Reporter,* January 31, 2010, http://www.hollywoodreporter.com/news/indian-themed-comedies-new-tv-20131.

23. Quoted in Jignya Sheth, "Desi Making Waves," *ABCD Lady*, July 2005, http://www.abcdlady.com/2005-07/art5.php.

24. Lowe, *Immigrant Acts*, 8.

25. For a comprehensive account of the politics of creating "Latino/a" consumers, see Arlene Davila, *Latinos Inc.: The Making and Marketing of a People* (Berkeley: University of California Press, 2000).

26. Barbara Kiviat, "Chasing Desi Dollars," *Time Magazine*, July 6, 2005, http://www.time.com/time/magazine/article/0,9171,1079504,00.html.

27. South Asian American Policy and Research Institute, *Making Data Count: South Asian Americans in the 2000 Census with Focus on Illinois*, 2005, 2. http://saapri.org/research.html.

28. Maira, *Desis in the House*, 10. Further, while it is true that of those who migrated from India to the United States between 1965 and 1977, 83 percent held advanced degrees, it is also important to note the shift in this pattern during the late 1980s. As Vijay

Prashad notes, "of the Indians who migrated to the U.S. between 1987 and 1990, a fifth had no high school education, a tenth remain unemployed and a fifth live in poverty." Vijay Prashad, "Dusra Hindustan," *Seminar*, no. 538 (2004), http://www.india-seminar.com/2004/538/538%20vijay%20prashad.htm.

29. Kumar, *Gandhi Meets Primetime*.

30. Rajinder Kumar Dudrah, "Zee TV-Europe and the Construction of a Pan-European South Asian Identity," *Contemporary South Asia* 11, no. 2 (2002): 169.

31. Maira, *Desis in the House*, 55.

32. Anandam Kavoori and Christina A. Joseph, "Bollyculture: Ethnography of Identity, Media and Performance," *Global Media and Communication* 7, no. 1 (2011): 30.

33. For a detailed consideration of the commodification of Indian culture in America, see Sunaina Maira, "Henna and Hip-Hop: The Politics of Cultural Production and the Work of Cultural Studies," *Journal of Asian American Studies* 3, no. 3 (October 2000): 329–69, and "Temporary Tattoos: Indo-Chic Fantasies and Late Capitalist Orientalism," *Meridians* 3, no. 1 (2002): 134–60.

34. Hamid Naficy, *The Making of Exile Cultures: Iranian Television in Los Angeles* (Minneapolis: University of Minnesota Press, 1993), 144.

35. Tsing, *Friction*, 57.

36. Nandini Raghavendra, "Bollywood, US Body to Counter Piracy," *Economic Times*, March 19, 2010, http://articles.economictimes.indiatimes.com/2010-03-19/news/28491589_1_counterfeiting-and-piracy-film-industry-ficci-frames.

CONCLUSION

1. Nitin Govil, "Thinking Nationally," in *Media Industries*, ed. Holt and Perren, 133.

2. Saskia Sassen, "Locating Cities on Global Circuits," in *Global Networks, Linked Cities*, ed. Saskia Sassen (New York: Routledge, 2002), 1–38; Michael Curtin, "Thinking Globally." S. V. Srinivas's brilliant analysis of the circulation and reception of Hong Kong films in the state of Andhra Pradesh speaks to the importance of looking beyond the "national" and examining regional and/or translocal media circuits. S. V. Srinivas, "Hong Kong Action Film in the Indian B Circuit," *Inter-Asia Cultural Studies* 4, no. 1 (2003): 40–62.

3. Morley and Robins, *Spaces of Identity*, 6.

4. Ibid., 31.

5. David Harvey, *The Condition of Postmodernity: An Enquiry into the Origins of Cultural Change* (Malden, Mass. Blackwell, 1991).

6. Birla, *Stages of Capital*, 10.

7. Hari Kunzru, *Transmission* (New York: Penguin, 2004).

8. Personal interview, October 15, 2005.

9. Sundaram, *Pirate Modernity*, 97.

10. Brian Larkin, "Degrading Images, Distorted Sounds: Nigerian Video and the Infrastructure of Piracy," *Public Culture* 16, no. 2 (Spring 2004): 297.

11. VSNL was incorporated in 1986 as a public sector organization providing a range of communication services. In 2002, the Indian government privatized VSNL. The privately held Tata Group now holds a controlling stake in VSNL.

12. The moderator of the group informed me that over the last two years, over 50 percent of new subscribers have been non-Indians. A look at the conversations in the newsgroups indicates, however, that it is fans of Indian origin who participate the most. Non-Indian fans are lurkers for the most part and have yet to assert their presence in the group.

13. S. V. Srinivas, "Devotion and Defiance in Fan Activity," in *Making Meaning in Indian Cinema*, ed. Vasudevan, 305. Sara Dickey provides the only other sustained analysis of fan activity surrounding cinema. Dickey locates fan activity at the intersection of the formal realm of politics and civil social activity (charity work, blood donation campaigns, and other "social services"). Building on work that examines relationships between the construction of stardom and the politics of mobilization, Dickey provides a very useful ethnographic account of this aspect of fan activity in Tamilnadu. However, she ignores the possibility of fan activity that might not necessarily be "public" in the sense of there being a neighborhood fan association that meets at street corners, at tea shops, or outside cinema halls. Indeed, her analysis circumscribes fan activity in Tamilnadu as that defined by working-class (often lower caste) male youth in visible, public spaces. See Sara Dickey, *Cinema and the Urban Poor in South India* (Cambridge: Cambridge University Press, 1993).

14. S. V. Srinivas, "Film Culture: Politics and Industry," *Seminar*, no. 525 (2003), http://www.india-seminar.com/2003/525/525%20s.v.%20srinivas.htm.

15. Ibid.

16. Ibid.

17. Ibid.

18. Ashish Rajadhyaksha, "Viewership and Democracy in the Cinema," in *Making Meaning in Indian Cinema*, ed. Vasudevan, 267–96.

19. For a discussion of how the "fan" is constructed by film narratives, see Ratheesh Radhakrishnan, "Looking at Mohanlal: Spectatorial Ordering and the Emergence of the 'Fan' in Malayalam Cinema," *Deep Focus* (July–December 2002): 29–38.

20. A detailed exploration is beyond the scope of this chapter, but we must also note that the emergence of the multiplex as the preeminent mode of exhibition in urban India since the early 2000s further complicates this notion of "spectatorial rights."

21. Lawrence Liang, "Cinematic Citizenship and the Illegal City," *Inter-Asia Cultural Studies* 6, no. 3 (2005): 371.

22. S. V. Srinivas, "Devotion and Defiance in Fan Activity," 314.

23. The term "rasika," derived from an aesthetic theory (*rasa*) of performance, connotes a highly developed sense of appreciation of various "high art" forms. Rasika can be roughly translated as "connoisseur."

24. Chatterjee, *The Politics of the Governed*, 38.

25. Ibid., 47.

26. Ibid., 40.

27. Ibid.

28. T. S. Subramanian, "Another Actor in Politics," *Frontline*, October 7, 2005.

29. S. V. Srinivas, "Devotion and Defiance in Fan Activity." Kamma is a powerful caste group in the southern states of Andhra Pradesh and Tamilnadu.

30. Liang, "Cinematic Citizenship and the Illegal City," 380.

Agarwal, Vandana, and Bonita Baruah. "FMs Have Always Made Budget Speeches Dil Se." *Times of India*, February 27, 2005.

Aiyar, V. Shankar. "Badshah in the Red." *India Today*, April 26, 1999.

Ali. "Thank You, DD." *Screen*, September 5, 1986.

Alter, A. A Passage to Hollywood," *Wall Street Journal*, February 6, 2009.

Andreeva, Nellie. "Indian-Themed Comedies a New TV Trend." *Hollywood Reporter*, January 31, 2010. http://www.hollywoodreporter.com/news/indian-themed-comedies-new-tv-20131.

Anjaria, Jonathan Shapiro. "Street Hawkers and Public Space in Mumbai." *Economic and Political Weekly* 41, no. 21 (2006): 2140–2146.

Appadurai, Arjun. "Disjuncture and Difference in the Global Cultural Economy." *Public Culture* 2, no. 2 (Spring 1990): 1–24.

———. "Spectral Housing and Urban Cleansing: Notes in Millennial Mumbai." *Public Culture* 12, no. 3 (2000): 627–51.

Athique, Adrian, and Douglas Hill. *The Multiplex in India: A Cultural Economy of Urban Leisure*. New York: Routledge, 2009.

Awasthy, G. C. *Broadcasting in India*. New York: Allied Publishers, 1965.

Bajpai, Shailaja. "How Doordarshan Spends Rs. 133 Crores." *TV and Video World*, February 1985.

Bamzai, Kaveree. "Hot, Hip, Huge: Bollywood's Firecracker Year," *India Today*, November 14, 2005.

Bamzai, Kaveree, and Sandeep Unnithan. "Corporatization of Bollywood: Show Business." *India Today*, February 24, 2003.

Barnouw, Erik, and S. Krishnaswamy. *Indian Film*. New Delhi: Oxford University Press, 1980.

Bayly, Chris. *Rulers, Townsmen, and Bazaars: North Indian Society in the Age of British Expansion, 1770–1870*. Cambridge: Cambridge University Press, 1983.

BBC News: World Edition. "*Kaante* Revives Bollywood." January 6, 2003. http://news.bbc.co.uk/2/hi/entertainment/2632445.stm.

Bentsen, Cheryl. "Don't Call It Bollywood." *CIO Magazine*, December 1, 2000.

Bhadkamkar, Ulka. "Networks at War over Ratings of Hindi Film Songs." *Pioneer*, March 23, 1994.

Birla, Ritu. *Stages of Capital: Law, Culture, and Market Governance in Late Colonial India*. Durham: Duke University Press, 2009.

Business Line. "Corporatisation Will Kill the Soul of Filmmaking." March 16, 2003. http://www.thehindubusinessline.in/2003/03/16/stories/2003031601660300.htm.

———. "Film Accorded Industry Status." October 19, 2000. http://www.indiaserver.com/businessline/2000/10/19/stories/141918re.htm.

———. "Film Industry Told to Set Its House in Order." March 15, 2003.

———. "Sops Set Film Industry on a Roll." March 2, 2000.

Business Standard. "Film Industry Demands More Revenue." April 25, 1985.

Business Today. "The New Marketing Mantra." April 16, 2005.

Caldwell, John. *Production Culture: Industrial Reflexivity and Critical Practice in Film and Television.* Durham: Duke University Press, 2008.

Castells, Manuel. *The Rise of Network Society.* Berkeley: University of California Press, 1996.

Chakravartty, Paula. "The Democratic Politics of Telecommunications Reform in India, 1947–1997." Ph.D. dissertation, University of Wisconsin-Madison, 1999.

Chakravarty, Sumita S. *National Identity in Indian Popular Cinema, 1947–1987.* Austin: University of Texas Press, 1993.

Chandran, Rina. "CII to Host Film Marketing Summit." *Business Line,* January 10, 2003.

Chatterjee, Partha. *The Politics of the Governed: Reflections on Popular Politics in Most of the World.* New York: Columbia University Press, 2004.

Chopra, Anupama. "Stumbling toward Bollywood." *New York Times,* March 22, 2009. http://www.nytimes.com/2009/03/22/movies/22chop.html.

Comaroff, Jean, and John L. Comaroff. *Millennial Capitalism and the Culture of Neoliberalism.* Durham: Duke University Press, 2001.

Cullity, Jocelyn. "The Global Desi: Cultural Nationalism on MTV India," *Journal of Communication Inquiry* 26, no. 4 (2002): 408–25.

Curtin, Michael. "Media Capital: Towards the Study of Spatial Flows." *International Journal of Cultural Studies* 6, no. 2 (2003): 202–28.

———. *Playing to the World's Biggest Audience: The Globalization of Chinese Film and TV.* Berkeley: University of California Press, 2007.

———. "Thinking Globally: From Media Imperialism to Media Capital." In *Media Industries: History, Theory, and Method,* edited by Jennifer Holt and Alisa Perren, 108–19. Malden, Mass.: Wiley-Blackwell, 2009.

Daga, Anshuman. "Dotcom Firm Plays Patriotic Card." *New India Times,* August 24, 2001.

Damodaran, Harish. *India's New Capitalists: Caste, Business, and Industry in a Modern Nation.* New York: Palgrave Macmillan, 2008.

Das, Sibabrata. "Bollywood Banks on Corporate Route to the Big League." *Indian Television,* March 21, 2006. http://www.indiantelevision.com/special/y2k6/film-finance.htm.

Das Gupta, Surajeet. "How Bollywood Makes Money." *Rediff,* May 27, 2006. http://www.rediff.com/money/2006/may/27spec1.htm.

Datta, Pallab. "@India.com: The Frontiers of the New Economy." *India West* 25, no. 17, February 25, 2000.

Dave, Shilpa, LeiLani Nishime, and Tasha G. Oren, ed. *East Main Street: Asian American Popular Culture.* New York: NYU Press, 2005.

Davila, Arlene. *Latinos Inc.: The Making and Marketing of a People.* Berkeley: University of California Press, 2000.

Deccan Herald. "Licenses for Private Internet Providers before Nov 7." November 2, 1998.

Desai, Jigna. *Beyond Bollywood: The Cultural Politics of South Asian Diasporic Film.* New York: Routledge, 2004.

Dey, Sudipto. "Bollywood Goes to the Classroom." *Economic Times,* November 10, 2003.

Dhawan, Radhika. "Dotcom Survivors." *Business World,* May 14, 2001.

Dickey, Sara. *Cinema and the Urban Poor in South India.* Cambridge: Cambridge University Press, 1993.

D'Monte, Darryl. *Ripping the Fabric: The Decline of Mumbai and Its Mills*. New Delhi: Oxford University Press, 2002.

Dossani, Rajiq, and Martin Kenney. "Creating an Environment for Venture Capital in India." *World Development* 30, no. 2 (2002): 227–53.

Dubey, Rajeev. "Family Support." *Business World*, June 3, 2002.

Dudrah, Rajinder Kumar. "Zee TV-Europe and the Construction of a Pan-European South Asian Identity," *Contemporary South Asia* 11, no. 2 (2002): 163–81.

Dutt, Srikant. "India and the Overseas Indians." *India Quarterly* 36 (1980): 307–35.

Dwyer, Rachel, and Divya Patel. *Cinema India: The Visual Culture of Hindi Film*. New Delhi: Oxford University Press, 2002.

Economic Times, The. "Sharp Hike in TV Film Rates." November 29, 1982.

Fernandes, Leela. "The Politics of Forgetting: Class Politics, State Power, and the Restructuring of Urban Space in India." *Urban Studies* 41, no. 12 (2004): 2415–30.

Financial Express, The. "From Hong Kong to Bollywood via K Sera Sera and Ram Gopal Varma." September 9, 2003. http://www.financialexpress.com/news/from-hong-kong-to-bollywood-via-k-sera-sera-&-ram-gopal-varma/88054.

———. "IDBI Outlines Norms for Film-Financing." March 31, 2001. http://www.financialexpress.com/fe/daily/20010331/fc031005.html.

Free Press Journal. "Plan for Socially Relevant TV Films." May 28, 1982.

Gairola, Manoj. "Panel Clears Norms for Private Gateways." *Economic Times*, April 13, 1999.

Ganti, Tejaswini. *Producing Bollywood: Inside the Contemporary Hindi Film Industry*. Durham: Duke University Press, 2012.

———. *Bollywood: A Guidebook to Popular Hindi Cinema*. New York: Routledge, 2004.

———. "Casting Culture: The Social Life of Hindi Film Production in Contemporary India." Ph.D. dissertation, New York University, 2000.

Ghosh, Ahona, E. Kumar Sharma, and Nitya Varadarajan. "The New New Bollywood." *Business Today*, October 23, 2005.

Ghosh, Amitav. "The Diaspora in Indian Culture." *Public Culture* 2, no. 1 (1989): 73–78.

Ghosh, Indranil. "Spreading the Net." *Business India*, September 7–20, 1998.

Gillespie, Marie. *Television, Ethnicity, and Cultural Change*. London: Routledge, 1995.

Gladwell, Malcolm. "The Coolhunt." *New Yorker*, March 17, 1997.

Gopalan, Lalitha. *Cinema of Interruptions: Action Genres in Contemporary Indian Cinema*. London: British Film Institute, 2008.

Gopinath, Gayatri. *Impossible Desires: Queer Diasporas and South Asian Public Cultures*. Durham: Duke University Press, 2005.

Goswami, Manu. *Producing India: From Colonial Economy to National Space*. Chicago: University of Chicago Press, 2004.

Govil, Nitin. "Size Matters," *BioScope: South Asian Screen Studies* 1, no. 2 (2010): 105–09.

———. "Something to Declare: Trading Culture, Trafficking Hollywood and Textual Travel." Ph.D. dissertation, New York University, 2005.

Hall, Stuart. "Cultural Identity and Diaspora." In *Identity: Community, Culture, Difference*, edited by Jonathan Rutherford, 223–237. London: Lawrence & Wishart, 1990.

Hansen, Thomas Blom. *Wages of Violence: Naming and Identity in Postcolonial Bombay*. Princeton: Princeton University Press, 2001.

Harvey, David. *The Condition of Postmodernity: An Enquiry Into the Origins of Cultural Change*. Malden, Mass.: Blackwell, 1991.

Hilmes, Michele. *Hollywood and Broadcasting: From Radio to Cable*. Urbana: University of Illinois Press, 1990.

Hindu, The. "Compulsory Study of Music." September 29, 1957.

———. "Focus, Please (Indian Movies)." September 23, 1998.

———. "Vividh Bharati: New Programme over All India Radio." September 29, 1957.

Holt, Jennifer. *Empires of Entertainment: Media Industries and the Politics of Deregulation, 1980–1996*. New Brunswick: Rutgers University Press, 2011.

Holt, Jennifer, and Alisa Perren, ed. *Media Industries: History, Theory, and Method*. Malden, Mass.: Wiley-Blackwell, 2009.

India Abroad Daily. "Film Industry Becomes Eligible for Bank Finance." October 18, 2000. Accessed March 4, 2006. http://www.indiaabroaddaily.com/2000/10/18/18filmfin.html.

India Brand Equity Foundation. "India Knowledge Centre." Accessed September 4, 2010. http://www.ibef.org.

"Indian Entertainment Industry Focus 2010: From Dreams to Reality," report commissioned by the Confederation of Indian Industry (CII) and developed by KPMG Consulting.

Indian Express, The. "Finally an Industry." May 12, 1998. http://www.expressindia.com/ie/daily/19980512/13250064.html.

———. "Internet Users Take Pot Shots at VSNL." December 8, 1996. Accessed via http://www.cscsarchive.org, October 18, 2006.

Indian Television. "Bollywood Producers Need Specialised Marcom Consultants." January 14, 2003. http://www.indiantelevision.com/special/y2k3/valuecreation3.htm.

———. "Need a Hit? It's All about Marketing and Communications." January 14, 2002. http://www.indiantelevision.com/special/y2k3/valuecreation.htm.

Jain, Kajri. *Gods in the Bazaar: The Economies of Indian Calendar Art*. Durham: Duke University Press, 2007.

———. "More than Meets the Eye: The Circulation of Images and the Embodiment of Value." *Contributions to Indian Sociology* 36, no. 1–2 (2002): 33–70.

Jenkins, Henry. *Convergence Culture: Where Old and New Media Collide*. New York: NYU Press, 2006.

———. "Why Mitt Romney Won't Debate a Snowman." In *Satire TV: Politics and Comedy in the Post-Network Era*, edited by Jonathan Gray, Jeffrey P. Jones, and Ethan Thompson, 187–212. New York: NYU Press, 2009.

Juluri, Vamsee. *Becoming a Global Audience: Longing and Belonging in Indian Music Television*. New York: Peter Lang, 2003.

Kaur, Naunidhi. "The Dreams of a Diaspora." *Frontline* 20, no. 2, January, 13-21, 2003. http://www.frontlineonnet.com/fl2002/stories/20030131008112700.htm.

Kavoori, Anandam, and Christina A. Joseph. "Bollyculture: Ethnography of Identity, Media and Performance." *Global Media and Communication* 7, no. 1 (2011): 17–32.

Kazmi, N. "Holier Than Thou." *Times of India*, November 10, 1996.

Khan, Nasima. "Dual Deal." *India Today*, January 21, 2002, 28–32.

Khanna, Parag. "Bollystan—The Global India." *Globalist*, December 3, 2004. http://www.theglobalist.com/printStoryId.aspx?StoryId=4279.

Kiviat, Barbara. "Chasing Desi Dollars." *Time Magazine*, July 6, 2005. http://www.time.com/time/magazine/article/0,9171,1079504,00.html.

Kohli, Vanita. "Look, Here's a Booming Market." *Business World*, February 7–21, 1999.

Kripalani, Manjeet, and Ron Grover. "Bollywood." *Business Week*, December 2, 2002.

Krishnan, Sanjay. "Narayana Murthy's 5-Pt Plan for Film Sector." *Rediff*, April 8, 2005. http://www.rediff.com/money/2005/apr/08murthy.htm.

K Sera Sera Productions Limited. *Draft Red Herring Prospectus*, September 29, 2005. Accessed September 4, 2010. http://www.sebi.gov.in/dp/kseradraft.pdf.

Kudaisya, Gyanesh. "India's New Mantra: The Internet." *Current History*, April 2001.

Kumar, Shanti. *Gandhi Meets Primetime: Globalization and Nationalism in Indian Television*. Urbana: University of Illinois Press, 2006.

———. "Mapping Tollywood: The Cultural Geography of 'Ramoji Film City' in Hyderabad." *Quarterly Review of Film and Video* 23, no. 2 (2006): 129–38.

Kunzru, Hari. *Transmission*. New York: Penguin, 2004.

Lakshman, Nandini, and Ronald Grover. "Why India's Reliance Is Going Hollywood." *Business Week*, June 18, 2008. http://www.businessweek.com/print/globalbiz/content/jun2008/gb20080618_504190.htm

Lall, M. C. *India's Missed Opportunity: India's Relationship with the Non-Resident Indians*. Ashgate: Aldershot, 2001.

Larkin, Brian. "Degrading Images, Distorted Sounds: Nigerian Video and the Infrastructure of Piracy." *Public Culture* 16, no. 2 (Spring 2004): 289–314.

———. *Signal and Noise: Media, Infrastructure, and Urban Culture in Nigeria*. Durham: Duke University Press, 2009.

Lelyveld, David. "Upon the Subdominant: Administering Music on All-India Radio." *Social Text* 39 (1995): 111–27.

Liang, Lawrence. "Cinematic Citizenship and the Illegal City." *Inter-Asia Cultural Studies* 6, no. 3 (2005): 366–85.

Lorenzen, Mark, and Florian Arun Taube. "Breakout from Bollywood? The Roles of Social Networks and Regulation in the Evolution of Indian Film Industry." *Journal of International Management* 14 (2008): 286–99.

Lowe, Lisa. *Immigrant Acts: On Asian American Cultural Politics*. Durham: Duke University Press, 1996.

Maira, Sunaina. *Desis in the House: Indian American Youth Culture in New York City*. Philadelphia: Temple University Press, 2002.

———. "Henna and Hip-Hop: The Politics of Cultural Production and the Work of Cultural Studies." *Journal of Asian American Studies* 3, no. 3 (October 2000): 329–69.

———. "Temporary Tattoos: Indo-Chic Fantasies and Late Capitalist Orientalism." *Meridians* 3, no. 1 (2002): 134–60.

Majumdar, Neepa. *Wanted Cultured Ladies Only! Female Stardom and Cinema in India, 1930s–1950s*. Urbana: University of Illinois Press, 2009.

Malik, Iqbal. "TV Film Contracts: Cause for Concern." *Indian Express*, September 28, 1981.

Mallapragada, Madhavi. "Home, Homeland, Homepage: The Web, Transnationalism, and Indian-American Identities" (Ph.D. dissertation, University of Wisconsin-Madison, 2003).

Mani, Bakirathi, and Latha Varadarajan. "'The Largest Gathering of the Global Indian Family': Neoliberalism, Nationalism, and Diaspora at Pravasi Bharatiya Divas." *Diaspora: A Journal of Transnational Studies* 14, no. 1 (2005): 45–73.

Mankekar, Purnima. "Brides Who Travel: Gender, Transnationalism, and Nationalism in Hindi Film." *Positions* 7, no. 3 (1999): 731–62.

———. *Screening Culture, Viewing Politics: An Ethnography of Television, Womanhood, and Nation in Postcolonial India.* Durham: Duke University Press, 2000.

Marcus, George. *Ethnography through Thick and Thin.* Princeton: Princeton University Press, 1998.

Marcus, George, and Michael Fischer. *Anthropology as Cultural Critique: An Experimental Moment in the Human Sciences.* Chicago: University of Chicago Press, 1986.

Marshall, P. David. "The New Intertextual Commodity." In *The New Media Book*, edited by Dan Harries, 69–82. London: British Film Institute, 2002.

Masand, Rajeev. "Bollywood Inc?" *Indian Express*, April 28, 2002.

Mayer, Vicki, Miranda Banks, and John Caldwell, ed. *Production Studies: Cultural Studies of Media Industries.* New York: Routledge, 2009.

Mazumdar, Ranjani. *Bombay Cinema: An Archive of the City.* Minneapolis: University of Minnesota Press, 2007.

Mazzarella, William. *Shoveling Smoke: Advertising and Globalization in Contemporary India.* Durham: Duke University Press, 2003.

McDowell, Stephen, and Karthik Pashupati. "India's Internet Policies: Ownership, Control, and Purposes." In *Internet in Asia*, edited by Sankaran Ramanathan and Jorg Becker, 53–70. Singapore: Asian Media Information and Communication Center, 1999.

McMillin Divya C. "The Global Face of Indian Television." In *Reorienting Global Communication: Indian and Chinese Media Beyond Borders*, edited by Michael Curtin and Hemant Shah, 118–38. Urbana: University of Illinois Press, 2010.

Mehta, Monika. "Globalizing Bombay Cinema: Reproducing the Indian State and Family." *Cultural Dynamics* 17, no. 2 (2005): 135–54.

———. "Selections: Cutting, Classifying, and Certifying in Bombay Cinema." Ph.D. dissertation, University of Minnesota, 2001.

Miniwatts Marketing Group. "India: Internet Usage Stats and Telecommunications Market Report." Last modified April 9, 2011. http://www.internetworldstats.com/asia/in.htm.

Mishra, Vijay. *Bollywood Cinema: Temples of Desire.* New York: Routledge, 2002.

Mitra, Amit. "Framing Indian Media's Progress." *Picklemag: Indian Entertainment Biz Guide*, March 2009.

Moorti, Sujata. "Uses of the Diaspora: Indian Popular Culture and the NRI Dilemma." *South Asian Popular Culture* 3, no. 1 (2005): 49–62.

Morley, David, and Kevin Robins. *Spaces of Identity: Global Media, Electronic Landscapes and Cultural Boundaries.* New York: Routledge, 1995.

Mozumder, Suman Guha. "Desi Television Comes Alive." *India Abroad*, January 7, 2005.

Nadkarni, Sunaya. "Fardeen Koena Caught on MMS." *IBNLive*, November 8, 2005. http://ibnlive.in.com/news/fardeen-koena-caught-on-mms/809-8.html.

Naficy, Hamid. *The Making of Exile Cultures: Iranian Television in Los Angeles.* Minneapolis: University of Minnesota Press, 1993.

Nagdev, Vinod, Atul Dev, and Iqbal Malik. "Doordarshan's Great Leap Forward." *TV and Video World*, September 1984.

Nandgaonkar, Satish. "Producers Fret as *In Mumbai* Gets Set to Beam Blockbusters." *Times of India*, February 2, 1996.

Nandy, Ashis, ed. *The Secret Politics of Our Desires: Innocence, Culpability, and Indian Popular Cinema*. New York: St. Martin's Press, 1998.

Nigam, Aditya. "Imagining the Global Nation: Time and Hegemony." *Economic and Political Weekly* 39, no. 1 (2004): 72–79.

Niranjana, Tejaswini. *Mobilizing India: Women, Music, and Migration between India and Trinidad*. Durham: Duke University Press, 2006.

Ong, Aihwa, and Stephen J. Collier. *Global Assemblages: Technology, Politics, and Ethics as Anthropological Problems*. Malden, Mass.: Wiley-Blackwell, 2004.

Ortner, Sherry B. "Studying Sideways: Ethnographic Access in Hollywood," in *Production Studies*, edited by Vicky Mayer, Miranda Banks, and John Caldwell, 175-189. New York: Routledge, 2009.

Overdorf, Jason. "Bigger than Bollywood." *Newsweek*, September 9, 2007. http://www.thedailybeast.com/newsweek/2007/09/09/bigger-than-bollywood.html.

Padmanabhan, Arvind. "Of Incubators, Angel Investors, and Venture Capitalists." *India Abroad*, April 14, 2000.

———. "Surfing for Success." *India Abroad*, April 14, 2000.

Pagano, Penny. "FCC OK's Plan to Let Host of TV Stations on Air." *Los Angeles Times*, September 10, 1980.

Pahwa, Nikhil. "Rajshri.com Is a Multiplex with Unlimited Seats," *Paid Content*, November 10, 2006. http://paidcontent.org/tech/rajshricom-is-a-multiplex-with-unlimited-seats-rajjat-a-barjatya-md-rajshri.

Patil, S. K., ed. *Report of the Film Enquiry Committee*. New Delhi: Government of India Press, 1951.

Pendakur, Manjunath. "New Cultural Technologies and the Fading Glitter of Indian Cinema." *Quarterly Review of Film and Video* 11 (1989): 69–78.

Pendakur, Manjunath, and Jyotsna Kapur. "Think Globally, Program Locally: Privatization of Indian National Television." In *Democratizing Communication? Comparative Perspectives on Information and Power*, edited by Mashoed Bailie and Dwayne Winseck, 195-217. Creskill, N.J.: Hampton Press, 1997.

Pillai, Swarnavel Eswaran. "Tamil Cinema and the Major Madras Studios (1940–57)," Ph.D. dissertation, University of Iowa, 2010.

Pitroda, Sam. "An Experiment at Nation-Building." *Silicon India*, September 2000.

———. "Taking Silicon Valley Culture to India." *Silicon India*, April 2000.

Prakash, Gyan. *Mumbai Fables*. Princeton: Princeton University Press, 2010.

Prasad, M. Madhava. *Ideology of the Hindi Film: A Historical Construction*. New Delhi: Oxford University Press, 1998.

Prasad, Madhava. "This Thing Called Bollywood." *Seminar*, no. 525 (2003). http://www.india-seminar.com/2003/525/525%20madhava%20prasad.htm.

Prashad, Vijay. "Dusra Hindustan." *Seminar*, no. 538 (2004). http://www.india-seminar.com/2004/538/538%20vijay%20prashad.htm.

———. *The Karma of Brown Folk*. Minneapolis: University of Minnesota Press, 2001.

Punathambekar, Aswin. "Bollywood in the Indian-American Diaspora: Mediating a Transitive Logic of Cultural Citizenship." *International Journal of Cultural Studies* 8, no. 2 (2005): 151–75.

Purie, Aroon. "Hype and Hardsell." *India Today*, February 13, 2006.

Radhakrishnan, Ratheesh. "Looking at Mohanlal: Spectatorial Ordering and the Emergence of the 'Fan' in Malayalam Cinema." *Deep Focus* (July–December 2002): 29–38.

Raghavendra, Nandini. "Bollywood, US Body to Counter Piracy," *Economic Times*, March 19, 2010, http://articles.economictimes.indiatimes.com/2010-03-19/news/28491589_1_counterfeiting-and-piracy-film-industry-ficci-frames.

Rai, Amit. *Untimely Bollywood: Globalization and India's New Media Assemblage*. Durham: Duke University Press, 2009.

Rajadhyaksha, Ashish. "The 'Bollywoodization' of the Indian Cinema: Cultural Nationalism in a Global Arena." *Inter-Asia Cultural Studies* 4, no.1 (2003): 28–34.

———. "The Curious Case of Bombay's Hindi Cinema: The Career of Indigenous 'Exhibition' Capital." *Journal of the Moving Image* 5 (2006).

———. *Indian Cinema in the Time of Celluloid: From Bollywood to the Emergency*. Bloomington: Indiana University Press, 2009.

———. "Viewership and Democracy in the Cinema," in *Making Meaning in Indian Cinema*, edited by Ravi Vasudevan, 267–96. New Delhi: Oxford University Press.

Rajadhyaksha, Ashish, and Paul Willemen. *The Encyclopedia of Indian Cinema*. New Delhi: Oxford University Press, 1994.

Rajagopalan, Sudha. *Indian Films in Soviet Cinemas: The Culture of Movie-Going after Stalin* (Bloomington: Indiana University Press, 2008).

Ram, Anjali. "Framing the Feminine: Diasporic Readings of Gender in Popular Indian Cinema." *Women's Studies in Communication* 25 no. 1 (2002): 25–52.

Rao, Madanmohan. "Riding the Net Train in India: Internet Development Evokes Global Aspirations in India." *Little India*, February 1, 1998.

Raval, S., and A. Chopra. "The Plot Thickens." *India Today*, January 22, 2001.

Ray, Rajat Kanta. *Industrialization in India: Growth and Conflict in the Private Corporate Sector, 1914–1947*. New Delhi: Oxford University Press, 1979.

Rediff. "NRIs All Set for Diasporic Meet," January 8, 2003. http://www.rediff.com/money/2003/jan/08pbd.htm.

Sadanandan, Smita. "Back to films." *Hindu*, June 14, 2004. http://www.hindu.com/mp/2004/06/14/stories/2004061402110100.htm.

Saha, Prajjal. "Online Movie Trailers Gain Prominence." *Agency Faqs*, May 25, 2004.

Santanam, Murli. "Video Biz: Now Is the Time." *TV and Video World*, September 1988, 62–65.

Sassen, Saskia. "Locating Cities on Global Circuits," in *Global Networks, Linked Cities*, edited by Saskia Sassen, 1–38. New York: Routledge, 2002.

Saxenian, Anna Lee. *Regional Advantage: Culture and Competition in Silicon Valley and Route 128*. Cambridge: Harvard University Press, 1996.

———. "Silicon Valley's New Immigrant Entrepreneurs." *California Public Policy Institute*, 1999.

Schuker, Lauren. "Spielberg, India's Reliance to Form Studio." *Wall Street Journal*, September 20, 2008.

Scott, A. J. *On Hollywood: The Place, the Industry*. Princeton: Princeton University Press, 2005.

Screen. "Changing Face of Cinema." July 29, 2005. http://www.screenindia.com/fullstory.php?content_id=10858.

Shankar, Arun. "Dot.coms: Will They Make It?" *Business India*, November 11–24, 2002.

Shankar, Shalini. *Desi Land: Teen Culture, Class, and Success in Silicon Valley*. Durham: Duke University Press, 2008.

Sharma, E. Kumar. "The Truth behind Sify's Mega-Deal." *Business Today*, February 7, 2000.

Sheth, Jignya. "Desi Making Waves." *ABCD Lady*, July 2005. http://www.abcdlady. com/2005-07/art5.php.

Shoesmith, Brian. "Changing the Guard: The Transition from Studio-Based Film Production to Independent Production in Post-Colonial India." *Media History* 15, no. 4 (2009): 439–52.

Shoesmith, Brian, and Noorel Mecklai. "Religion as Commodity Images: Securing a Hindu Rashtra." In *Hindu Nationalism and Governance*, edited by John McGuire and Ian Copland. New Delhi: Oxford University Press, 2007.

Shukla, Archana. "Bollywood Gears Up with Filmi Marketing Formulas." *Economic Times*, September 27, 2003. http://articles.economictimes.indiatimes.com/2003-09-27/ news/27550157_1_film-maker-film-marketing-ram-gopal-varma.

Shukla, Archna, and Sagar Malviya. "Business Majors Script New Plot for Bollywood." *Mint*, November 15, 2007.

Siegel, Tatiana, and Anne Thompson. "DreamWorks, Reliance Close Deal." *Variety*, September 19, 2008. http://www.variety.com/article/VR1117992505.

Silicon India. "Homeward Bound." June 2000.

———. "Start-Up Fever in India." February 2000.

Singh, Abhay, and Nabeel Mohideen. "*Krrish*, Bollywood Blockbuster, Pummels *Superman* in India." *Bloomberg News*, August 22, 2006.

Singh, Amardeep. " 'Names Can Wait': The Misnaming of the South Asian Diaspora in Theory and Practice." *South Asian Review* 28, no. 1 (2007): 13–28.

Singh, Avtar. "Is Anyone Not Setting Up a Dotcom?" *Man's World*, May 2000.

Singh, Bhrigupati. "The Problem." *Seminar*, May 2003.

Singhvi, L. M. *Report of the High Level Committee on the Indian Diaspora*. New Delhi: Ministry of External Affairs, 2000. Accessed August 2, 2010. http://www.indiandiaspora. nic.in/contents.htm.

Sinha, Mrinalini. *Colonial Masculinity: The "Manly Englishman" and the "Effeminate Bengali" in the Late Nineteenth Century*. Manchester: Manchester University Press, 1995.

Sinha-Kerkhoff, Kathinka, and Ellen Bal. " 'Eternal Call of the Ganga': Reconnecting with People of Indian Origin in Surinam." *Economic and Political Weekly* 38, no. 38 (2003): 4008–21.

Sircar, Ajanta. "Love in the Time of Liberalization: *Qayamat Se Qayamat Tak*." *Journal of Arts and Ideas*, no. 32–33 (1999): 35–60.

Sontag, Deborah. "I Want My Hyphenated-Identity MTV." *New York Times*, June 19, 2005.

South Asian American Policy and Research Institute. *Making Data Count: South Asian Americans in the 2000 Census with Focus on Illinois*, 2005, 2. http://saapri.org/research. html.

Srinivas, S. V. "Film Culture: Politics and Industry." *Seminar*, no. 525 (2003). http://www. india-seminar.com/2003/525/525%20s.v.%20srinivas.htm.

———. "Hong Kong Action Film in the Indian B Circuit." *Inter-Asia Cultural Studies* 4, no. 1 (2003): 40–62.

———. "Devotion and Defiance in Fan Activity," in *Making Meaning in Indian Cinema*, edited by Ravi Vasudevan, 297-317. New Delhi: Oxford University Press.

———. *Megastar: Chiranjeevi and Telugu Cinema after NTR*. New Delhi: Oxford University Press, 2009.

——. "Making of a Peasant Industry: Telugu Cinema in the 1930s–1950s," *BioScope: South Asian Screen Studies* 1, no. 2 (2010): 169–88.

Subramanian, Nithya, and Ratna Bhushan. "Bollywood Logs On to the Net." *Business Line*, August 5, 2003.

Subramanian, T. S. "Another Actor in Politics." *Frontline*, October 7, 2005.

Sundaram, Ravi. "Beyond the Nationalist Panopticon: The Experience of Cyberpublics in India." In *Electronic Media and Technoculture*, edited by John Caldwell, 270–94. New Brunswick: Rutgers University Press, 2000.

——. *Pirate Modernity: Delhi's Media Urbanism*. New Delhi: Routledge, 2010.

Swaraj, Sushma. "Keynote Address on Entertainment, Ethnic Media, and Diasporic Identity." Speech at Pravasi Bharatiya Divas, New Delhi, January 9, 2003. Accessed April 6, 2007, http://www.indiaday.org/pbd1/pbd-sushmaswaraj.asp.

Syed, Siraj. "Video Pirates: Copyright Thieves." *TV and Video World*, June 1987, 74–79.

Tan, Lili. "Bollywood Gets Booed," *Asia Media*, April 11, 2003. http://www.asiamedia.ucla.edu/article.asp?parentid=9195.

Times Group, The. *Kaante: The Film*. Last modified 2001. http://kaante.indiatimes.com.

Times of India. "*Filmfare* Is Now in Cyberspace." October 6, 1996.

Tinic, Serra. *On Location: Canada's Television Industry in a Global Market*. Toronto: University of Toronto Press, 2006.

Tripathi, Dwijendra. *The Oxford History of Indian Business*. New Delhi: Oxford University Press, 2004.

Tsing, Anna. *Friction: An Ethnography of Global Connection*. Princeton: Princeton University Press, 2005.

TV and Video World. "Doordarshan's Winner: Manju Singh Makes Waves with 'Show Theme.'" September 1984.

——. "The Indian Experience on US TV." December 1987.

——. "Serial Bazaar." April 30, 1988.

Uberoi, Patricia. "The Diaspora Comes Home: Disciplining Desire in DDLJ." *Contributions to Indian Sociology* 32, no. 2 (1998): 305–36.

Upadhya, Carol. "A New Transnational Capitalist Class? Capital Flows, Business Networks and Entrepreneurs in the Indian Software Industry." *Economic and Political Weekly* 39, no. 48 (2004): 5141–51.

Vadodera, N. E. *BJP Foreign Policy Agenda for the Future*. New Delhi: Bharatiya Janata Party Publication, 1994.

Vasudevan, Ravi. "The Meanings of 'Bollywood.'" *Journal of the Moving Image* 7 (2008).

——. *The Melodramatic Public: Film Form and Spectatorship in Indian Cinema*. New York: Palgrave Mcmillan, 2011.

Vasudevan, Ravi S., ed. *Making Meaning in Indian Cinema*. New Delhi: Oxford University Press, 2000.

Velayutham, Selvaraj. "The Diaspora and the Global Circulation of Tamil Cinema." In *Tamil Cinema: The Cultural Politics of India's Other Film Industry*, edited by Selvaraj Velayutham, 172–88. New York: Routledge, 2008.

Venugopal, Arun. "Obit, MTV-Desi." *SAJAforum* (blog), February 18, 2007. http://www.sajaforum.org/2007/02/obit_mtv_desi.html.

Verma, V. "1986 Brings Hope for the Future." *Screen*, January 3, 1986.

"Victim of Ad Hocism, A." *Filmfare* 27, no.9, May 16–31, 1978.

Virdi, Jyotika. *The Cinematic ImagiNation: Indian Popular Films as Social History*. New Brunswick: Rutgers University Press, 2003.

Viswanathan, Vidya. "India Internet World." *Business World*, September 27, 1999.

———. "Masters of the Web." *Business World*, May 24, 1999.

Wallia, Kaajal. "Bollywood Spawns Film Marketing." *Times of India*, March 5, 2002.

Yang, Anand. *Bazaar India: Peasants, Traders, Markets and the Colonial State in Gangetic Bihar*. Berkeley: University of California Press, 1998.

Yudice, George. *The Expediency of Culture: Uses of Culture in the Global Era*. Durham: Duke University Press, 2005.

ABOUT THE AUTHOR

Aswin Punathambekar is Associate Professor of Communication Studies at the University of Michigan–Ann Arbor. He is the co-editor, with Anandam P. Kavoori, of *Global Bollywood* (NYU Press, 2008).